1495

The Catholic Ethic
and the
Spirit of Capitalism

THE
CATHOLIC
ETHIC
and the
SPIRIT
of
CAPITALISM

MICHAEL NOVAK

THE FREE PRESS
A Division of Macmillan, Inc.
New York

Maxwell Macmillan Canada
Toronto

Maxwell Macmillan International
New York   Oxford   Singapore   Sydney

The Free Press
A Division of Macmillan, Inc.
866 Third Avenue, New York, N.Y. 10022

Maxwell Macmillan Canada, Inc.
1200 Eglinton Avenue East
Suite 200
Don Mills, Ontario M3C 3N1

Macmillan, Inc. is part of the Maxwell Communication Group of Companies

Printed in the United States of America

printing number
1   2   3   4   5   6   7   8   9   10

Library of Congress Cataloging-in-Publication Data

Novak, Michael.
    The Catholic ethic and the spirit of capitalism / Michael Novak.
        p.   cm.
    Includes bibliographical references and index.
    ISBN 0-02-923235-X
    1. Sociology, Christian (Catholic)   2. Capitalism—Religious aspects—Catholic Church.
3. Catholic Church—Doctrines.   4. Social justice.   I. Title.
BX1753.N66   1993
261.8'5—dc20   92-32151
                                                                                                              CIP

In homage to
Pope John Paul II

In memory of
my father, Michael J. Novak (1910–1992)

In many ways, the Catholic man of the middle classes was like his Protestant opposite number. He too believed in being frugal, respectful, clean, time-saving, prudent. Yet, the self-made man of Catholic France was in fact relatively free of the fearful anxieties which Weber has ascribed to the Protestant Saint of the sixteenth and seventeenth centuries. He had little taste for agonizing self-reexamination, living on the boundaries in unending quest of the assurance of election.

BENJAMIN NELSON

"Of many Saints we read that they were very rich. They climbed up on this tower, on this mountain, and they were nearer to God. The more they had, and climbed up on it, the higher they were and the nearer to heaven, grateful to God for it and thanking him for it and loving him the more for it" [Blessed Giordano da Rivalto, 1304]. In this idea, that the evil lies not in possession of wealth but in making it the end of life, all the scholastics are agreed, from St. Thomas to St. Antonino of Florence, and Cardinal Gaetano. Their teaching was reasserted in the Encyclicals of Leo XIII and Pius XI.

AMINTORE FANFANI

CONTENTS

PREFACE

THE JAPANESE HAVE PROVED CONCLUSIVELY that in order to embody the spirit of capitalism, human beings do not have to be Protestant. A good thing, too, since many of us who are Jewish, Catholic, or secular chafe under having to describe what moves us as a "Protestant" ethic.

Moreover, the newest frontiers of capitalism today lie in two great regions of the globe—Eastern Europe and Latin America—whose cultures are Catholic (including Russian Orthodox) rather than Protestant. This book was conceived and written for, and in solidarity with, the peoples of those regions, among whom in recent years I have been privileged to spend much time. As a Roman Catholic, I share keenly in their current spiritual struggles and their worldly hopes—which are so crucial to the shape of the twenty-first century. But I have also written for those in America who are trying to make a fresh start on the problems the United States now faces, such as those of race, ethnicity, and the urban "underclass."

During the past 15 years more than a dozen Catholic nations, from the Philippines through Latin American and Poland, have become democracies. Samuel Huntington of Harvard has described this "third wave" of democratization as "the Catholic wave." These nations, and others like them, are now struggling to build dynamic economies. It is these same countries, I argue, that constitute the third wave of *capitalism rightly understood.*

The collapse of socialist economics has obliged those on the left to seek a new language for their ideals. But it also has obliged those both in the center and on the right to focus their energies on reducing world poverty.

After the death of socialism, Pope John Paul II asked in *Centesimus Annus* (1991) what sort of system we should propose to Eastern Europe and the Third World. As the Pope knew firsthand, socialism, having failed to inspire love or creativity, died because of its inadequate hold on the human spirit. A philosophy of basic needs is not enough; human beings are not cattle. Sufficiency of food, shelter, and employment will not satisfy the hunger of the human spirit. Free human beings want to form governments framed by their own consent, and economies empowered by their own personal initiative and creativity.

This lesson is a warning to capitalist societies as well: The fact that, of all known and existing systems, only capitalist societies deliver the goods satisfies neither the inquiring mind nor the thirsting soul.

The only long-lasting foundation for a capitalist society is a moral, spiritual, and religious one. The German sociologist Max Weber (1864–1920) called attention to such a foundation in 1904, in *The Protestant Ethic and the Spirit of Capitalism.* Since Weber did not hit the mark exactly, either in grasping the essence of modern capitalism or in articulating the relevant Christian ethic, a fresh start suitable for the coming century seems called for. I have named the ethic we are looking for "the Catholic ethic," though this should be understood in the small "c" sense of the word as well as the large. Since practically all the words needed to define this new ethic can be understood within the framework of other Christian traditions, including the Protestant, I debated calling it "the Christian Ethic." But this choice would have had three disadvantages: It would have muffled important differences between Max Weber's thesis and my own; in particular, it would have obscured the vital contribution to the Christian tradition made by the Catholic ethic as a counterbalance to the Protestant ethic; and, perhaps most important, it would have left out the Jewish tradition, with its strong emphasis on creativity and imagination, which the larger concept of "catholic" includes. It was Judaism, after all, that taught the human race that all things have their origin in one single Creator, Who calls all humans to participate in His creative work as history proceeds.

At the inmost heart of a capitalist system, for instance, is confidence in the creative capacity of the human person. As Catholic theology teaches, and as experience verifies, such confidence is well-placed. Each person is made in the image of God, the Creator. Each is called to be a co-creator and given the vocation to act creatively. Every co-creator is free, that is, expected both to assume responsibility and to show initiative.

Among citizens who are no longer merely subjects of king or emperor but rather sovereigns in their own right, a new habit is summoned up: enterprise. Enterprise in this sense is a moral and intellectual virtue that prompts them to be alert and discerning with respect to projects to be launched and goods and services to be provided. For the things they want and need, such citizens are taught by the Jewish and Christian testaments to act for themselves, rather than look to the state. They themselves must set in motion the procedures required to bring about the goals they desire. They learn to live as free men and women, responsible for their own destiny. While before God they may drop to their knees, before the world they stand erect and responsible.

This book differs from *The Spirit of Democratic Capitalism.* In 1981, when I was writing that book, I had not yet seen the link between capitalism and creativity, the crucial point in the Catholic ethic.

Not only did I devote few words to papal social thought, but three groundbreaking encyclicals of Pope John Paul II (*Laborem Exercens, Sollicitudo Rei Socialis*, and *Centesimus Annus*) had not yet endorsed so many possibilities for a new ethic of capitalism. As the last act of a play often changes the meaning of what went before, so in particular *Centesimus Annus* in 1991 cast new light on the preceding hundred years of papal social thought.

Finally, although I had written that "the death of the socialist idea is the most unreported fact of our era," I did not foresee the spectacular and cascading collapse of communism in 1989. After the dark days of 1979–81, the political drama of the decade of the 1980s was very high. For global significance, it may rival any decade in centuries. Many new data must now be accounted for.

The most important new idea in this book is that behind the political and economic progress of the advanced societies much more has been at work than our economists, on both right and left, have noticed. This profound dynamic can best be brought to light by a Jewish–Christian anthropology that stresses "the creative subjectivity of the human person," such as that advanced by Pope John Paul II, most notably in *Centesimus Annus*. (The attentive reader will note that I keep saying "person" rather than "individual" to mark an important distinction, as will be clarified in chapter 7.) Instead, the voice of social analysis we most commonly hear in Western culture today is materialistic, external, more suitable for brute animals than for self-conscious humans— sometimes a vulgar Marxism, as Raymond Aron called it; at other times, a vulgar utilitarianism. This omnipresent secular voice is quite inept at explaining us to ourselves. By contrast, a Jewish and Christian anthropology begins with the Book of Genesis itself: Yahweh created humans in His image. Errant, yet called to be like our Creator in creativity, imagination, and generosity, we human beings need to be addressed both in our weakness and in our as-yet-unfulfilled destiny.

Again, another concept to which I devote new attention in this book is civil society. Indeed, in what I take to be one of the most important theoretical breakthroughs in this book, I reinterpret social justice as the distinctive virtue of free persons associating themselves together, cooperatively, within a free society. I delink social justice from an uncritical reliance on the blind leviathan of the state and link it, instead, to the concrete intelligence operative in individuals and their free associations within "the civic forum" (as the Czechs and Slovaks so neatly put it in their revolt against the totalitarian state). The role of the state, I argue, is to strengthen the fertile and creative actions of civil society, not to derogate from them or (God forbid) supplant them. This recommendation is of course controversial. But it does lay out, I believe, the best road to a future more humane than the one the blood-soaked and misbegotten twentieth century brought us.

Thus, the thesis of this new book may be stated in a single sentence: *Out of the crucible of a hundred-year debate within the Church came a fuller and more satisfying vision of the capitalist ethic than Max Weber's "Protestant ethic."* Not only is this Catholic (and catholic) ethic more appropriate for the realities of the present moment, but also it offers inspiriting guidance for the future. And its emergence is particularly timely for the young leaders of Eastern Europe and Latin America—many of whom have, as it happens, Catholic roots. Alexis de Tocqueville would surely have attributed its happy appearance in Pope John Paul II to a benign and caring Providence.

A word of caution is in order, however. When I write here of the intra-Catholic development of "the Catholic ethic," I intend especially the limited sphere of Catholic social teaching, and of the encyclical tradition in particular. For the Catholic ethic, fully considered, is a many-splendored realm of many mansions, going far beyond worldly and temporal matters. In its variegated unfolding it includes many schools of spirituality, from the contemplative to the most active; the traditions of many religious orders; and many newly germinating lay initiatives. Of all that, I am looking only at a relatively small slice—the elemental order of political economy and cultural ethos. Within this more-or-less-worldly dough, the life of God's grace works as leaven.

The Catholic tradition concerns matters far richer than mere political economy and long antedates the emergence of modern capitalism (and shall no doubt long outlive the latter). No other religious tradition has wrestled so long with, or been so reluctant to come to terms with, the capitalist reality. So it should not be too surprising that many of the hard-won—and now most useful—terms for understanding capitalism spring from the struggles of that tradition against itself.

Thus the story that this book tells is one of moral struggle. Which, since such struggle is the daily lot of all of us, is wonderfully reassuring.

INTRODUCTION
More Than the Protestant Ethic

Besides the earth, man's principal resource is man
himself. His intelligence enables him to discover the
earth's productive potential and the many different
ways in which human needs can be satisfied. It is his
disciplined work in close collaboration with others
that makes possible the creation of ever more extensive
working communities which can be relied upon to
transform man's natural and human environments.
Important virtues are involved in this process such as
diligence, industriousness, prudence in undertaking
reasonable risks, reliability and fidelity in interpersonal
relationships as well as courage in carrying out
decisions which are difficult and painful, but necessary
both for the overall working of a business and in
meeting possible setbacks.

POPE JOHN PAUL II, *Centesimus Annus*

IT WAS MAX WEBER'S GREAT ACHIEVEMENT to discern that the
humdrum and often drab work of economics, grubby and messy
as it sometimes is, has a religious underpinning. His emphasis on
spirit is even more obvious to scholars today. It is not easy to
explain the spectacular economic success of the Japanese in purely
material terms. Compared to the Brazilians, whose natural resources are abundant and whose living space is vast, 140 million
Japanese live densely crowded on the coastal plain of tiny islands
in which natural resources are few and sources of energy virtually
nil. Nonetheless Japan is rich, Brazil is poor. Clearly, the capacity

of the Japanese for organization, discipline, hard work, invention, and enterprise is not a negligible economic good. To have pointed to certain forms of the human spirit was the great strength of Weber's thesis; to have limited these to Calvinism was its weakness.

Indeed, although many have taken it as gospel, the "Protestant" emphasis embodied in Max Weber's *The Protestant Ethic and the Spirit of Capitalism* (1904) was from the first inexact. Weber's father, for example, had a rather relaxed "Mediterranean" attitude toward the inherited family business.[1] He was content to do as little as necessary to keep it going, and to turn away from it for as much leisure and easy living as he could. It was a Calvinist uncle, rather, who was for Max Weber the immediate exemplar of the so-called Protestant ethic, a man driven both by a grander vision of (to use the word common at the time) "increase" and a passion for innovation, improvement, and work. Thus, even in Weber's own family there were highly visible variations among Protestant traditions.

MAX WEBER'S LIMITS

Several difficulties in Weber's thesis can be distinguished.

First, Weber's definition of the Protestant ethic is never clearly stated; it is hard to reproduce it in a few terse lines so that one can test it empirically. It appears to rest, rather, on a general impression of the situation in Europe at the end of the nineteenth century: that the Northern "Protestant" countries were both more heavily industrialized and more prosperous than the Southern "Catholic" countries. So widespread and powerful was this impression that Weber thought the burden of proof lay on those who disagreed with his thesis rather than upon him.[2] Moreover, by "Protestant" Weber was scarcely thinking of the Anglican tradition, or even the Lutheran one; he in fact seemed to mean "Calvinist" or, even more precisely, "Puritan." And (as Calvinist theologians who reject Weber's attribution of capitalism to Calvinism delight in showing) he clearly meant something in the end quite anti-Christian in spirit: the singleminded pursuit of an increase of capital (monetary wealth) as an *end in itself*, not as a means; as a kind of discipline of self-denial, not for glory or pleasure. To make this as intimidating as a knight's glittering sword, he added three further characteristics: a sense of *duty* toward the acquisition of wealth for its own sake; religious *asceticism* in avoiding luxury, pleasure, and consumption; and a sense of *calling*, such that work was undertaken soberly, conscientiously, and industriously.

Obviously, the appearance of a new body of human beings shaped by these four inner imperatives manifested something rather larger than an accidental outbreak of business astuteness; these imperatives arrived (he says) as an entirely new ethos. Today, however, more than a century after its alleged appearance, do many real human beings actually share in such an ethos, at least in the West? Does the "ethos" so identified miss too many vital elements necessary to "real existing capitalism" today, spread to so many quarters of the world?[3]

To grasp the problems inherent in Weber's hypothesis—even in its own time, let alone for today—the reader will be well served by a review of three passages from Weber's work. A moment's reflection on each passage is worth the effort, since the phrase "Protestant ethic" is used frequently in the press, and often erroneously:

> A specifically bourgeois economic ethic had grown up.
> With the consciousness of standing in the fullness of
> God's grace and being visibly blessed by Him, *the
> bourgeois business man*, as long as he remained within
> the bounds of formal correctness, *as long as his moral
> conduct was spotless and the use to which he put his
> wealth was not objectionable, could follow his pecuni-
> ary interests as he would* and feel that he was *fulfilling
> a duty* in doing so. The power of *religious asceticism*
> provided him in addition with sober, conscientious,
> and unusually industrious workmen, who clung to
> their work as to a life purpose willed by God.[4]

> The peculiarity of *this philosophy of avarice* appears to
> be the ideal of the honest man of recognized credit,
> and above all the idea of *a duty of the individual to-
> ward the increase of his capital, which is assumed as an
> end in itself*. Truly what is here preached is *not simply
> a means* of making one's way in the world, but a pe-
> culiar ethic. The infraction of its rules is treated not as

foolishness but as forgetfulness of duty. That is *the essence of the matter. It is not mere business astuteness*, that sort of thing is common enough, *it is an ethos. This* is the quality which interests us.[5]

In fact, the *summum bonum* of this ethic, the earning of more and more money, combined with the strict avoidance of all spontaneous enjoyment of life, is above all completely devoid of any eudaemonistic, not to say hedonistic, admixture. It is thought of so *purely as an end in itself*, that from the point of view of the happiness of, or utility to, the single individual, it appears entirely transcendental and *absolutely irrational*. Man is dominated by the making of money, by *acquisition as the ultimate purpose of his life*.[6]

Explicitly, Weber is not here describing all forms of "the capitalist spirit," but only one fairly narrow and limited kind. Nor is he purporting to describe all forms of the Protestant ethic, not even all forms of Calvinism. Indeed, the great economic historian Jacob Viner stresses how narrow Weber's thesis actually is, compared to the way so many commentators casually treat it.[7] Further, Viner finds that for the precise link that Weber alleges between capitalism and Protestantism—the doctrines of calling and predestination—the evidence that Weber gives is weak; indeed, after a sustained search of Protestant writers, Viner finds in them *no* support for Weber's thesis. Nonetheless, Viner notes, no analyst of the nineteenth century denies that *most* of the Protestant territories were economically more successful than *most* of the Catholic territories. But was this due to Protestant doctrine? Viner finds no one who thinks so. Some argue, rather, that being in business and trade makes for an inquiring mind, a large imagination, and a zest for innovation. Thus, particularly for those sects or persons that struggle in minority status, business offers both one of the few ways to survive, and a specialization that steadily rewards innovation, efficiency, and excellence.

The daily grind implied by this sort of capitalist spirit, furthermore, did not really appeal to Weber, any more than it attracts many today. On the contrary, Weber was rather an admirer of hot-blooded Teutonic knights and their heroic grandeur, who dreaded being confined in the "iron cage" of capitalist rationality.

In this vein, Viner comments, Weber's thesis has been picked up "by leftists of many varieties who embraced it as an *exposé* of the unattractive origins of modern capitalists"; by Protestants to beat up on Catholics, and vice versa; "and in pre–World War Germany, following a lead given by Max Weber himself, as an ingredient in the chauvinistic denigration of the Anglo–American world as a whole."[8] His colleagues in later years described Weber as "a modern incarnation of Dürer's knight between death and the devil," "one of the few truly aristocratic types from the German history of the turn of the century," "a duke who moved into battle at the head of his vassals," "a giant resurrected warrior from the forests of Germany."[9] All this helps us to understand Weber's ambivalence about his subject. Weber saw an admirable discipline in the Protestant ethic, but dreaded its steely grip upon modern Europe, which in his eyes was choking out the romantic glory of the knightly past:

> The Puritan wanted to work in a calling; we are forced to do so. For when asceticism was carried out of monastic cells into everyday life, and began to dominate worldly morality, it did its part in building the tremendous cosmos of the modern economic order. This order is now bound to the technical and economic conditions of machine production which today determine the lives of all the individuals who are born into this mechanism, not only those directly concerned with economic acquisition, with irresistible force. Perhaps it will so determine them until the last ton of fossilized coal is burned. In Baxter's view the care for external goods should only lie on the shoulders of the saint like "a light cloak, which can be thrown aside at any moment." But fate decreed that the cloak should become a housing hard as steel.[10]

Weber's Protestant ethic is, in any case, no Christian ideal. His "philosophy of avarice" and "housing hard as steel" (or "iron cage," in the Talcott Parsons translation) do not represent a humane ideal. So it is not difficult to see why many scholars have heavily qualified Weber's hypothesis, even beyond Weber's own qualifications—which were many. Indeed, after all these qualifications, it is not clear how much of it still lives. In addition, Weber's thesis bumps against several other inconvenient facts.

First, Weber had great difficulty finding Protestant theologians who advised their readers to interpret their Christian duties in the world as he did. Weber's chief sources (and they are few) are from what might be called pastoral exhortations by ordinary ministers close to the people in the pew. Ironically, too, he is reduced to citing that bon vivant from Philadelphia, Benjamin Franklin, as an exemplar of the Calvinist ethic, despite the fact that it was not as a Puritan, but quite the opposite, that the worldly Franklin saw himself. Even his emphasis on hard work, ambition, regularity, and good habits had more the ring of common sense than of Calvinist injunction.

Second, in the present day, many Calvinist theologians and historians rather angrily deny that John Calvin should in any respect be held responsible for (as they see it) the "evils" brought by capitalism into this world. In Europe especially, many (if not most) Calvinist churches, denigrating capitalism, lean toward Christian socialist or social democratic parties.

Third, in the United Kingdom, for example, highly Calvinist parts (i.e., Scotland) were for a long time the most economically retarded and least capitalistic parts.

Moreover, as Hugh Trevor-Roper has pointed out, many of the first capitalist centers appeared in such Catholic cities as Liège, Lille, and Turin.[11] And many of the first capitalist families in Europe (for capitalism was first of all a family affair) were Catholic, Jewish, freethinking, and—in any case—not Calvinist.[12]

To summarize: The complex of attitudes that Weber identified as Protestant actually was shared by many others besides Calvinists. Its tonalities and lineaments were rather more various, subtle, and diverse than he suggests. Furthermore, Calvinists today do not usually recognize themselves in his portrait. Calvinist Geneva, for example, took a tough line against interest, banks, and capital investment for some generations after the death of Calvin.

Finally, although Weber's "philosophy of avarice," making the acquisition of wealth both a duty and an end in itself, has supplied much ammunition to such later foes of the capitalist ethic as R. H. Tawney in England, Robert N. Bellah in America, and Amintore Fanfani in Italy, it is far too extreme to stand as a credible account of the capitalist ethic in actual practice. By Weber's own testimony, the Calvinist ethic imposed many moral constraints upon capitalist behavior. On the point of avarice, for example, Weber derided the common charge that capitalism is fed by greed (he calls this a "kindergarten" notion) and pointed out that, compared to earlier forms of economy, capitalism dampens the fires of greed, and through encouraging thrift and investment even acts as a restraint upon it.[13]

Moreover, the overwhelming majority of poor people on this planet at the end of the nineteenth century had room for nobler motives than avarice. Like magnets, centers of capitalism drew hordes of immigrants, refugees, and the dispossessed, who found in it the one system that gave hope of a better life.

Again, human psychology itself suggests that the steely and avaricious singlemindedness hypothesized by Weber is bound to be rare. Religious and humanitarian habits of the heart told against it, but so also did the attraction of a well-rounded personality, not to mention (more powerful perhaps than either) the siren lure of pleasure.

There is no doubt Weber was onto something, nonetheless.[14] Capitalism is not an economic system only; its reality cannot be explained solely in terms of objective economic techniques. What needs to be explained is not private ownership of the means of production, the existence of markets, and profit or accumulation. These three characteristics, which form the substance of definitions of capitalism in most English-language dictionaries, are quite ancient in origin, and most assuredly precapitalist. For example, the commandment given by Yahweh to Moses, "Thou shalt not steal," long ago presupposed the legitimacy of private property. And Aristotle, Cicero, and Thomas Aquinas had long since praised regimes of private property, as well as virtues such as "liberality," "magnificence," and "magnanimity" that presuppose ample means.[15]

What Weber set out to explain is something quite different; something that arrived considerably later than the Protestant Reformation; something added to the world many centuries after markets, private property, and profit had already grown silver with respectability and bent with age. To put it simply, Weber detected something new, a novel *Geist* or spirit or cultural inspiration, some new complex of social attitudes and habits. He may have erred in calling it Protestant. But he did not err in identifying a moral and cultural dimension internal to capitalism. In an entirely different key, Adam Smith had done the same a century before, in *The Theory of Moral Sentiments*.

For capitalism is not a set of neutral economic techniques amorally oriented toward efficiency. Its practice imposes certain moral and cultural attitudes, requirements, and demands. Cultures that fail to develop the required habits cannot expect to eat broadly of capitalism's fruits.

Ironically enough, the path to the capitalist prosperity so often depicted today in the colors of mere worldliness—mammon, materialism, hedonism, consumerism—passes in actual practice through a set of practical disciplines of a most unworldly coloration, a kind of secularized monasticism regimented by the clock, demanding self-sacrifice and exacting the submission of blood-pounding passions and sensual pleasures to the rigors of mental discipline as life-plan and career-line triumph over instinct. There is no way around this. Even without the Puritan agonies of conscience[16] that Weber describes, hard work is hard work. The capitalist way requires, as well, a respect for the larger political and cultural orders within which humane practices and the rule of law are established. And these orders impose virtues beyond mere economic prudence.

Today, the formerly socialist nations of Eastern Europe (including the former USSR) are confronting, quite directly, the need to develop the moral and cultural habits necessary to undergird their dreams. Indeed, they have had to learn three hard lessons. First they discovered that having work, housing, hospital care, and education supplied for them by "the authorities" was not enough; they wanted governments formed by their own consent. Then they discovered that democracy alone was not enough: The people will not be happy merely to vote every two years or so; they want and demand an economic system that enables families to "better their condition." It is not utopia they are asking for— just tangible progress. But the third lesson, the hardest lesson, is that they cannot have *either* democracy *or* capitalism unless they acquire the appropriate moral habits *and* (of course) adapt both their institutions and their laws.

For more than 70 years the people of the former USSR were discouraged from showing initiative, enterprise, or economic ambition. Market activities between consenting adults were criminalized. Envy was so mightily reinforced (under the guise of equality) that enormous social pressure is *still* brought to bear upon anyone who succeeds more than his fellows. Many remember the devastation wreaked on the *kulaks* (successful farmers) under Stalin. Such psychological leveling still holds most people back. But so also do habits of dependency on the state, learned over three generations. Although many in the formerly socialist countries still find the term "capitalism" morally hard to swallow, they see very well that their revolution carries with it a heavy set of new moral demands.

In pointing to the cultural dimension of capitalism, therefore, Weber earned an immortal place in intellectual history. This is so for two reasons. First, he identified something new in economic history and glimpsed (even if he did not accurately describe) its moral and religious dimensions. Second, he suggested in advance why Marxism, both as an explanatory theory and as a vision of paradise, was doomed to fail: Its resolute materialism excluded the human spirit.

THE HUMAN SPIRIT

In our day, no one can deny the role of the spiritual dimension in human affairs. Anyone who lived through the Iranian Revolution of 1978 and the "miracle" of the Revolution of 1989 in Central and Eastern Europe would have to be dull indeed to overlook in world affairs the power of the human spirit. On a certain Monday the Shah of Iran had the fourth most powerful army in the world, and by the following Friday that army, under the religious influence of the Ayatollah, had laid down its arms. As late as the summer of 1989, two young men were killed trying to reach the Berlin Wall, which looked as solid and indestructible as ever. And yet by that Christmas virtually every member of the Warsaw Pact had broken free not only from Soviet control but also from Communist government, and the Berlin Wall was joyously torn down.

Similarly, "capital" (*das Kapital*) no longer means primarily cattle, land, or even those material things that are the instruments of production. Its primary meaning is "human capital"—the human mind, inventiveness, knowledge, skill, know-how, enterprise, a capacity for organization, habits of cooperation, and initiative. It may be said that Weber pointed to this cultural dimension of capitalism. But it cannot be said that he perceived either the central importance of human capital or the specific nature of capitalist intelligence. He emphasized "rationality" (the calculating sort that proceeds on iron rails) but overlooked, or minimized, invention and the zest for the new, the free, the flexible. He thought that the essence of capitalist reasoning lay in calculative rationality—the arithmetic of means and ends.

In this, Weber was wide of the mark, as Hayek, Schumpeter, Kirzner, and others were later to show.[17] The heart of capitalism, as they demonstrated, lies in discovery, innovation, and invention. Its fundamental activity is insight into what needs to be done to provide a new good or service. The distinctive materials of capitalism are not numbers already assembled for calculation by the logic of the past. On the contrary, its distinctive materials are new possibilities glimpsed by surprise through enterprising imagination. Thus have new technologies been born and entire new industries (automobiles, airplanes, moving pictures, electronics, computers) been created. The chief moral virtues of capitalism are creativity, cooperation, and the other virtues of building purposive communities. Weber feared that capitalism would perish of predictability. Capitalism, instead, is full of serendipity—discovery and surprise. Who would have predicted that libraries of information could be contained on bits of silicon derived from grains of sand? Or that fiber optics would render copper wires obsolete?

Weber also overlooked the role of democracy in framing capitalism, guiding it, and making it fruitful. At one level, democracy solves crucial problems of legitimate and peaceful succession, so that long-run investments may go forward. At a deeper level, democratic procedures empower majorities to temper the autonomous will for gain-and-gain-alone that Weber feared in capitalism left to itself. Since the human being is a political as well as an economic animal, to view capitalism in a vacuum devoid of politics is to abstract from reality. Indeed, Peter Berger has assembled much empirical evidence to show that capitalism is a necessary (even if not sufficient) condition for democracy.[18] In 1900, of course, there were only 13 democracies in the world; Weber lacked a sufficient number of cases from which to derive such empirical correlations.[19]

Yet it is not only Weber's theory of capitalism that now seems inadequate. When one looks at the actual practice of capitalist societies, libertarian theories also seem finally inadequate. Some very good minds have been satisfied by Milton Friedman's account of capitalism as the system best suited to ensuring liberty.[20] Many others are less moved by such accounts or, finding them quite helpful as far as they go, press beyond them to deal with further questions. Liberty is but one value in the human moral quiver, and a rather equivocal value at that, susceptible to diametrically opposed meanings and many self-destructive and socially destructive uses. Libertarian accounts seem to many too "thin." Religious people often find in them an arid absence of religion, or even a lightly veiled hostility to religion. To their ears, libertarians seem to be singing off-key.

For such reasons, it does not seem idle to suppose that a fresh interpretation of the capitalist spirit—and a fresh statement of its ideal—might stimulate others to see that its lived reality is far richer than conventional interpretations suggest. In a pluralistic world, no one account is likely to satisfy all.

TOWARD A CATHOLIC ETHIC

In this book I wish to offer a vision of how the Catholic ethic may undergird, correct, and enlarge the spirit of capitalism. To be in favor of capitalism, or to make it work well, one need not be a partisan of the Protestant ethic in a narrow sense. And one need not be a Protestant to present a potent theory of capitalism. Jewish writers have presented Jewish approaches to capitalism.[21] Several British historians have uncovered materials that locate the cultural roots of modern capitalism much farther back in European history than the Reformation.[22] They have located these roots not only in papal support for a transnational, single-market empire after the coronation of Charlemagne in the year 800 A.D., but even as far back as the way of life of Benedictine monasteries in the fifth century.

Yet the history that I wish to recount is not that earlier one. Rather, it is the story of Catholic (especially papal) social thought since 1891, when Leo XIII's encyclical letter *Rerum Novarum* led the modern papacy onto new terrain: a pointedly social concern for the moral effects on families and individuals of the new ethos of the industrialized age. Over the next 100 years, papal social thought developed rather rapidly under a self-imposed pressure to work out a theological ethic adequate to the "new things" of modern political and economic life. This tradition, often ignored in the wider world, has begun to attract fresh attention from both left and right, as one by one the simpler ideologies of the twentieth century have lost credibility.

During *Rerum Novarum*'s centenary year (1991), for example, some 4,000 conferences were called worldwide to reflect on the first century of modern papal social thought. This tradition is rich and complex, since it has tried to interweave eternal truths with perceptive readings of each historical moment, to blend together several different cultural traditions and intellectual disciplines, and to grow and change with hard experience. The appearance of the 100th-anniversary encyclical *Centesimus Annus* (on May 1, 1991) provided a brilliant and (to some) surprising end to the early part of the story. No doubt, Leo XIII condemned socialism—and, more damaging still, assessed it as "futile"—while merely criticizing capitalism. This asymmetry[23] suggested a certain toleration of at least some features of capitalism (most notably, of private property). Still, Leo XIII's coolness to the capitalism of 1891 led many to question whether Catholicism could ever get "inside" capitalism, or would choose forever to remain outside it, like a nagging stepmother at the doorway. *Centesimus Annus* provided a surprising answer.

Moreover, this recent positive assessment of "the market economy," "the business economy," or "the enterprise economy" by a Catholic pope may have come just in time for Latin America, as well as for Eastern Europe. For as David Martin brilliantly documents in *Tongues of Fire*, the rapid growth of a certain kind of evangelical Protestantism in Latin America is producing a phenomenon much in line with Max Weber's thesis.[24] These millions of new Protestants seem to gain sudden confidence that they can be "different" from others around them, gain control over their own passions, lives, and circumstances, and begin acting with worldly competence in matters of enterprise, business, and work. The economic success of these new Protestants is quite striking, although Catholics who also form small communities of prayer, moral conversion, and joint action are reaping similar fruits.[25]

This social upheaval is eerily analogous to the Protestant and Catholic Reformations some 450 years ago. But in any case, Latin America is for the first time experiencing the birth-pangs of a genuine grassroots "people's capitalism." Indeed, it seems about to break away at last from the patrimonial mercantilism inherited from the Spanish and Portuguese Catholic aristocracy. Pope John Paul II's Catholic ethic of capitalism will soon be getting its first large-scale test.

A PREVIEW

Somewhat like all Gaul, this book is divided into three parts: Part One deals with the inherited situation and the founding documents of modern papal social thought. Part Two brings onstage Pope John Paul II's "new birth of freedom." And Part Three turns to the future, under the title "Next?"

Part One begins with a chapter on Amintore Fanfani's *Catholicism, Protestantism and Capitalism* (1935), whose thesis is that capitalism is incompatible with Catholicism. This slender book, something of a classic, is a good place to start reading up on this subject, since it is in some ways a more thorough endorsement of Weber's thesis than even Weber might have liked. In effect, Fanfani virtually *blames* capitalism (or at least what he means by the term) on Protestantism. Weber, by contrast, was not averse to paying Protestantism a kind of compliment; a certain excitement and approbation, perhaps despite himself, sometimes crept into Weber's prose. Wasn't it a good thing that Protestant countries were more "progressive," "modern," and "advanced" than Catholic (read "Latin") countries? Naturally, Fanfani did *not* accept the characterization of Protestant countries as "more advanced." That term implies a more-or-less transcendent measure of progress and decline. Fanfani questioned the implied standard.

Fanfani's definition of capitalism, however, never satisfied me, even in those student years during which I first read his book. Earlier in this century, the Latin countries of Europe (Italy, Spain, Portugal) did seem to be anticapitalist in philosophy as well as precapitalist in fact. One sometimes encountered there a wall of ignorance, even of antipathy, against Anglo–American "Protestant" cultures. Studying in Italy in 1956–58, I experienced a comedy of mutual misunderstanding. Even today, one needs to confront the rather common Latin Catholic bias against capitalism and to discern its target quite precisely. Only in taking the trouble to do this can one see just how far the Catholic intellect has come in the years since 1935.

Following the chapter on Fanfani, I turn to Pope Leo XIII's

encyclical of 1891, *Rerum Novarum*, the first of the modern papal treatments of "the social question" and, most notably, of socialism and its "liberal" alternative, the market economy. My primary emphasis is on Leo XIII's predictions—even before any socialist state actually existed—about the futility of socialism. These predictions are paired with testimonies from those who nearly a century later reflected on their sad experiences under existing socialist states. My aim in this second chapter is not only retrospective, however; the reader is asked to cast eyes forward to the unfinished business of democratic and capitalistic societies, a subject to which we return in the last part of the book.

Chapter 3 takes up a central concept in papal social thought, "social justice," a term that entered the canon of papal thought via Pius XI's *Quadragesimo Anno* of 1931. The definition given to social justice in that encyclical was vague and unsatisfying. I offer a new and—I think—practical definition, designed to rescue it from certain powerful objections (from Friedrich Hayek, for example). This new definition puts the emphasis on "civil society," not on the "state," and thereby gives rise to a new approach to government and social activism which I call "the civil society project."

In Part Two, there follow two chapters on the social thought of Pope John Paul II. Eastern Europeans often say that no other single person was so central to the sudden collapse of Communism in the "miracle year" of 1989 as this Polish pope, who ascended to the papacy in 1978.[26] As early as 1963, in the debate on religious liberty at the Second Vatican Council, Karol Wojtyla (then the Archbishop of Krakow) signaled his commitment to human liberty. How that vision came to include economic as well as religious and political liberty is part of our story.

In Part Three, I apply this new "Catholic ethic," especially the civil society project, to several social perplexities of the near future, including the parlous condition of the world's poor, ethnicity and race, and the new factor in cultural ecology—the omnipresent media of communications.

PART ONE

WHICH SYSTEM?

Leo XIII to Pius XI (1891–1931)

CHAPTER 1

CATHOLICS AGAINST CAPITALISM

And hence it is, that to feel much for others, and little
for ourselves, that to restrain our selfish, and to
indulge our benevolent, affections, constitutes the
perfection of human nature; and can alone produce
among mankind that harmony of sentiments and
passions in which consists their whole grace and
propriety.

When the happiness or misery of others depends in
any respect upon our conduct, we dare not, as self-
love might suggest to us, prefer the interest of one to
that of many. The man within immediately calls to us,
that we value ourselves too much and other people too
little, and that, by doing so, we render ourselves the
proper object of the contempt and indignation of our
brethren.

ADAM SMITH

SHORT OF STATURE, DAPPER, QUICK OF MOVEMENT, AND EXCEED-
INGLY INTELLIGENT, Amintore Fanfani has more than once been
the Prime Minister of Italy, and since 1948 one of the leading lights
of the Christian Democratic Party. For nearly a dozen years he
had gone into exile during the Fascist government of Benito Mussolini. During that time in exile, like so many others among the
future leaders of postwar Europe, Fanfani wrote a book for which
he first became famous—in his case, *Catholicism, Protestantism*

and Capitalism (1935). His thesis was that Catholicism is incompatible with capitalism. I remember reading that book as an undergraduate; it made a deep impression on me. Despite the fact that I was determined then to be a man of the left, it gave me pause.

Fanfani's resistance to capitalism has been common among Catholic intellectuals—lay persons as well as clergy—for several generations. Less approving of Protestantism than even Max Weber was, they embrace Weber's argument all too willingly. Many have been quite happy to dismiss capitalism as a Protestant phenomenon.

Ironically, too, this anticapitalist attitude is fairly common even among Catholics who are, like Fanfani, not only anticommunist and antisocialist, but very much in favor of private property, enterprise, savings, and investment. They would find it hard to imagine an economic system without a market; they oppose a command economy. Despite all this, however, they could never bring themselves to support capitalism. The very word rubs them the wrong way; the connotations it conjures up offend them. While they might hesitate to call themselves "anticapitalist," since to their ear that would sound more ideological than they would like to appear, they certainly reject *something* for which they use the word "capitalism." They would not want to be caught supporting or—God forbid—praising it.

But what is the *something* that they so dislike? Many years ago, in trying to figure that out, I found Fanfani's little classic extremely helpful. And here, exactly, is how Fanfani describes the capitalist spirit:

> In summary . . . the capitalist spirit is that attitude
> adopted by a man towards the problems of wealth, its
> acquisition and use, when he holds that wealth is simply a means for the unlimited, individualistic and utilitarian satisfaction of all possible human needs. A man
> governed by this spirit will, in acquiring wealth,
> choose the most effectual means among such as are
> lawful, and will use them without any anxiety to keep
> the result within certain limits. In the use of wealth he
> will seek individualistic enjoyment; to the acquisition
> and enjoyment of goods he will recognize one limit
> only—hedonistic satiety.[1]

Fanfani himself senses that this description is but an intellectual construct. A little later he writes:

> To some it may seem as if what we have defined as
> the spirit of capitalism were an imaginary category,
> since no agent in the capitalistic world of to-day
> would now dream of justifying his mode of action by
> similiar arguments.[2]

To this objection he replies with a quote from Max Weber, to the effect that today the Weltanschauung is such that (among those in business), "the man who, in the actions of his life, does not adapt himself to the conditions indispensable to success under the capitalistic system, is left behind or goes under." But this is not convincing. To succeed in business in the United States it is by no means necessary to adopt the so-called capitalist spirit defined above by Fanfani. On the contrary: Many in commerce and industry *do not* in fact apply themselves to their work in the fanatical spirit Fanfani describes. And such persons are by no means "left behind," nor do they "go under." The real existing capitalist economy functions quite well, independent of the extremist spirit defined by Fanfani.

FANFANI'S ITALY

When I was an undergraduate, Fanfani, Alcide de Gasperi, Luigi Sturzo, Guido Gonella, and other founders of Christian Democracy in Italy (as well as their counterparts in France, Germany, and Latin America) were heroes of mine.[3] They were awakening European Catholicism from its social slumbers. They were imagining a new social order based upon the activities of the Catholic laity in the world of economics and politics. Still, Fanfani's thesis even then seemed too stark. Capitalism may go well enough with Protestantism, he suggested (like many Italians of his education he thought of the Protestant spirit as foreign, arid, insufficiently humanistic). I thought that Fanfani too little understood the world beyond the European continent, and particularly the United States and Great Britain. His image of capitalism—remarkably Mediterranean—seemed remote from my own experience. He forced me to confront quite early in my life the extent to which the

concrete world of Anglo–American experience is different from
that of Latin Catholicism.

I lived in Rome during 1956–58, just after graduation from
college, and fell in love with Fanfani's Italy—with the brilliant
sunlight, the ruins of the Forum, the tiny hilltop villages, the
ancient towers and fortresses, the wines of Orvieto and Frascati,
and (for me) an entirely new world of *pasta, calamari,* and *pros-
ciutto e melone*. Italy was then a predominantly agricultural land,
with quite turbulent and fascinating political and economic traditions. I followed the Christian Democratic Party in Italy as best
I could, observed the theory and practice of the organizations of
"Catholic Action," listened to the Communists and Socialists. In
those days, as a seminarian, I wore a cassock. In Trastevere—just
outside the walls of the Vatican—little children once or twice spat
at me and playfully called me "cockroach." The anticlericalism in
the air was very different from what I had known in America.

One part of Fanfani's thesis especially troubled me. His claim
that capitalism is closer in spirit to Protestantism than to Catholicism did not speak altogether well for Catholic nations, whose
records both in democratic institutions and in economic development seemed oddly inferior to those of Protestant (or, as I
preferred, "pluralist") nations. Perhaps Fanfani was wrong about
capitalism; if so, his errors would be damaging both to poor nations and to Catholic social action. However admirable might be
the stress of the Christian Democrats on democracy, their failure
to grasp the nature of the free economy would impede economic
development in Latin Europe and Latin America, and in the end
undercut democracy.

European writers sometimes seem to pay too much attention
to abstract theory in their speculations, while overlooking the
lived, commonsense world of actual experience—which often is
quite different from theory. This tendency became very clear in
the "Americanist" controversy at the turn of the century, in which
some Europeans tried to render the American experience in caricatures which falsified the lived reality. And Rome condemned
the caricature.[4] What if Fanfani had similarly misdiagnosed the
lived reality of capitalism?

This early intuition became stronger in me as I watched the
titanic struggle of the American Jesuit John Courtney Murray to
articulate the lived experience of religious liberty in the United
States, in the very teeth of an abstract Roman "thesis" of official

unity between church and state. During my college and graduate years Murray's writings were under a cloud, and he was silenced—but the argument went on around him.

Murray's struggle and my disquiet with Fanfani's inquiry into the "spirit" of capitalism led me, eventually, to my own inquiry into the lived reality of the American political economy, which I called *The Spirit of Democratic Capitalism*.[5] I linked my researches on this subject to the tradition of Christian Democracy as expressed in the work of Jacques Maritain, having done so first in a paper delivered, happily enough, in Italy.[6]

Fanfani's work helped me in two respects—one negative, one positive. Positively, he helped me to interpret capitalism from a *Catholic* point of view, looking rather less at the individual than at the many communities of daily life (families, religious traditions, ethnic groups, and local associations). Negatively, Fanfani's work put me on guard against the classic Catholic *mis*interpretations of capitalism. For one thing, Fanfani overemphasized the role of the individual in Protestant experience, as even Protestant thinkers are sometimes wont to do, underemphasizing Protestantism's strong associative and social aspects. Protestant cultures are not notably lacking in immense capacity for association, a respect for law and common orderliness; nor are Catholic cultures, including Italy and Spain (and even France), notably bereft of strong expressions of rampant individualism, social divisiveness, resistance to law (as if it were an impediment to liberty), and a certain contempt for pragmatic cooperation across ideological lines. Observation taught me that some Latin cultures are in some respects more given to individual will, self-assertion, and pure self-interest apart from a sense of the common good than are some Protestant cultures. In short, things are not always as books and abstract theories portray them. Fanfani gave a caricature of the capitalist spirit. Simultaneously, he idealized certain aspects of Catholic doctrine whose lived reality, in Italy at least, was in fact not like the ideal.

In particular Fanfani, like Max Weber before him, tried to grasp the spirit of capitalism without seeing it as an aspect of *political* economy. That is, he tried to abstract the economic system from its lived incarnation within the political system of democracy, as well as within cultures that highly value common law, the principle of association, and social cooperation. This abstraction enabled him to treat the capitalist spirit in a denuded way, quite false to its lived reality. To argue, as he does, that the capitalist spirit

sees material wealth, and only material wealth, as the highest aim
of humankind; that the capitalist self is entirely atomic and individualistic; and that self-interest is limited to strictly monetary
measures, is to remain far outside the lived reality of Christian,
Jewish, and humanistic life within such nations as the United
States.[7] Not to mention how far it is, even, from a clear understanding of Adam Smith's ideal of "sympathy."[8]

MEAN, PETTY, SELFISH, AND MATERIALISTIC

One plausible rejoinder from Fanfani blocked my way for some
time: One *can* point to authors such as Ayn Rand. There does
indeed seem to be an antithesis between the frank atheism and
egoistic individualism of Ayn Rand and the Catholic spirit.[9] But
Ayn Rand by no means speaks for the capitalist spirit. In a pluralistic culture hers is but one voice. Hers is not the voice of Adam
Smith, John Stuart Mill, Abraham Lincoln (whose words on "the
just and prosperous system" of "free labor" are too often
neglected[10]), Frank Knight, Wilhelm Roepke, or even such severe
libertarians but large-minded reformers as Milton Friedman.

A similar rebuttal from Fanfani also blocked my way for a
time. If one picks up almost any textbook in economics today,
one will likely find an abstract view of markets, individual interests
calculated in strictly monetary ways, and "laws" and statistical
aggregates directed solely to economic factors apart from political,
moral, and cultural considerations. But the authors of these textbooks not only admit this; they call attention to it. They know
that economics, as an autonomous science, abstracts from the thick
reality of concrete life. But so does theology. Does anyone think
that in the *Summa Theologica* of St. Thomas Aquinas (or in the
theological textbooks we used at the Gregorian University in Rome
circa 1956–58) one will find accurate, concrete accounts of actual
Christian life in the thirteenth (or twentieth) century in Italy?
Sciences are constituted by their formal, necessarily abstract perspective, and by studiously neutral and exact terminology. By
contrast, the knowledge practiced by a confessor and counselor
of souls or by a businessman, statesman, and man of affairs is of
a substantially different order. To exercise scientific knowledge in
the real world is a practical art which requires attention to partic-

ular and contingent matters quite beyond the scope of scientific abstraction.

Thus there are two habits of economics—a scientific one, and a prudential one. The former is practiced by academics, the second by persons of all walks of life living in the real world. There is also a distinction within academic economics itself—between positive (formal models) and normative (political economy). Again, this is not unlike the distinction between speculative and practical theology—"I would rather feel compunction than know how to define it," writes the author of *The Imitation of Christ*. Many persons who do not know the science of economics are amazingly good at the arts of economic activism. Thus one does not go to academic economics in order to glimpse the spirit of capitalism; one goes to economic activists and practitioners, to entrepreneurs and shopkeepers, to inventors and creators of new goods and services. The spirit of capitalism is a practical spirit.

To read Fanfani on the spirit of capitalism is to learn that its principles are mean, petty, selfish, materialistic, narrow, grasping. In this light, he denigrates even its admitted virtues, such as self-denial, abstention from consumption, and moral discipline. If this were all there is, one would hardly expect capitalist nations to produce so many artists, visionaries, pioneers, and creators in every field. One would scarcely expect such unprecedented outpourings of public philanthropy and so many voluntary, public-spirited campaigns (against tuberculosis, to "save the whales," the Red Cross, and all the rest). Nor would one expect so much risk-taking and the itch to chance everything on opening new frontiers. One would not even expect the honesty, candor, and courtesy that one typically encounters among Anglo–American peoples. In fact, the capitalist spirit is creative, open, spontaneous, cooperative, and liberal in the sense of being innovative, generous, and experimental. Fanfani describes the capitalist as if he were a tight-fisted Scrooge, a miser, a possessive, crotchety, and asocial individual.

In fact, precisely during the age of capitalism the miser began to *disappear* from literature. When there are new horizons for creative investment and when reward is commensurate with imagination and risk, to hoard is not simply evil—it is also foolish. Considering the daring and unprecedented creativity of capitalism in building up the continent of North America (especially when compared to the Catholic systems in Latin America during the same period),[11] would it not be more just to describe the spirit of capitalism as bold, extroverted, imaginative, and venturesome? For capitalism engenders in its own fashion much the same romantic zest for exploration and risk as that associated with the Catholic Baroque culture of Latin Europe. The quiet difference is that the former was rather more free of state control, and regarded wealth less as a matter of *taking* than of creating. Capitalists value not only industry but imagination as well.

The truth is, of course, that there are at least *two* different spirits of capitalism. First, there is the transformation that Max Weber experienced in his own family. One generation was relaxed, easygoing, content to make a good living; the next began to seek out more efficient, more imaginative, and more profitable methods of operation. In that transition mercantilism passed over into capitalism. On the whole, this new spirit of capitalism remained within the orbit of cautious prudence. The family firm did not so much invent new goods or services; its aim was to create greater wealth through innovative and rationalized methods of operation. Its novel idea was that the sustained application of creative intellect could produce greater wealth. This new spirit is typically embodied, for example, in the family businesses of Europe specializing in such diverse products as fine wines, cheeses, breads, lace, and millinery. Contrary to the romantic critique, this bourgeois spirit often exhibits classical standards and a high sense of excellence and reliability.

But the still more daring and bold spirit of capitalism, properly so-called, is not that of the innovative shopkeeper and enterprising family producer (a new spirit different enough from what went before), but that of the inventor of new goods and services. It is no accident that the age of invention coincides with the birth of capitalism. By embedding into law the concept of patents and copyrights, which recognized original ideas as a form of intellectual property, capitalist societies forged a practical nexus between science and commerce. More swiftly than in any earlier era, ideas were quickly placed in practical service, to the improvement of daily life. This second spirit of capitalism may be called the spirit of invention. It is adventurous and pioneering. Its ideal is innovation in both goods and services.

In classical Europe a noble regard for goods valued for themselves, with no further utility, was thought to show true virtue. To practice the liberal arts—to contemplate beauty—was regarded as purer virtue than working for a living or engaging in other such "servile" labor; aristocrats of the spirit should not appear to sweat. By contrast, work for a purpose, pragmatic work on things merely useful (*utile*) to society, was regarded as inferior. In the United States, as Tocqueville noted,[12] but also in Great Britain (and, later, in Germany and Sweden), serious people began to contemplate the useful as a highly regarded service to their fellow humans. They began to think of being practical and of making useful improvements as virtues in their own right, and not inferior virtues either.

In this context, the spirit of capitalism came to seem to many exciting, romantic, almost esthetic. As Oscar Handlin notes, the romance of spanning the whole continent of North America by a functioning railroad, even across vast stretches where paying customers were few, destroyed the fortunes of many a romantic dreamer, while virtually all who built railroads North–South, in more secure and limited confines, prospered.[13] A man could dream of building new cities, creating whole new industries, achieving great things never even imagined before. From such dreams, there came in time to be ironclad steam-driven ocean vessels, self-propelled carriages, telephones, airplanes, television, computers. The spirit of capitalism came thus to be linked to the spirit of invention and creativity.

To believe that all the motivations of great industrialists and commercial pioneers were monetary, self-regarding, and materialistic is to fall prey to the very materialism Fanfani wishes justifiably to excoriate. Such industrial and commercial pioneers often took great pleasure in their creativity; they regarded themselves as artists, prided themselves on their intuitions and hunches, and gloried in the beauty of many of the things they produced. This was true not only of the first movie moguls and the founders of great newspapers, but also of those who built new factories—or whole new industries—and skyscrapers, and airplanes, and so on. These romantics had the misfortune, however, to enter upon the world's stage at a moment when many European intellectuals were preaching pernicious doctrines quite hostile to the actual capitalist spirit. Four of these must be delineated—and will be, after a word of explanation to establish their context.

During the nineteenth century the new business class supplanted the power of the old aristocracy that for centuries had supplied patronage for intellectuals. This new business class, in

Europe as in America, became anathema to the rising intellectual class of artists, journalists, professors, literary personages, and the like who derided the *nouveaux riches*, and especially the vulgar Americans. Marx wrote of "class struggle" between proletarians and the bourgeoisie; even more significant may have been the class struggle between the intellectuals and the business class. Matthew Arnold writing about "philistines," Max Weber about the "iron cage," Marx about "the cash nexus," Upton Sinclair about "the jungle," and Fanfani about the irrationality of infinite growth— all these and many others traded caricatures about an entire class of fellow citizens they scarcely knew, roundly despised, and felt not so obscurely threatened by.

The century between 1850 and the recent present was not, in this respect, the intellectuals' finest hour. Many of them were taken in by the preposterous claims of socialist economics because they already believed in their hearts a caricature of capitalism, a caricature which rested on such unexamined doctrines as the following:

1. *Materialism.* Positivist philosophers were saying that only material causes count, even as inventors were demonstrating that creative *ideas*, not labor, are the greatest sources of wealth. The "labor theory of value" (first in Ricardo and later in Marx) was an intellectual error of monstrous proportions. The intellectual breakthrough represented by the steam engine alone should have demonstrated the point. But intellectuals, oddly, were mesmerized more by the noise and grease of the locomotive and the rigidity of steel rails than by the spiritual genius and creative imagination that gave birth to their possibility.

2. *Darwinism.* Just as Darwinism taught those of little (and therefore dangerous) learning that the fundamental process of natural evolution is "the survival of the fittest," capitalist economies were prompting inventions and improvements that systematically came to the assistance of the neediest: eyeglasses for those of weak eyesight, lamps for those in darkness, new medicines for the ill, mechanical aids to replace brute human strength, and ever-greater ease of transport. Life became softer, even as intellectuals described it in terms of the jungle. The spirit of capitalism may in fact be portrayed more accurately as leading to excessive comfort than as reincarnating the law of survival. Moreover, the clamor of the intellectuals for reform more often than not met with success, just

as most of the readers of their books, and theatergoers attending their satirical lampoons, came (as they did themselves) from the ranks of the bourgeoisie they affected to despise. Many businessmen, it is true, did have recourse to vulgar Darwinism ("It's a jungle out there"), but that association falsified, and so did not reveal, the entire spirit of capitalism.

3. *Individualism.* Undeniably, both in its bourgeois spirit of excellence and in its "animal spirits" a market system gives rein to the creative individual. Historians properly link "the Age of the Individual" to both Protestantism and capitalism. Just the same, one must not be simpleminded about such pat schemes. It is true that, from the Renaissance on, Europe discovered the glory of the individual as never before. The even older tradition of the "freehold" in England liberated former serfs and made individuals owners—that is, sovereigns of their own estates.[14] The historical emergence of personal dignity was beautifully treated by Jacques Maritain with respect to the arts in *Creative Intuition in Art and Poetry*, and with respect to politics in *The Person and the Common Good*.[15] But its very novelty blinded intellectuals to the simultaneous emergence of new forms of community. Ernst Troeltsch and Tönnies, of course, noted the historic gravitational shift from *Gemeinschaft* to *Gesellschaft*.[16] But I do not think *anyone* has grasped clearly enough the spiritual ideal behind the new forms of voluntary association—the new communitarian ideal—involved in liberal societies.[17]

The most distinctive invention of the spirit of capitalism is not the individual as much as it is many individuals joining together in creative enterprise. It is, for example, the joint stock company, the corporation; or again, the credit union, as well as insurance funds and pension funds; and finally, the market itself, considered as a social mechanism obliging all who participate in it to practice a sensible regard for others. Correlatively, political life and moral–cultural life in liberal societies also catalyze an explosion of voluntary associations. Not only are business enterprises incorporated; so also are political parties, foundations, church groups, beneficial societies, artists' unions, and many other forms of social organization.

Life in liberal societies is far from being as individualistic and atomic as many liberal, utilitarian theories are. In actual practice, such societies exhibit the most highly and complexly organized forms of life in all of human history. To be sure, their vital principle is no longer merely birth, kinship, and other involuntary "organic" ties such as had been the chief forms of social unity in the past. The new principle is that of covenant, compact, and voluntary participation. This new social principle cannot fairly be said to be either unevangelical or unbiblical. On the contrary, especially among the early American divines and their forebears in England and the Netherlands, those who first articulated its principles were deeply persuaded of its biblical basis.[18]

Some say that today these voluntary associations are fraying. But is "excessive individualism" the cause of this fraying, as some charge, or a disregard by urban planners and builders (big businesses and government) for small, organic neighborhoods, parishes, and families? Were sheer individualism the culprit, wouldn't we see a greater sense of personal responsibility, self-control, and accountability? Instead, the individual with strong inner self-guidance appears to be disappearing. In our cities, growing thousands seem unable to cope with such elementary responsibilities as learning how to read, completing their (free) schooling, staying off drugs, and waiting for marriage before having children. In the loss of a sense of individual responsibility the plight of many today seems to be worse than before the emergence of the welfare state. Rather than an excess of emphasis on individual responsibility, a false sense of community, anchored in the state, seems the worse affliction of advanced societies.

In practice, capitalist nations have been exceedingly open to arguments for the welfare state (even incautiously so) because they in fact live by an ethos of interdependence and social bonding. The very experience of "the global village" grew from the telegraph, telephone, television, computer, airline, and fiber-optic industries, which supplied its technological base. Closer at hand, most capitalist activities are associative, not individualistic. Hardly any business enterprise can be conducted by one individual alone; and, of course, *none* can succeed in isolation. Business activities are inherently relational. Trust is at the core of voluntary activities, and habits of mutual regard are normal among fellow workers.

Much more could be said about all these points. The attribution of radical, atomic individualism to capitalism *as a lived reality* is much too simplistic. Going to meetings and taking part in evening activities are capitalist passions. Indeed, one eminently social fruit of the capitalist spirit is the creation of new wealth sufficient to maintain a large universe of not-for-profit organizations and voluntary associations. Capitalist parents bring up their children to take part in more activities than one parent alone can drive them to. Marriage sometimes seems to be, essentially, a transportation service.

4. *Limits and the unlimited.*   Fanfani writes that in the pre-capitalist period the unlimited enrichment of the individual was held to be unlawful. Thus, he holds, a desire for personal enrichment was morally senseless, since each person was thought to have a strictly limited number of needs, these to be satisfied in the measure demanded by his station in life.[19] Maybe. But it is truly difficult for a tourist in France, Italy, or Germany to believe that the vast wealth ostentatiously displayed in the palaces, castles, and residences of European aristocracy in the precapitalist era exhibits "a strictly limited number of needs" or is as morally noble as Fanfani here suggests. While the Stoic principle of sufficiency is no doubt part of the substratum of European Catholic thought on which Fanfani here draws, Adam Smith's insight into "the nature and the causes of the wealth of nations," which in 1776 opened up new horizons of social possibility, did not of itself (as Max Weber saw) negate Stoic—or even Puritan—restraint.

In a world with very little economic growth, a desire for greater personal wealth was regarded as a dangerous *cupiditas*, tempting its subject to corruption, threatening the existing social order, and taking from others their "rightful" share. From this earlier understanding of the world as a narrowly limited zero-sum game, first America and then all humanity began to glimpse the new possibility of economic development. Only much later, in 1971, was this new vision adopted by Pope Paul VI as a Catholic imperative: "Development is the new name for peace."[20] Smith's subject, like the Pope's, was the wealth of nations, not the wealth of individuals. After only a 200-year effort, it is still far too early to set limits on the rise of the world's poor. Fanfani fails to grasp this social dimension, too, of the capitalist vision. His time horizon (in 1935) was far too short.

WEALTH IS A MEANS, NOT AN END

Finally, Fanfani's main confusion lies in failing to note the equivocations hidden in the word he makes central: "unlimited," as in "the unlimited pursuit of wealth." In precapitalist ages, he holds, moralists had to discriminate not only between lawful and unlawful means (as do capitalists) but also between "lawful and unlawful *intensity* in the use of lawful means."[21] Fanfani argues that the capitalist, precisely *qua* capitalist, cannot make such a discrimination; his unlimited concentration is, and can only be, upon the *single* moral criterion of producing wealth without limits. But in the real world this is absurd. The capitalist is also a human being. To imagine someone so utterly fixated upon producing wealth, and that alone, is not to imagine the ideal sketched by Adam Smith, John Stuart Mill, Paul Samuelson, Milton Friedman, or any other exponent of a capitalist ethic.[22] Even Max Weber, as we have seen, took pains to show how, more than earlier systems, capitalism of its own nature restrains greed.[23] Fanfani's abstract conception of the capitalist is a figment of thought; if any person in concrete life lived out such a conception, he or she would speedily be branded, even by his or her peers, a fanatic. Indeed, if anyone violated the law in pursuit of such illicit passion, that person would be put in jail—like Ivan Boesky. Fanaticism surely exists. Indeed, religion too has known (and suffered from) its own fanatics. But to define the spirit of Catholicism—or of capitalism—by its fanatical exhibitions would simply be unjust.

There is an important difference, furthermore, between these two views: that human ambitions may run *beyond* every limit, and that the future is not limited by the present, but *open*. "Unlimited," then, may refer either to a (foolish) refusal to accept the limits of being human or, in a quite different and more fruitful way, to a realistic awareness of the indeterminacy of the future. The former is an aberration; the latter, a healthy and creative realism. As for "intensity" in the pursuit of lawful means, one may agree with Fanfani that the precapitalist era was less striving, more relaxed, more tolerant of limits and oppression of every sort, whereas the liberal spirit constantly discerns new possibilities that are worth urgent and sustained striving. The capitalist spirit *is* more intense than the tradition-cherishing preliberal spirit. One speaks, indeed, of an "awakening" on all continents today—a new energy. Is this to be despised? It is certainly not so foreign to Catholicism as Fanfani seems to suggest. It is in fact implicit in all notions of humane economic development.

Fanfani's tendency to caricature capitalism is most nakedly visible in his chapter "Catholicism and Capitalism." His account of the social ethics and moral ideals of Catholicism up to 1935 is, on the whole, a moving one. It fails to show, however, that a serious Catholic could not fulfill Catholic morality to its fullest within the context of a liberal society. Fanfani seems to forget that such a society is *pluralist*: Many diverse persons and diverse communities help to shape it and to bring to it their own convictions, finding ample space within it to create realities suffused with their own vision. Instead, he imagines that a person of pure capitalist spirit (as if there were such) must necessarily be antireligious, antisupernatural, and at heart amoral.

Fanfani pictures the capitalist spirit as absolutist, totalistic, pervading the whole of a person's being. And, given the definition he ascribes to such a spirit, such a capitalist person—driven and materialistic—*would indeed* be a deformed and pitiable creature. In reality, no doubt, there *are* some such. One would however expect to encounter rather more of them on the Continent (especially in highly atheistic, laicist, and secularist circles, wherein Comtian positivism has created an almost total spiritual vacuum). Anglo–American culture seems far less hostile to religion, rather more philanthropic, and not nearly so positivistic.

"Capitalism," Fanfani writes, "has one principle: individual economic utility."[24] This would seem to imply that it cherishes no art, no philanthropy, no public-spiritedness, no sense of citizenship, no morals, no larger vision, no romance, no care for personal or humane company and social relations, no ideals, no sense of service to one's fellow human beings. Such a monstrous abstraction, were it true, would create figures fit only for ridicule, and could not possibly win the allegiance of the human spirit. But *is* it true—true to the millions of persons of industry and commerce who fill our churches and synagogues, build our art galleries, engage in so many fields of human service, and try to infuse their daily work with Jewish and Christian ideals? Such ideals are not, in the Catholic scheme, as antihumanistic or antinatural as some of the Puritan attitudes abstractly described by Max Weber seem to be. They are generous ideals, which spring from the generosity of the Creator himself. *Bonum est diffusivum sibi*: "The mark of goodness is to diffuse itself outward" (as, hearing a good story, we can hardly wait to share it with others).

Fanfani imagines capitalism as a closed system, an end rather than a means. Surely, most of us who find liberal societies, on the whole and with all their faults, humane and decent, do not regard the economic part of our lives as an end in itself; or the imperatives of our economic system, loose as they are, as "closed." (It must not be forgotten that approximately a third of all employed persons in the United States work in the nonprofit, educational, governmental, and other noncommercial, nonindustrial parts of the economy. And that the effort and initiative of the risk-taking capitalist creates the wealth that enables the nonprofit sector to thrive.)

Fanfani writes:

> To discover a principle on which to base criticism of a system like that of capitalism within that system is impossible. Criticism can only come from another order of ideas, from a system that would direct social activity towards non-capitalistic ends. This Catholicism does when its social ethics demand that ends must converge in a definitely non-capitalistic direction. Not that Catholicism rejects economic rationalization, or that it wishes this to be brought about by principles foreign to the economic order, but it holds that such rationalization should be bounded by the other principles that order life.[25]

Catholicism is not alone in regarding economic life as a means, as secondary, to a fully human life; so also Protestantism, Judaism, and humanism—and so also Adam Smith, Abraham Lincoln, John Stuart Mill, and many others.

Fanfani's short book of 1935 is a *locus classicus* of anticapitalist sentiment among Catholic intellectuals. It helps to explain why Catholic nations were long retarded in encouraging development, invention, savings, investment, entrepreneurship, and, in general, economic dynamism. In the name of Catholic ideals, this anticapitalist spirit is blind to its own prejudices. It doesn't grasp the great differences between the Continental world and the Anglo–American world. It fails to state correctly the capitalist ideal. It fails also to see some of the faults and underdeveloped parts in Catholic social thought circa 1935.

There is much of value in Fanfani's book. It helps us to reflect on some of the changes that have entered the world since the invention of a dynamic, developing economy. Had Fanfani lived in a democratic, pluralistic, and capitalist society during his youth, he would almost certainly have recognized the remoteness of his own descriptions of the capitalist spirit. One says this with some confidence, if only because a thinker considerably admired by

Fanfani, Jacques Maritain, had such an experience in the United States during and after World War II, and came to see how abstract and inadequate his own earlier ideas had been.[26]

Maritain discovered that the processes of democracy in the political order *do* modify the processes of capitalism in the economic order, by bringing to bear the will of the majority for reform.[27] Further, a Jewish and Christian culture, not to mention a generous Anglo–American humanism, also modifies the actual practices of capitalism, by directing it to humane ideals, setting limits to what is permitted, and suffusing both collaborative work and individual initiative with moral and religious significance. The concrete reality of such a threefold system of political economy is quite different from Fanfani's abstract conception of its economic system alone.

THE CATHOLIC SPIRIT SLOWLY AWAKENS

In Pope John Paul II's *Laborem Exercens* (1981), a distinction is drawn between "early" and "reformed" capitalism. There is much evidence, however, that even the early capitalism of the pre–World War II era, for all its faults and injustices, was never so bleak for ordinary people, nor so detached from Jewish–Christian inspiration, as the conventional wisdom of anticapitalist intellectuals suggests.[28] The bulk of this evidence lies in the actual improvements in the conditions of daily life wrought by the new order of political economy. There was much suffering and poverty among the early urban poor who had flocked to industrial centers, but there were also—and for the first time—newspapers and widely distributed books to chronicle this suffering, and an ample supply of "bourgeois" sentiment and compassion to appeal to for its amelioration. By contrast, in precapitalist periods there had not been nearly as many chronicles of the sufferings of the poor in *rural* settings— as more recently described, for example, in Carlo Levi's *Christ Stopped at Eboli*. It is the glory of capitalism that during the past century it did, in fact, beneficently transform the conditions of life for the vast majority of both Europeans and Americans.

In fact, anyone who visited Italy in the 1930s or 1940s, and revisited the same rural areas some 50 years later, could detect this transformation vividly. The narrow, winding roads of yore, often blocked by sheep or oxen, have been replaced by valley-arching *autostrada* as impressive as the ancient aqueducts. Shiny new automobiles are everywhere. The prosperity of the hilltop cities positively glistens. Italy is alive with entrepreneurship. And today contemporary appeals go out daily to the newly affluent (who were themselves, and within living familial memory, among the desperately poor) that they should come to the assistance of those in the Third World who have as yet shared only a few of the benefits of similar economic progress.

Indeed, there is undeniable irony in the fact that the Catholic spirit, over many centuries, did far less to lift the tyrannies and oppression of the preliberal era than did the capitalist spirit in which Fanfani detects only moral inferiority.

There is a second irony. Fanfani tried so hard in 1935 to sketch the antagonism between the capitalist spirit and the Catholic ethic that he failed to show how the two properly require each other. Better than the Protestant ethic, with its theoretical emphasis on the individual (even though, in practice, itself richly associative), the Catholic ethic brings to light the social dimensions of the free economy. Through its sacramental love for the senses—for incense, holy water, brilliant vestments, the taste of bread and wine, and glorious music—the Catholic spirit is rather more attuned to creation and to the goodness that the Creator himself saw in the world. In these respects, it also expresses better than the ascetic Protestant spirit the creative, healing, humanly beneficial aspects of liberal societies. There is a tendency in Protestant thought (and in some forms of Catholic Jansenism) to stress crisis, sin, brokenness; to prefer plainness and lack of sensory stimulation. A desert, a wasteland, Pilgrim's Slough of Despond—all these are more acutely attuned to a Protestant sense of the lostness of this world, apart from Christ. Both Judaism and Catholicism offer a readier tongue, a larger stock of similes, for expressing joy, delight in the senses, and the sheer fulfillment involved in creativity. Important facets of capitalism—its sociality, its creativity—are scarcely brought to consciousness by the Protestant ethic.

As I said at the beginning, as a youth I owed a great deal in my own intellectual awakening to Fanfani's attempt to describe the spirit of capitalism. Better than Max Weber or R. H. Tawney, he placed in focus, as an alternative ideal, the Catholic ethic. If I came eventually to see many more lines of intersection between the capitalist spirit and the Catholic ethic, as both are actually lived out in the real world of our time, it is because I have been privileged to learn about their mutuality from the American experiment. These lessons have now been replicated in Italy and in many other places around the world, in a quite amazing diversity of ways. And this adaptability to cultural diversity is indeed yet another of capitalism's unsuspected strengths.[29]

Fanfani was quite correct that the capitalist spirit articulated by Max Weber was inadequate. Yet he himself failed to grasp the largeminded "Christian anthropology" that could bring into a single vision the threefold dynamic of human creativity—in morals (and culture), in politics, and in economics—that now moves the world. The Catholic tradition, in argument with itself, was however already brooding over its dissatisfactions with the existing order, and its longing for something better.

CHAPTER 2

SOCIALISM, NO! CAPITALISM? MAYBE: LEO XIII

WE HAVE SEEN THAT, quite slowly over the past 100 years, under the pressure of real experiences and concrete observations, some faulty theories inherited from the past have been discarded. Experience is always a good teacher, and keeps nudging theories until they hew closer to the truth. The starting place for Catholic social thought 100 years ago was hardly sympathetic to "liberal capitalism." Not long before, Pius IX, in his *Syllabus of Errors* (1864), had expressly rejected reconciliation with liberalism, progress, and modernity. This lack of sympathy lingered until our own time. But a process of self-correction had been and was underway.

Pius IX began his papacy (1846–78) as a liberal, but became embittered by the murders, riots, and other excesses of those in Italy who called themselves liberals. (Causing a riot even during his funeral procession, such "liberals" tried to throw his body into the Tiber.) Then the quiet and scholarly Vincenzo Gioacchino Pecci was elected Pope, at the age of 68, and chose the name Leo XIII. Having learned to love the liberal society from a brief stint in Belgium as a papal diplomat, and having lived more than three decades (1846–78) in virtual exile as bishop of the out-of-the-way diocese of Perugia (he was made cardinal in 1853), Leo XIII surprised many who expected his papacy to be brief and unspectacular.

As Pope, mild of manner as always, frail in body and hardly

expected to live long, Leo was in spirit the lion his name suggested. When one well-wisher early in his pontificate expressed the traditional wish, "May you live a hundred years," the elderly but bright-eyed Leo shot back: "Why set limits to Providence?" He outlived most of his electors, conducting an active and innovative pontificate (1878–1903) that lasted into the new century.

Leo XIII regretted the isolation into which Pius IX had pushed the Church by his hostility to the world of his time (for all its faults, the world of the nineteenth century was surely *not* at the nadir of European history). And he determined to chart a new course. He took as his master, and recommended as teacher par excellence for the whole Church, that "first Whig" (as both Lord Acton and Friedrich von Hayek have designated him), St. Thomas Aquinas, who more than any other championed a synthesis of faith and reason, grace and nature, Christianity and humanism. And in 1891 he issued the letter to the whole world,[1] *Rerum Novarum*, the first text of modern papal social thought, the magna carta of the Catholic vision of "the reconstruction of the social order." That document, although not without faults, turned out to be prophetic.

In announcing a conference in 1991 to mark the centenary of *Rerum Novarum*, a brochure from St. Edmund's College in Cambridge, England, could speak of "Four Revolutions": the industrial revolution, the liberal–capitalist revolution, the socialist revolution, and a yet-to-be-seen "Christian transformation of society." The same brochure contained the following description of the present situation:

> In the century since [1891], capitalism seemed to go into decline, while socialism was in the ascendancy. In the last 20 years, however, capitalism has regrouped and risen again; now Marxism and socialism seem to be in decline.[2]

This thumbnail sketch of recent history raises certain serious questions.

First, why did Marxism and socialism fail?

Correlatively, as the American exponent of Marxist thought, Robert Heilbroner, recently asked,[3] why did so few intellectuals or academics, particularly of the center and the left, predict this failure? On these points, much can be learned today from those who have lived under Marxist and socialist systems. Their accounts stunningly confirm the predictions made by Leo XIII in 1891.

Second, where did the "liberal–capitalist revolution" find the capacity to renew itself? Part of the answer may lie in the marriage of capitalism to a democratic political system, and part may lie in its openness to the religious and humanistic ideals, aspirations, and habits of a Jewish and a Christian people. Scholars need to explore further the openness of capitalism to change, since the dictionary definitions of capitalism, like the descriptions made of it by its ideological opponents, seem oddly wide of the mark.

Third, supposing that, as the most practical and liberating social ideal, most of the human race will now be "stuck" with the capitalist model for the foreseeable future, how can these capitalistic societies be brought into closer accord with Jewish, Christian, and humanistic visions of the good life?

Each of these three questions must be faced squarely if we are to develop a practical Christian ethic of capitalism for the grievous problems that await us at every turn—problems of poverty, problems of ethnicity (nationalism) and race, and the special problems of a culture of liberty. These eminently practical problems will be addressed more fully at the end of this inquiry. We need to look first to Leo XIII's analysis of similar problems already on hand before the twentieth century began.

WHY DID SOCIALISM FAIL?

The life of Vincenzo Gioacchino Pecci (1810–1903) spanned not only almost all of the nineteenth century, but the start of the twentieth too. Born of a family of the lower nobility in the village of Carpeneto, this tall man of aristocratic bearing went for the most part unnoticed between 1846 and 1878 as the humble bishop of Perugia. Although made a cardinal in 1853, he was hardly a favorite at the Vatican, after revealing that his sympathies during the Roman Revolution of 1848 did not lie with the harsh defenders of the papal states, and for later not strongly resisting the annexation of Umbria by the new Italian state in 1860. However, his long period out of favor with Pius IX gave the learned and energetic bishop—a man accustomed to setbacks and not given to bitterness—plenty of time to study.

Pecci's older brother, a Jesuit seminary professor, encouraged him to plunge forthwith into the writings of St. Thomas Aquinas, a figure long out of favor in Italian seminaries except in adulterated textbook form. The humanism that Fr. Pecci found in Aquinas, as well as the depth and breadth of his vision, confirmed the future bishop in his dissatisfaction with the ecclesiastical status quo, whose word to modernity was: *Anathema*! By 1877, Cardinal Pecci had come to think the Church of the nineteenth century should engage the world of its time as St. Thomas Aquinas had engaged the turbulent world of the thirteenth century, during which Italy was invaded from the north by the German King Frederick II (1194–1250) and from the south by Islamic philosophy. So it happened that the Bishop of Perugia issued a pastoral letter at the beginning of 1877 and again in 1878 recommending a more generous address by Catholics to the world around them.

These pastoral letters drew such notice beyond Italy that at the death of Pius IX in February 1878, the non-Italian cardinals favored a man who had been distant from the politics of Rome— and helped to elect Pecci to the papacy. Determined to reorganize the whole of the Church's intellectual life—from biblical studies to philosophy, from the relations of church and state to "the labor question"—Leo XIII defied predictions, conducted an energetic papacy right into his ninety-third year, and advanced an old literary form for papal teaching addressed to the Church around the whole world: the encyclical. Of these long, doctrinal letters we can linger here on only one, *Rerum Novarum* ("The Spirit of Revolutionary Change," also called "The Condition of Labor"), addressed to the great economic question that, in effect, the United States of America had put to Europe.

As Hannah Arendt points out, the success of the United States in making its poor relatively prosperous had awakened the social conscience of Europe.[4] Long inured to the poverty of the vast majority of its citizens, most of them in rural areas, Europe was slowly shamed by the fact that, in America at least, the poor were with relative speed moving *out of* poverty. Provoked by the new vistas that the Industrial Revolution had opened up, and the vast movement of families from the countryside to the city, a new social ideal—that poverty should no longer be accepted as a norm—swept Europe, not only under the banners of communists and socialists, but also under the impulse of trade unionism and many bourgeois circles of reform. Leo XIII was eager to speak, and in a positive way, to this maelstrom of ideas. He consulted broadly (with the American Cardinal Gibbons of Baltimore, for instance, who urged him to be sympathetic to labor unions, so many of whose leaders and rank-and-file in America were devout Catholics) and sought out knowledgeable experts.

After the reign of Pius IX, it had seemed to many impartial observers (ambassadors from abroad in Rome, for example) that the Catholic Church was at last in its death throes. Following the secularization enforced by the French Revolution, and under the assault of anticlericalism in Italy and Germany, the state of Catholic learning was at one of its lowest ebbs in centuries. Many colleges and seminaries had been taken over by the state, many libraries disbanded. Thus Leo XIII had to make do with what was available. Nonetheless, *Rerum Novarum*, from its first appearance on May 15, 1891, caught the attention of editorialists and parliamentarians throughout the Christian world. It led to many movements for social reform, both in the voluntary and in the state sector. Indeed, in many places it made possible the first organized alternative to socialism.

Joseph Schumpeter (to cite one worthy commentator) paid a great compliment to what he called the "political Catholicism" of *Rerum Novarum*, pointing out that the encyclical reinforced the foundation on which a number of intelligent priests in Germany had created a much-needed political party for Catholic workers (the German Center Party). In other places, for want of such an alternative, the workers had been left naked to the appeal of the socialist parties, into which they were being swept in large numbers. At the end of the nineteenth century, Schumpeter wrote:

> The Catholic Church was on the continent of Europe the object of legislative and administrative attacks from hostile governments and parliaments. . . . What could not have been expected was that these attacks everywhere ended in retreat and that they left the Catholic Church stronger than it had been for centuries. Political Catholicism arose from a renaissance of religious Catholicism. Looking back, we see not merely a reassertion of the Catholic standpoint by people who had never abandoned it; we also see a change of attitudes among people who had; around 1900 it was a common observation to make that in a Catholic family the old and elderly were laicist and liberal and the youngsters,

believers and "clerical." . . . Political Catholicism
from the first stood for social reform.[5]

In any case, Leo XIII opened up *Rerum Novarum* with a
withering set of predictions about Europe's budding socialist
movement. He wrote, for example:

> The *Socialists* . . . in endeavoring to transfer the pos-
> sessions of individuals to the community, strike at the
> interests of every wage earner, for they deprive him of
> the liberty of disposing of his wages, and thus of all
> hope and possibility of increasing his stock and of bet-
> tering his condition in life.
>   What is of still greater importance, however, is
> that the remedy they propose is manifestly against jus-
> tice. For every man has by nature the right to possess
> property as his own. This is one of the *chief points of
> distinction* between man and the animal creation. (#3)

In 1891 the Pope was using the term "socialism" in a very
broad sense, easily understood by ordinary Catholic parishioners
throughout Europe and elsewhere who were being proselytized
by socialist labor unions and parties—sometimes under the name
of socialism, but at other times under the label of communism.[6]
The mixed economies and the welfare state that came into existence
mainly after World War II were as yet nowhere in sight. In *Rerum
Novarum*, Leo XIII listed at least ten reasons why the program
of socialism in the older sense would prove futile—and, a century
later, his words seem to have been remarkably prescient.

At the same time, Pope Leo was sharply critical of many of
the beliefs, customs, and abuses that he observed in the practices
of liberal capitalist nations (then relatively few in number). He
criticized capitalism severely, although not by that name, which
never occurs in the encyclical. His approach to socialism was not
at all symmetrical to his criticism of capitalism. He did not criticize
socialism or recommend its reform; he condemned it. He condemned it because it is against natural justice, against nature,
against liberty, and against common sense. In order to get beyond
the liberalism of the day and to reconstruct the social order, the
Pope judged it especially necessary to distinguish his own ideal of
a reconstructed order from that of the socialists.

Among the good factors in capitalist and precapitalist societies that Leo XIII judged to be violated by socialism were three principles: private property, personal initiative, and natural inequality. On *private property*, the Pope writes: "Nature confers on man the right to possess things privately as his own."[7] And he adds: "In seeking help for the masses this principle before all is to be considered as basic, namely, that private ownership must be preserved inviolate."[8] Further: "To own goods privately is a right natural to man, and to exercise this right, especially in life in society, is not only lawful but clearly necessary."[9]

On *personal initiative*, *Rerum Novarum* supplies these texts: "Clearly the essential reason why those who engage in any gainful occupation undertake labor, and at the same time the end to which workers immediately look, is to procure property for themselves and to retain it by individual right as theirs and as their very own."[10] "Would justice permit anyone to own and enjoy that upon which another has toiled? As effects follow the cause producing them, so it is just that the fruit of labor belongs precisely to those who have performed the labor."[11] "If incentives to ingenuity and skill in individual persons were to be abolished, the very fountains of wealth would necessarily dry up; and the equality conjured up by the socialist imagination would, in reality, be nothing but uniform wretchedness and meanness for one and all, without distinction."[12]

Concerning *natural inequality*, Leo XIII concludes succinctly:

> Therefore, let it be laid down in the first place that in civil society the lowest cannot be made equal with the highest. Socialists, of course, agitate the contrary, but all struggling against nature is in vain. There are truly very great and very many natural differences among men. Neither the talents, nor the skill, nor the health, nor the capacities of all are the same, and unequal fortune follows of itself upon necessary inequality in respect to these endowments. And clearly this condition of things is adapted to benefit both individuals and the community; for to carry on its affairs community life requires varied aptitudes and diverse services, and to perform these diverse services men are impelled most by differences in individual property holdings.[13]

To which he later adds: "While justice does not oppose our striving for better things, it does forbid anyone to take from another what is his and, in the name of a certain absurd equality, to seize forcibly the property of others; nor does the interest of the common good permit this."[14]

Before rushing onward, the reader should note how often the words "right," "rights," and "natural right" occur in these texts. In the premodern, Thomistic foundation of Catholic thought, the word "right" (*ius*) does not have the same meaning that modern thought after Hobbes and Locke has given it. In the modern sense, rights are universal; in the ancient sense, they may accrue to a person in a certain office or station. In the modern sense, absolute rights are invoked apart from virtues practiced or duties met, whereas in the ancient sense rights cannot so easily be pulled out from a much larger moral tissue and texture. Yet here Pope Leo XIII appears to be straddling both traditions, medieval and modern. We shall return to this question.

In any case, although Leo XIII's charges against socialism form a pretty devastating list, it is not hard to match them against the charges leveled by those who have lived under socialism for the last several decades. Kevin Acker has compiled a list of such testimony[15] from which we glean the following:

> Several German intellectuals and politicians had hard words for the fellow citizens who flung themselves on the West German shops as soon as they could. . . . These could only be the words of people who have forgotten, or never knew, the personal humiliation inflicted by the permanent lack of the most elementary consumer goods: the humiliation of silent and hostile lines, the humiliation inflicted upon you by sales people who seem angry to see you standing there, the humiliation of always having to buy what there is, not what you need. The systematic penury of material goods strikes a blow at the moral dignity of the individual. (Bulgaria)[16]

> For 50 years it was said that this was public property and belonged to everyone, but no way was ever found to make workers feel they were the co-owners and masters of the factories, farms and enterprises. They

felt themselves to be cogs in a gigantic machine. (USSR)[17]

We cannot talk of freedom unless we have private property. (USSR)[18]

We categorically favor the concept of private initiative. The economic foundation of totalitarianism has been the absolute power derived from the monopoly on property. We shall never have political pluralism without economic pluralism. But some of those who still have Communist leanings try to equate private initiative with 'exploitation' and maintain that the emergence of rich entrepreneurs would be a catastrophe. In the same way they try to play on the feelings of those who are lazy and would therefore envy the wealthy, and those who—having once enjoyed the privileges of the Communist system—are afraid of the effort of working. (Romania)[19]

The totalitarian system has a special bacterial property. The system is strong not only in its repressive police methods, but, more, in the fact that it poisons people's souls and demoralizes them. (Czechoslovakia)[20]

Listen again, with these passages in mind, to two of Leo XIII's extended predictions about socialism:

The *Socialists*, working on the poor man's envy of the rich, endeavor to destroy private property, and maintain that individual possessions should become the common property of all, to be administered by the State or by municipal bodies. They hold that, by thus transferring property from private persons to the community, the present evil state of things will be set to rights, because each citizen will then have his equal share of whatever there is to enjoy. But their proposals are so clearly futile for all practical purposes, that if they were carried out the working man himself would be among the first to suffer. Moreover they are

emphatically unjust, because they would rob the lawful possessor, bring the State into a sphere that is not
its own, and cause complete confusion in the community.[21]

A few paragraphs later, after some further fencing, the Pope once
again opens up with a slashing thrust:

The Socialists, therefore, in setting aside the parent
and introducing the providence of the State, act
against natural justice, and threaten the very existence
of family life. And such interference is not only unjust, but is quite certain to harass and disturb all
classes of citizens, and to subject them to odious and
intolerable slavery. It would open the door to envy, to
evil speaking, and to quarreling; the sources of wealth
would themselves run dry, for no one would have any
interest in exerting his talents or industry; and that
ideal equality of which so much is said would, in reality, be the leveling down of all to the same condition
of misery and dishonor. Thus it is clear *that the main
tenet of Socialism, the community of goods, must be
utterly rejected*; for it would injure those whom it is
intended to benefit, it would be contrary to the natural rights of mankind, and it would introduce confusion and disorder into the commonwealth.[22]

This prediction, even one hundred and more years later, seems
inspired.

Nonetheless, there is one major criticism of socialism which
Leo XIII did not make; Ludwig von Mises formulated it some 30
years later.[23] One of the most important functions of a market
system is to communicate information vital to everyone. Without
market systems, economic actors are blind. They cannot know
what people want, or how much of it they want, or how much
they are willing to pay for it; and they cannot know the costs that
lie behind raw materials, labor, and goods or services. A "planned"
system is an exercise in pretense. Its prices are arbitrary; someone
just makes them up.

In the Soviet economy, Heilbroner reports, the State Committee on Prices had responsibility for setting prices on more than

24 million items.[24] A person assigned as a "planner" to set prices on a certain sector of goods could carry in a briefcase papers concerning hundreds of items to be decided on each day. It proved impossible to deal with so many prices, even monthly. Individual planners or functionaries were reduced to blind guesswork. Nothing related rationally to anything else, except in the mind of the planner. And even this relation left out of account the sweat, the desires, and the effort that real human beings were interested in investing in their purchases or sales. The whole economy was based on make-believe, pursued in the name of rationality.

As Hayek has pointed out, the fatal conceit of socialism lies in its mistaken view of reason.[25] In the name of rationality, socialism misconstrues the nature of practical intelligence as it actually operates in society. Socialism imagines that society works from the top down, like a pyramid, and through a more-or-less geometric form of reason, as if from a few goals (which operate as premises) a planner can deduce practical directives, which in turn will guide every individual action. This indeed is a form of rationality. But, as St. Thomas Aquinas (following Aristotle) stressed, there is more than one kind of rationality, and it is a sign of wisdom to choose the appropriate kind for each field of inquiry. In the practical affairs of society, one must allow for the *contingency* inherent in temporal events, and also for the *liberty* of individual human agents. In such a field the appropriate form of rationality is prudence (practical wisdom, *phronesis*), not geometry. This is why so many writers rebelling against socialist rule, such as Dostoevsky, Orwell, and Zamyatin, protested against the "2 × 2 = 4 man."[26]

Freedom is a necessary condition for the exercise of practical wisdom, since individuals must activate their own capacities for practical reasoning and make their own choices. Without reliance on prudence, individuals could not act freely. A planned or directed society is necessarily coercive, and those who favor it should admit this openly. Regarding ideas, individuals need freedom of both inquiry and discourse. Regarding economic choices, they require a free market. Obviously, reflections of this sort lay behind Leo XIII's arguments in favor of private property, long-term family incentives, and the limited state.

Yet Leo XIII neither defended nor attacked the free market. He neither described its many important functions nor pointed out why it is necessary to a free society governed by practical wisdom and charity. In the ruins of Catholic intellectual life from which Leo XIII had to begin (whole libraries, monasteries, and seminaries having been confiscated, dispersed, or destroyed after the French Revolution), and in the antagonism toward modernity given so much vigor by Pius IX, no systematic view of modern economic questions was available in Roman circles.

Even into the mid–twentieth century, Italy remained a predominantly agricultural economy still locked in the customs and methods of a past that went back to the time of the Romans. Politics, not economics, was on the mind of its nineteenth-century leaders struggling to build a unified state. Indeed, Prof. Anthony Waterman argues that the Roman scholars around Leo XIII lacked sophistication in the extended arguments concerning markets that had agitated British religious life for a century before 1891; their main points were simply not considered.[27] Thus, Leo was especially concerned about the condition of workers and the poor—but, like many others, did not grasp how much they suffered from the lack of competition in markets. He saw the excessive power of relatively few employers, but knew no cure for such monopoly except in government.

Whereas he dwelt little upon markets, Leo's grasp of the fundamental importance of private property to the free society was admirable. As Eastern European reformers today can see, a regime of private property limits the power of the state. But so also does a regime of market exchange. The alternative is an authoritarianism vast enough to control every exchange of private property. Indeed, most Eastern Europeans now dread total political control over free markets. In terms as clear as Bohemian crystal, the Finance Minister of Czechoslovakia said in 1989: "We want a market economy without any adjectives. Any compromises will only fuzzy up the problems we have." Vaclav Klaus became justifiably famous for his intellectual forthrightness: "To pursue a so-called third way is foolish. We had our experience with this in the 1960s when we looked for socialism with a human face. It did not work, and we must be explicit when we say that we are not aiming for a more efficient version of a system that has failed."[28]

A market economy is important not only for political freedom; it is also important for morals. A market economy inculcates a type of mentality quite different from that of a command economy.

In place of passivity and obedience, it awakens the life of active virtue. Anatoly Sobchak, the mayor of what was then Leningrad, put the alternative in 1990 quite clearly:

> For decades in our country, we have fostered a beg-gar/consumer mentality: the state will provide and de-cide everything for you—poorly, perhaps, but provide equally for everyone, give you all the basic necessities. And this parasitic mentality is very widespread here. Yet a market economy, in order to function, requires a very different type of mentality: enterprise, initia-tive, responsibility, every person solving his own problems. The government does nothing more than create the conditions in which one can employ one's initiative and enterprise; the rest is up to the individ-ual.[29]

If markets are to serve liberty and morality in this way, com-petition within each market area needs to be insisted upon, not narrowed. Access to markets must be universal, legally accessible to all. Not fully exploring the ways in which markets may be used as tools, especially for the amelioration of the lot of the poor, Leo XIII did not attend to an important argument against socialism, one whose force in history would prove decisive.

He was not alone. While virtually all Western economists know from their work that markets are more efficient than command economies, some were willing to suspend judgment concerning the Soviet experiment—and consistently lent it much more cre-dence than it deserved. To the softer thinkers it seemed intuitively plausible that an economy under political control from above just might be more "rational" than one in which every person simply thinks and chooses for himself. There might be, so it was thought, less duplication, less wastage, less concern with (by someone's standards) trivialities and more concern with basic needs. And intellectuals were especially tempted by the proposition that mem-bers of their own class, given authority, might fashion a more rational and more moral social order than would free citizens alone, left to their own choices. Once theoreticians of the left and center succumbed to this conceit (particularly in an intellectual environ-ment driven by the left, in which the "mixed economy" merely moves more slowly than the left but in the same general direction), it was exceedingly difficult for them to energize their native skepticism. Those who rejected this conceit root and branch, by contrast, were more likely to spot the inevitability of failure.

But why were such persons, the scholars of the "right" named by Heilbroner (Hayek, von Mises, Friedman, and others), treated so dismissively by their leftward peers? Those who knew which way history might be moving—toward greater rationality from above—could dismiss such dissenters as malcontents who preposterously wanted to set the clock back (as if history moves forward as rigidly as a clock's inner mechanical wheels). In other words, the rationalistic conceit disallowed challenge from outside. Those who embraced it claimed to have rationality all to themselves. Their consciences were not uneasy, therefore, when they accused those to their right of irrational and unworthy motives (protecting the interests of the rich, for example). They never imagined that their *own* motives might be suspect, and that *they* might be protecting the interests of the politically powerful. Their consciences were clean, and their core conceit was untroubled by doubt. That is why the sudden collapse of the moral prestige of socialism surprised them. One must credit Heilbroner for the honesty to admit it.

WORKERS, YES! CAPITALISM? MAYBE

It is a paradox that in the 20th century the ideas of socialism have not been realized in the socialist countries, but in other countries, the capitalist countries. In the countries which call themselves socialist, socialism has been distorted to the degree where it causes disgust (Yuri Afanasyev, USSR).[30]

The reasons for the failure of socialism are many and manifest. What are the reasons for the success of capitalism in reforming itself from within? Sympathizers with socialism are not the only ones who hold capitalism in low regard. Down through the ages, aristocrats have shown considerable contempt for persons of commerce.[31] Aristocrats could afford to be (or not to be) concerned with things for their own sake, and in any case to look down on grubby utilitarian efforts requiring sweat. More generally, especially in Latin cultures, traditionalists have thought of capitalism as crass, vulgar, and uncivilized. In Latin America there is even a saying, "Liberalism is sin." From both the left and the right, there were many reasons for misjudging capitalism.

From the point of view of *Rerum Novarum*, by contrast, the European economy of 1891 had three saving features, even though it was in need of reconstruction. The saving features were these: At least liberal capitalism allowed for private property, the *sine qua non* of a society of personal self-determination; it allowed for—even insisted on—the limited state; and it created a significant degree of "civic space" within which free associations such as labor unions, social clubs, schools, and religious organizations could thrive. (Leo was to become known as "the pope of free associations.")

Nonetheless, Leo XIII judged that the liberal–capitalist society of 1891 was founded on at least two serious errors. First, liberalism misconceived the human person, thinking each to be radically individual and isolated from others, except through artificial social contract. Second, it assumed that all human beings are equal, without paying sufficient heed to the weakness and helplessness of many who could not be expected to compete with others on equal terms. In this respect, the new liberal order left too many at the mercy of too few: "The present age handed over the workers, each alone and defenseless, to the inhumanity of employers and the unbridled greed of competitors."[32]

Far from being wholly antagonistic to "the present age," however, Leo XIII was determined, even before becoming Pope, to reach out for as many points of contact with it as seemed permissible and wise—or at least to make a beginning in this direction. As far as is known, he never read Adam Smith, John Stuart Mill, or other British political economists directly. Nonetheless, admiration for Smithian concepts, and even allusions to certain phrases of Smith's, are visible in the text of *Rerum Novarum*.[33] Ernest Fortin supposes that members of Leo XIII's circle of Italian experts consciously but more-or-less uncritically assimilated texts of Locke and Smith (on private property, e.g.) to texts from the medieval tradition, without noting important differences.[34]

For example, *Rerum Novarum* speaks of property rights as "sacred,"[35] whereas the traditional Thomistic and Aristotelian justification for property rights was both conditional and pragmatic, as was that of John Stuart Mill, who was chary of the term "sacred.''[36] Aquinas, for example, also argued from the lessons of experience that a regime of private property has beneficial consequences, whereas ownership-in-common breeds characteristic abuses. Further, Aquinas held, the right to private property also entails duties to the poor, and is justified by its utility for the common benefit.[37] The Thomistic position is not altogether far from that of John Stuart Mill. *Rerum Novarum*, in saying that property rights are "sacred," goes beyond both—perhaps to intensify its argument against socialism, or perhaps (as Fortin thinks) uncritically.

We have already noted the frequency with which Leo XIII invokes "natural rights," "natural justice," and "rights from nature." According to the followers of that other Leo, the Chicago philosopher Leo Strauss (1899–1973), the modern doctrine of natural rights stems from Thomas Hobbes and John Locke and is rooted in an anthropology wholly opposed to that of St. Thomas Aquinas and the entire premodern tradition. The moderns suppose (not without some evidence) that man by nature is vicious, *homo homini lupus*, and that human life is "solitary" and "brutish." From motives of terror, atomic individuals consent to form the state. By contrast, Aristotle and Aquinas hold that humans are by nature social, not solitary, and that the state is a natural expression of this social nature.

One might argue that it would be more difficult than some Straussians may suppose for the moderns to begin their philosophical reflection *tabula rasa*. More may be going on in the depths of Hobbesian and (particularly) Lockean thought than these authors were aware of; the extent of their debts to the past is difficult to plumb. In any case, by a kind of *via negativa*, Hobbes and Locke came to say many important things about the dignity of the free person.

However that may be, Leo XIII seemed determined to wrest such concepts as natural justice and natural rights away from the pessimistic, wholly secular modern tradition. This he could not do clearly and by direct inference from the intellectual matrix provided by Thomism. Moreover, institutions suitable to expressing the dignity of free human beings were not in evidence in the Europe of his experience. By 1891, however, Leo XIII was 81 years old, he had much yet to do, and the Church needed—the *world* needed—a more humane vision of society than either socialism was promising or capitalism was supplying. So he could not tarry for the niceties. He could not himself supply all the intellectual work of whose urgency he was painfully aware.

Well aware that "False conclusions concerning divine and human things, which originated in the schools of philosophy, have crept into the orders of the state and have been accepted by the common consent of the masses," Leo XIII in his second year as Pope issued the encyclical *Aeterni Patris* (1879) commending the study of St. Thomas Aquinas. Whereas Pius IX had reacted against modernity, progress, and liberalism with negative fury in the fiery anathemas of *The Syllabus of Errors* (1864), setting modernity and the past in as clearcut an opposition to one another as later would Leo Strauss, in self-conscious contrast Leo XIII reached back to the greatest premodern Doctor of the Church, Thomas Aquinas, and made the latter's work the recommended starting place for a fresh appropriation of the good modernity had accomplished, confident that its "false conclusions" (such as socialism) would be discerned by their fruits. Leo XIII was determined to close the breach between modernity and the medieval/ancient past—and, in particular, between the life of the Church and the life of the world. Thus, if the synthesis begun by Leo XIII in *Rerum Novarum* seems sometimes hurried and not quite satisfactory, and indeed if it has not yet been worked out all the way down to its depths, this is not because he failed to discern the problems. Leo XIII was nothing if not lucid.

A good example of one of his tentative attempts at the synthesis that does not quite succeed lies in Leo's novel approach to the Marxian concept of exploitation. Karl Marx reached the concept of exploitation through his theory of class conflict, his labor theory of value, and his theory of the expropriation by capitalist owners of the "surplus value" of the labor of workers. In a more subtle way, as Stephen T. Worland has demonstrated,[38] Leo XIII also worked from a theory of "exploitation" different from and deeper than that of Marx. Leo XIII rejected the theory of class conflict, the labor theory of value, and the theory of surplus labor. In his view, which echoes Smith in a beautifully balanced Latin, each class "needs the other completely: neither capital can do without labor, nor labor without capital. *Omnino altera alterius indiget: non res sine opera nec sine re potest opera consistere.*"[39]

The exploitation Leo feared was of a different order. He feared that the concrete pragmatism required by capitalism would in-

culcate habits of instrumentalist thinking at the expense of the
other habits, from the religious to the esthetic, necessary for full
human development. Everything might come to be judged according to a calculus of profit and loss, which would induce hard-
heartedness among powerful persons in society, truncate their
humanity, and warp their souls. In one sense, such tendencies in
humans are an old story; the Bible recounts many tales of hard-
heartedness, callousness, and cruelty. In another sense, though,
the institutions of liberal capitalism might inculcate such habits
more systematically and more broadly throughout the population.

This was a serious charge. It rested, however, on a hidden
premise: Liberal capitalism is a singleminded, unrestrained system,
subject to no checks and balances (from the civil law and from the
political and moral systems, for example). In such a tripartite
system, instrumentalist thinking may be restricted to those aspects
of life for which it is appropriate. It should be vigorously repelled
when it encroaches on other spheres. This institutional pluralism
disrupts rationalism; it encourages practical wisdom.

The rationalistic conceit at the heart of socialism, by contrast,
leads to social structures that are at the very least authoritarian,
and certainly monistic. All three powers—moral, political, and
economic—are concentrated in one set of institutions and one set
of hands. The economy is under political control, and both are
under ideological control. There follows the dictatorship of *ap-
paratchiks*.

In the classic texts of Marxism and socialism, accordingly, there
is little or no discussion of the separation of systems, the separation
of powers, checks and balances, and the "auxiliary precautions"
of which, at the very founding of the American constitutional
order, James Madison spoke so eloquently.[40] The socialist vision
in most of its forms has been caught up with the vision of shaping
"the new man," a man perfect in justice and thoroughly imbued
with the spirit of equality and comradeship.

This rationalistic conceit led to an errant optimism concerning
the condition of man, once the evil structures of capitalism were
removed. No such illusion is encouraged under democratic and
capitalist presuppositions. As Robert Heilbroner has lately noted:

> Radical views are inherently more optimistic than con-
> servative ones. Through radical glasses society always
> appears to fall far short of its potential, whereas

> through conservative ones it always expresses inescap-
> able and insistent needs of abiding human nature.
> Conversely, the conservative view is always darker
> than the radical. It is more concerned with avoiding
> catastrophe than with achieving unrealized possibili-
> ties. It cannot be progress-oriented or teleological in
> the way that radical thought must be.[41]

The American republic, as it happens, was born neither radical nor conservative in Heilbroner's sense. Its liberal capitalist order was brought to birth within an ethos thoroughly penetrated with a clear awareness of human weakness, fallibility, and vice—that is, of what in Christian theology is called original sin. The writings of James Madison and Alexander Hamilton echo the Puritan divines in this regard. But America was also born in hope (a Christian virtue, too), with faith in divine Providence, and with a sharp sense of progress made and yet to come. For such reasons the framers described themselves as neither liberals nor conservatives, but Whigs.

Thus, the two contrasting social visions, socialism and capitalism, are not symmetrical. Socialism is a *unitary* system. It *intends* to concentrate all powers in the hands of those who control the apparatus of the state. Even in its more moderate forms, the impulse of socialism is to bring the economy under political control and, in general, to enlarge the reach and to strengthen the hand of big government. By contrast, Whiggish liberal theory, as distinguished from socialism, retains a healthy fear of Leviathan, a worry about torture and tyranny flowing from the concentrated power of the state.

The constant liberal purpose, therefore, is to divide social systems, to divide the powers of the state, to divide offices and functions from top to bottom as thoroughly as possible, and to establish checks and balances. One purpose of this pervasive concern to limit and to divide government is to retain as large a civic space as possible for the voluntary action of individuals and their associations. The reason for this is the profound conviction that the most creative sources of virtue, intellect, and moral progress lie in spheres of private life[42] protected from state control. (By contrast, it was precisely this private sphere, in which he darkly imagined the inevitability of exploitation, that Marx sought to destroy.) The state is granted no right to make any laws restricting the free exercise of religion. Neither is it permitted to restrict the generation or the dissemination of information and ideas. The life of the spirit—of religion, science, the arts, morals, and culture—is kept free of state control.

The resulting moral and cultural vigor, in turn, provided a decisive check and balance to the economic system. Citizens were regarded as moral and cultural agents first and as economic agents only afterward. They were regarded as having moral and religious responsibilities that, in crucial places, took precedence over their economic projects. In the hot blood of its youth, of course, the new capitalist order often ran roughshod over religious and moral energies alike. But these quietly gathered their forces, and over the generations tamed the wildness of capitalism's youth. They could not have done so if they had not been ceded the important role of counterweight throughout the social system as a whole. Through the observance of the Sabbath, through the encouragement of philanthropy and compassion for the poor, through the "social gospel," through activism, and in many other ways the churches slowly disciplined the raw economic passions with which they were confronted. Indeed this process took time. Indeed its progress did not come without struggle.

In the United States today, religion is stronger than in any other developed country. (The U.S. has, for example, the world's largest and best organized prolife movement, centered in the churches.) In fact, American piety rivals that of even the most devout Third World countries. Yet however strong religion may be in America these days, the steady exclusion of religion from public life, abetted by a series of court decisions emphasizing the "no establishment" clause at the expense of the "free exercise" clause of the First Amendment, has palpably resulted in the reemergence of raw economic passions and "pocketbook issues" in public life. The battle to keep religious and moral values salient in public life must be joined over and over gain. Thus whole generations of clergymen, university professors, social workers, writers, and reformers, today as in the past, have introduced moral issues, movements of reform, and the social gospel into American public life.

They have not had to, and do not have to, rely on moral and cultural persuasion alone. For a second counterweight was also built into the system: the political power of the democratic state. In a democracy farmers, workers, and the poor outnumber the rich owners of factories and the captains of commerce by large numerical proportions. Moreover, in a highly diversified society the interests of citizens cannot be confined solely within the narrow banks of class analysis; this was Madison's point in *Federalist* Nos. 10 and 51.[43] The many have effective means of bringing about the slow but steady transformation of the institutions of the social order, until the latter produce progress that meets their approval. As a whole, working people and the poor tend to be socially conservative, not nearly as radical as intellectuals and middle-class reformers. Ordinary people seldom want revolution, since they fear disruption in the patterns of their daily lives, which are already hard enough. What pleases them best, therefore, is steady but measurable progress, which a pluralistic, democratic order is well-suited to provide. In recent decades, however, the advent of television (and computers) has given the intellectuals immense and disproportionate power over working people and the poor—often with devastatingly bad results that American society has not yet found a way of reversing.

Thus from two different directions, one moral–cultural and the other political, notable creative energies have arisen in the slow but steady transformation of liberal capitalism. From its founding in the late eighteenth century to (at this writing) the late twentieth century, the social system as a whole has consistently demonstrated a remarkable capacity for self-reform. Slavery was abolished; a civil rights revolution was conducted. By practically every measure available, the conditions of daily life from decade to decade have been quite considerably transformed. Even in the seventeenth century, John Locke had noted that "A king of a large fruitful territory [in a primitive land] feeds, lodges, and is clad worse than a day laborer in England."[44]

As liberal capitalist countries began to experience material progress during the nineteenth century, their standards for the life and health of the poor slowly rose, and the sense of compassion and civic responsibility shown by social reformers (and then mass movements) grew exponentially.

> For the distinctive feature of the success of market
> capitalism in Georgian England lay in its swelling
> bourgeoisie, in the thriving consumer economy of the
> "nation of shopkeepers," the intricate trading net-

works of small masters, artisans, journeymen, and the
expanding white-collar occupations.

Was not the critical victory wrought by capitalism
not the expropriation of the agrarian poor, but the se-
duction of the majority, as producers and as consumers, to become participants in a modernizing
economy that offered genuine opportunities for advancement and potential for personal betterment . . . ?
A wealth of historical studies have now documented
the growing range of goods and services, from mirrors
to magazines, clocks to chinaware, to which a substantial middling sector of British society had increasing access. Indeed, most economic historians now
emphasize that it was rising domestic consumption
levels that fueled the Industrial Revolution.[45]

In the twentieth century, after reform in the medical schools and
hospitals, and under the advance of knowledge about the causes
of disease, medical care improved dramatically. So did wages,
housing conditions, educational opportunity, and other facets of
life. Associations of middle-class reformers of all sorts flourished.
The churches used the available civic space to develop a remarkable
proliferation of institutions in the social sphere: schools, orphan-
ages, hospitals, musical societies, domestic clubs, athletic leagues,
and discussion groups. It may be doubted if any century surpassed
the nineteenth in the reach of its social reform, organized private
charity, civic responsibility, and voluntarism. Millions who came
to America poor were soon poor no longer, just as in Western
Europe standards of living reached by 1991 exceeded the wildest
fantasies of 1891.

So today we take for granted much that to John Locke and
Adam Smith would have seemed astonishing. This is certainly true
regarding the condition of the poor. Consider such things as welfare benefits (which in the U.S. are not counted in calculating who
is below the poverty line), and the following facts reported in a
study by the Heritage Foundation: that 38 percent of the American
poor own their own homes; that the average poor American is
more likely to own his or her own car than is the *average* Western
European; that 95 percent of the American poor have television
sets;[46] that the elderly among them are eligible for Medicare and
the younger for Medicaid; and even such trivial indicators as that

Reeboks are worn by many poor youngsters on schoolyard basketball courts. Boris Yeltsin stringently pointed out: "Some of what are, in the United States, called 'slums' would pass for pretty decent housing in the Soviet Union."[47]

Readers confronting such assertions as these, however, are quite likely to feel rising discomfort, not because these claims are untrue but because their minds have been trained to search out what has *not* yet been achieved, how much poverty and suffering have *not* yet been alleviated, and how much *backsliding* in other areas there may have been. Is our society becoming more unequal? Why do our students do poorly in international testing comparisons? What can be done in the drug-infested, high-crime areas of our cities? "Why, if we're doing so well," political scientist Aaron Wildavsky asks, "do we feel so bad?" Because the social dynamic inculcated in us by our system—and by Judaism and Christianity—instructs us to be discontented with the present; we know we should do better. Feeling bad (as long as it does not paralyze us) is our source of reform and renewal.

Still, detaching ourselves from our normal self-critical mode, it must be said coldly, because it is true as far as it goes: Never in the history of the North Atlantic peoples have so many been so free and so prosperous. Thus, Marx wrongly predicted that under capitalism we should see the accelerating immiseration of the poor. (Anyone who had collected a penny from every socialist who predicted the collapse of the capitalist order would today be rich.) Instead, the liberal capitalist order has experienced one resurgence after another.

The fundamental reason behind the capacity for self-reform in democratic capitalism lies in the independence of its moral–cultural order and its political order alike. Both operate effectively upon its economic system. Each of these three systems represents a different aspect of reality, and each of them is moved by certain organic laws that, when violated, exact considerable costs. Thus the system as a whole comes under three quite different reality checks. This tension places the system regularly in crisis, each becoming an opportunity for fresh restructuring.

Moreover, internal to capitalism itself lies another source of regeneration: its innovative spirit. Schumpeter discerned that the rationality of capitalism lies not in linear logic, but in the impulse of creativity.[48] Hayek showed that this creativity appears in practice as enterprise.[49] Israel Kirzner showed that at the heart of enterprise is the act of discovery.[50] Capitalism is a system rooted in the mind, and in this respect goes beyond all preceding economic systems. It is constituted by much more than (1) private property, (2) market exchange, and (3) profit (or accumulation), the three characteristics that formed the spine of traditional economies.

These are indeed preconditions of capitalism, but although they do figure in most dictionary definitions,[51] they do not identify its specific difference. Such dictionary definitions distinguish capitalism from Marx's idea of socialism, but not from traditional (precapitalist) market systems. They fail to identify the dynamic and creative element that distinguishes capitalism from the traditional market system. It is ironic that Mikhail Gorbachev should grasp the point that so many Westerners miss:

> The Soviet Union is suffering from a spiritual decline.
> We were among the last to understand that in the age
> of information technology the most valuable asset is
> knowledge, which springs from individual imagination
> and creativity. We will pay for our mistakes for many
> years to come.[52]

Capitalism has its origin in the human capacity for invention and innovation—the human capacity to create. For that reason, it has a profound interest in freedom of thought and expression. As any visitor to a trade fair may observe, a market functions as an efficient disseminator of information, skills, methods, and new possibilities. In addition, a market is an efficient instrument for taking useful goods and services from the research laboratory into immediate public use. The USSR was hardly scientifically backward—yet, lacking a vital marketplace, it failed to bring its research into the service of the common people. Similarly, the public success of the industrial revolution depended on the spirit of enterprise and the openness of the marketplace.

In summary: Capitalism is resurgent for two main reasons. First, a capitalist order was early embedded in a powerful moral–cultural system *and* a democratic political system, which together were able to direct it into fruitful channels and eventually to curb many abuses, real and potential. Second, the dynamic agency at the heart of capitalism is the creative capacity of the human mind. A capitalist order nourishes this innate capacity by means of a distinctive set of institutions, such as universal education, patent and copyright laws, easy access to legal incorporation, tax policies favorable to research and development, and associations for raising venture capital.

One of the most urgent tasks for nations that would become prosperous is to come to the support of the innovative practical mind; for example, to frame laws supporting the formation of many small businesses and undergirding their capacity to grow. In Eastern Europe the good news is that access to education has resulted in high levels of technical skill; the bad news is that habits of enterprise have atrophied for want of institutional support, as well as from being condemned as "criminal." However, the vitality of (e.g.) the black market shows that such skills persist. How could they not, since they are rooted in the natural propensity (discerned by Adam Smith, though not by Aristotle or Aquinas) "to truck, trade, and barter" and "to better the condition" of one's family. In Eastern Europe today, as in Latin America and North America, the key to dynamic growth from the bottom up lies in the small-business sector, not in the more glamorous large industries (which are necessarily more bureaucratic); here is where most new jobs are created. Here, too, a law of Christian theology makes itself felt: It is among humble things, often overlooked, that the most creative impulses are found.

TOWARD THE FUTURE

In *Rerum Novarum*, Leo XIII predicted with remarkable accuracy the futility of socialism. By his criticism of visible faults in liberal capitalist societies he set in motion currents of reform that ultimately contributed to social reconstruction. Nonetheless, for various historical and cultural reasons, neither Leo XIII nor any of his successors (until John Paul II) thoroughly analyzed the sources of regeneration and invention in democratic capitalist societies.

Even though the best hope of the poor on earth lies in the universal spread and deeper development of democratic capitalist systems, much fresh thinking is needed to deepen the present intellectual and moral foundations of democratic capitalist societies. Clear thinking is also needed if we are to bring swift and effective assistance to the poor. Those tempted to think that these problems are insoluble might ask whether the fault lies in the way we think about poverty—that is, in a trap of our own construction.

Within a Jewish and Christian horizon, the road toward an earthly approximation of the kingdom of God stretches very far into the future. There is no danger of confusing the sin, imperfection, and suffering that characterize democratic capitalist societies with the kingdom of God. For humans, given their liberty, do often what they should not do, and do not do what they should. What can at least be said, though, is that no existing alternative seems more adequately suited both to eliciting human creativity and to deflecting human weakness into watchfulness. It does the former by adding to the tinder of talent "the fire of interest," and the latter by assigning private interest to be a sentinel to public good.

Forty years later Pope Pius XI was to revisit *Rerum Novarum*—after the Russo–Japanese war of 1905, the First World War, the Communist Revolution in Russia, the rise of Mussolini in Italy, and in the midst of the Great Depression. Much had changed in the world, much of it for the better. But 1931 was nothing if not the beginning of an ominous decade. It was also the year in which the seemingly oxymoronic term "social justice" assumed its canonical form.

CHAPTER 3

SOCIAL JUSTICE REDEFINED: PIUS XI

The intellectuals' main idea, that social inequality
could be abolished through state planning and higher
public-sector spending, has slowly died.

The Economist

When I hear the word "social justice," I think of
regulation and redistribution imposed upon unwilling
citizens by state authorities. . . . You mean I'm
wrong?

A BYSTANDER

DESPITE THE GREAT DEPRESSION THAT HAD SPREAD WORLDWIDE
since the Wall Street crash of 1929, the seasoned and toughminded
Pope Pius XI issued an encyclical letter, in 1931, noting the progress that had been made since 1891. Much remained to be done.
The project of social reconstruction launched by Leo XIII still
faced grave challenges. Still, in law and in fact, the situation of
workers had clearly improved, and nearly all the advanced nations
(the only ones with an industrial proletariat) had inaugurated programs of social legislation. Labor unions effected many beneficial
changes in the lives of workers. The radio, the cinema, and the
automobile, as well as significant advances in the cure of many
common diseases, and in dental care and eyeglasses, along with
marked progress in marketing and agriculture, began to transform
the conditions of daily life.

On the negative side, especially in Germany, the aftermath of the First World War (1914–18) had encouraged the growth of great cartels, and banking in particular had become worrisomely concentrated. Pius XI denounced this dangerous economic centralization in no uncertain terms.[1] And he was right to do so: Just a few years later, the cartelization of the German economy made it far too easy for Hitler to capture the system by, in effect, bringing a small group of financiers and industrialists into one room. (The bitter memory of this swift conquest was not forgotten by the founders of the German "*Sozialmarktwertschaft*" after World War II. They took two key principles from Pius XI: to prevent monopolies, and to make sure that in the future there would be large numbers of midsized firms.)[2]

Yet Pius XI's longest-lasting contribution to Catholic social thought was a relatively new concept, social justice. This much-disputed term has by now become a commonplace in universal public discourse. It lay behind the postwar term "social market economy," as well as behind social democratic and reformist capitalist movements generally. But what does it *mean*? What did it mean to Pius XI? And does the concept still have a future? The person to interrogate first is the German Jesuit who played an important role in drafting the encyclical.

In his eightieth year, Oswald von Nell-Breuning, S.J., wrote in *Stimmen der Zeit* of the trepidation he had felt when, in 1931, at the age of 40, he had been given practically sole responsibility for the authorship of *Quadragesimo Anno*. In a nice touch, Nell-Breuning adds that, regarding the very few paragraphs actually penned by Pius XI (90–96), he himself was given authority as to whether they should be included, and where. Later, Nell-Breuning came to regret having included these lines, since in the public mind they linked the encyclical too closely to Mussolini's corporatist state.[3]

Nonetheless, what Pius XI clearly intended was not the corporatist state, ruled from the top down, but the rejuvenation of civil society by what Leo XIII had called "the principle of association."

RESCUING A VIRTUE

The frank revelation by Nell-Breuning of his own role in drafting *Quadragesimo Anno* makes all the more valuable his line-by-line interpretation of that encyclical in his book *Reorganization of Social Economy*. His discussion of the *locus classicus* of social justice, which has since become the unifying thread of Catholic social thought, sets forth the two roles of social justice—i.e., as a virtue and as a theory:

> The Encyclical *Quadragesimo Anno* has finally and definitively established, theologically canonized, so to speak, social justice. Now it is our duty thoroughly to study this concept—the spiritual foundation and supporting pillar of Christian solidarity, as it is called by Heinrich Pesch—according to the strict requirements of scientific theology, and to give it its proper place in the structure of the Christian doctrine of virtue on the one hand, and in the doctrine of right and justice on the other.[4]

Here, right at the beginning of his commentary, Nell-Breuning highlights the twofold role of social justice, first as a virtue, second as a theory of social order. And here, too, right at the beginning, a serious systemic problem rears its head.

To my knowledge, the late Nobel Prize winner Friedrich Hayek was the first to espy it. Six decades after *Quadragesimo Anno*, in the 1990s, no single economist had been accorded so much prestige, particularly in Eastern Europe, as this Austrian-born reviver of the classical liberal tradition. Robert Heilbroner, as we have seen, has complimented Hayek and Ludwig von Mises, both long despised by the economics establishment, for their prescience about the internal contradictions in socialist economic theory. Yet Hayek has produced in addition a series of magnificent studies of the evolution, traditions, and practices of the free society,[5] and also a devastating analysis of the concept of social justice.

Despite his Nobel Prize, Hayek was by no means part of the economic mainstream; for many years he was rejected as an outsider, a curmudgeon who refused to accept what most economists simply took for granted—growing state intervention on behalf of the welfare state, the accuracy of the interventionist theories of Keynes, and the outmodedness of the classical liberal tradition. An agnostic and frequent opponent of religious thinkers, whose work he (sometimes justifiably) found both fuzzy and exceedingly harmful to the poor they claimed to wish to assist, Hayek was often wrong on important philosophical issues. But he did write deeply and systematically about ethics and society, about politics and markets, and above all about the kind of laws and institutions indispensable to human liberty. In the sense of working ardently to build a more humane society, he was a great practitioner of social justice. His own generous practice in helping to shape new movements (the Mont Pelerin Society, the University of Chicago School of Economics, and a worldwide revival of "the tradition of liberty") makes his rejection of the concept of social justice all the more interesting. Indeed, Hayek himself sought some reconciliation between his own thought, which he called "liberal thought," and religious thought. For example, he proposed naming the Mont Pelerin Society for two Catholic thinkers, under the name "The Acton-Tocqueville Society," and in his opening address to its first meeting expressed the view that unless the breach between "true liberal and religious convictions" could be healed there was "no hope for a revival of liberal forces."[6]

The second volume of his trilogy, *Law, Legislation and Liberty*, under the title *The Mirage of Social Justice*, includes four penetrating thrusts into the heart of social justice, at least as the term is commonly employed.[7] To the best of my knowledge, these four assaults upon the conceptual underpinnings of social justice have never been intellectually rebutted. To go into all of them would take us too far afield, but the central charge may be briefly reported; it goes to the heart of Nell-Breuning's division of social justice into a virtue *and* a regulative principle of social order. The virtue of justice, Hayek trenchantly observes, is a habit of personal conduct. But "social justice," conceived of as a description of social outcomes which may not necessarily have been brought about by deliberate human decision, does not refer to *personal* moral conduct.[8] Too many writers, Hayek avers, confuse sentences about a state of affairs in society with sentences about a virtue proper to persons. For confusing these two meanings, Hayek roundly castigates John Stuart Mill. His strictures would seem to apply to Nell-Breuning's efforts as well.[9]

My reason for raising this difficulty is twofold. First, I want to display a meaning of "social justice" that escapes Hayek's critique—a new meaning that has special power in the domain of "civil society" as opposed to "state," and specifies a moral virtue preeminently necessary in free societies today. (This is the sense in which social justice is a virtue practiced even by Hayek himself.) Second, I want to show how the concept of social justice has for the precondition of its exercise a social order characterized by three sets of institutions: those of political, economic, and moral–cultural liberty. Indeed, the term social justice, while not exactly new, has come into common usage only during the era in which these three internally related institutions of liberty have appeared—the last 150 years.[10]

Some preliminary remarks are also in order. First, my aim is oriented toward the future development of social thought rather than toward a full account of intellectual history. Before we can have a complete history of the term "social justice," an enormous amount of intellectual labor is still very much in order. Today, however, the needs of the world's poor are quite urgent, and my own vocation (such as it is) lies rather in thinking about the future. Many questions might be asked of the historical materials I want briefly to present, but it is not my present purpose to pursue detailed historical inquiries.

Second, my own ideological proclivities are not implicated in the theory of social justice I mean to expound. If I am correct, this analysis will also be useful to those who strongly disagree with me in their assessment of the best available design for a social system. Both those who are more traditional and those who are more to the left than I should find my core analysis equally useful.

For candor's sake, however, let me characterize myself as a biblical realist, a participant in what I have identified as "the Catholic Whig tradition."[11] Others often describe me as a neoconservative in the precise American sense, signifying a former social democrat or democratic socialist who has broken with the left and glimpsed a better progressive ideal in the democratic capitalist and pluralist tradition. But, to repeat, acceptance of my analysis of social justice does *not* entail following me in my own particular commitments.

My plan is to proceed first by a brief historical conspectus, then to develop a fresh proposal, and finally to look toward the institutional implications of social justice for the transformation of social systems around the world, as we head into the twenty-first century.

CONCEPTUAL FOG

"Both social justice and social charity have been investigated but little by theology," writes Nell-Breuning in his commentary on *Quadragesimo Anno*. "Both are neither unknown nor new to it, even though the terms have been introduced but recently." Nell-Breuning is able to find, indeed, only one reference to social charity in papal documents before *Quadragesimo Anno*, and that in a personal but official letter of June 24, 1923. Nonetheless, he adds, "To extend and deepen the doctrine of social justice and social charity will be an important task of theology."[12] This challenge has not in all respects been met even today.

True enough, the term "social justice" has caught on; it has indeed been "canonized" and (as Hayek says, pointing to secular usage) has conquered public imagination: "The appeal to 'social justice' has . . . by now become the most widely used and most effective argument in political discussion. Almost every claim for government action on behalf of particular groups is advanced in its name, and if it can be made to appear that a certain measure is demanded by 'social justice,' opposition to it will rapidly weaken."[13] Social justice has become the chief battle cry of those who would expand the role of government, particularly in questions of redistribution.

Yet despite the centrality of the concept of social justice in Catholic thought, precise statements of the concept are exceedingly hard to find; indeed, even *discussions* of the concept are rare. The famous post–Vatican II encyclopedia, *Sacramentum Mundi*, has no entry under "social justice."[14] The discussion in Johannes Messner's magisterial text, *Social Ethics*, is disappointingly brief.[15] Aside from Nell-Breuning's commentary, the three best treatments I have discovered all agree that the term came into contemporary usage rather haphazardly and with an extraordinary lack of clarity. Two of these treatments offer a brief history of the term and, in the main, complement one another. One of these speaks of the term with at best faint praise amid considerable disparagement (Ernest Fortin),[16] while the other (Jean-Yves Calvez and J. Perrin)[17] puts the term in the best light it can muster. The third treatment, by Vincent Ferree, offers a highly stimulating interpretation, quite novel and idiosyncratic, which nonetheless offers an important clue about the path out of Hayek's trap.[18]

The confusion surrounding the term "social justice" is drily spelled out by Ernest Fortin. He summarizes in these words the way in which most people speak of social justice—which, since Fortin cites no one in particular, I would call "the vulgar view of social justice":

> As nearly as I can make out, social justice, in contra-distinction to either legal or distributive justice, does not refer to any special disposition of the soul and hence cannot properly be regarded as a virtue. Its subject is not the individual human being but a mysterious "X" named society, which is said to be unintentionally responsible for the condition of its members and in particular for the lot of the poor among them.

This concept makes complete sense, Fortin continues, "only within the context of the new political theories of the seventeenth century." It shifted attention away from virtue or moral character to new social structures that would guarantee the security and freedom of atomic individuals. "As such, it is of a piece with the modern rights theory." On the one side, it departed from traditional theories of virtue. On the other, it departed even from modern natural rights theory in emphasizing the need "to equalize social conditions,"[19] rather than personal responsibility.

Like Calvez, Fortin notes that the first author to use the term "social justice" was the Sicilian priest Taparelli d'Azeglio in his *Theoretical Essay on Natural Right Based on Facts* (1840). Fortin notes that the influence of this Catholic scholar on Leo XIII can be clearly traced, and Taparelli attempted to import the Enlightenment term "natural rights" into Catholic social thought by linking it to social justice.

However, what really laid the groundwork for this new concept of social justice was Rousseau's view that society corrupts the pure individual. Rousseau reformulated virtually all human problems in terms of the distinction between nature and history, as opposed to the classical distinction between body and soul. Fortin summarizes the consequences:

> If society and its accidental structures are the primary cause of the corruption of human beings and the evils

attendant upon it, they must be changed. Social reform takes precedence over personal reform; it constitutes the first and perhaps the only moral imperative.[20]

There is no doubt that Fortin is correct in describing the woolly
sloganizing to which "social justice" has become prey. Even the
communists found it useful for their propaganda, and socialists
use it unabashedly as the generic name for their own purposes.
To rescue the term from such ideological misuse is no easy task.
The first step is to disentangle its complicated history.

A BRIEF HISTORICAL OVERVIEW

The rough, unpolished idea behind the recently coined term "social
justice" skips across history like a rock skipping across a pond,
not breaking the surface for centuries at a time but then for some
years creating large ripples. In its classical appearances this underlying idea was variously referred to as legal justice (Aristotle)
and general justice (Aquinas).

In the fifth book of the *Nicomachean Ethics*, Aristotle needed
a term to express two insights: first, that there seems to be a habit
or virtue required for keeping the law, something like law-abidingness; and second, that it is better for the whole city if there are
many law-abiding citizens.[21] These observations suggest new moral
territory, something necessary for moral life, which Aristotle designated "legal justice." Still, Aristotle was not willing to call legal
justice a separate virtue. He thought of it, rather, as a general name
for all the virtues without whose practice the law would go unob-
served. He did not think of either legal justice or law-obeying
justice as requiring any new type of human act or habit. But he
did sense the presence of some larger concept, involving society
and law, beyond the individual virtues taken singly.

Aquinas sharpened Aristotle's insight. He saw that one's moral
life is radically affected by the condition of the city in which one
resides. Like Aristotle, Aquinas had vivid personal experiences of
civil war, flight, and exile (Aristotle as a young man, Aquinas as
a child). When the accustomed order fails, the worst in men often
comes out, and virtuous practice is rendered exceedingly difficult.
Therefore, if the existing order is reasonably just (there is no
paradise on earth), to defend it against disorder or unjust usur-

pation is a very great moral good. Thus a soldier who defends his city is practicing not simply the virtue of bravery but also the virtue of acting for the common good of the city. There is a type of act that is drawn into exercise specifically for the sake of the *civitas* as a whole—i.e., for the common good that surrounds and supports the good of individuals. Aquinas saw this virtue as a habit of justice whose direct object is not some other individual or discrete group, but rather the whole social order—as it were, the general good or the common good.[22] He called this specific virtue "general justice" and noted that it differs from other habits of justice by its object. He did not press the matter further. He did not ask whether this newly identified habit is exercised through any special and direct acts of its own, or whether it is always simply an accompaniment of some other virtue, such as the bravery of the soldier or the law-abidingness of the citizen.

During the nineteenth century, the term "legal justice" came to be used by German jurists in ways ("the letter of the law," "state laws") that brought that term into disrepute. The German controversy and the rise of the slogan "social justice" in the mid-nineteenth century is especially important for understanding Nell-Breuning's use of the term; Nell-Breuning expressly credits the term to one of his teachers, Heinrich Pesch, S.J. (1854–1925).[23]

Writing in the depth of the worldwide Depression (and an especially severe banking crisis in Germany), Nell-Breuning began drafting *Quadragesimo Anno* poignantly aware of massive social instability. As he worked on his text, Stalin was beginning to terrorize Ukraine, Hitler was on the rise in Germany, German banks were embroiled in scandals and inflation was staggering, Mussolini was arrogantly exercising in Italy what he described as "the totalitarian will," and Japan's warlords were plotting their expeditions overseas. Forty years earlier, Pope Leo XIII had spoken of "the spirit of revolutionary change" undercutting European institutions. By 1931, the widening dimensions of the "social question" had overflowed from politics and economics into the world of terrible new moral ideals such as Nazism, Fascism, Communism, and fashionable Western nihilism. The world faced a moral and religious crisis, deeper even than the highly visible economic crisis. This was far more true in 1931 than in 1891.

Pius XI grasped the moral challenge implicit in this generations-long sea change, and asked what claims justice makes upon humans in unstable times. He made an intensive effort to recover the idea that Thomas Aquinas had intended by the name "general justice" and, placing this new term in the context of rapid social change, gave it a new name, "social justice."[24]

A few words about the personality and background of Pius XI may illuminate his efforts. Poland gave the modern papacy one of its own sons in John Paul II in 1978 but, in an odd way, it also gave the world Pope Pius XI. Born Achille Ratti in 1857 in the little industrial town of Desio near Milan, the young Fr. Ratti (ordained in Rome in 1879) was a most unlikely candidate for the papacy. Quiet, studious, reclusive, his first assignment (after receiving three doctorates in three years) was as an instructor in the Milanese seminary. So scholarly was he that he was assigned to pursue historical research for 22 years, notably in paleography, at the Ambrosian Library in Milan (1888–1910). After that, he spent another eight years as vice-prefect of the Vatican Library in Rome, where he continued writing and publishing historical monographs, several on the history of Milan and one on the modern history of the Church in Poland.

At the age of 60, Ratti might have expected to continue such obscure scholarly work for the rest of his life—but the emergence of Poland as an independent country in 1918 presented a perplexity to the Vatican diplomatic corps, since the Vatican at that time had no expert on Poland. Someone then recalled Fr. Ratti's monograph; he was speedily consecrated a bishop and sent to Poland as Nuncio. In Warsaw from 1918 until mid–1921, he endured the communist siege of the city in 1920, worked closely with Josef Pilsudsky, and—in a way—midwifed modern Polish Catholicism (a work of enormous long-range consequences). The organizational abilities, leadership, and diplomatic astuteness of this sheltered scholar may have surprised many, but Pope Benedict XV took note and made Ratti the Cardinal Archbishop of Milan, Ratti's beloved city, that June. Barely had the new Archbishop established a Catholic university there—soon to become famous around the world—than Benedict XV died, and Cardinal Ratti was elected to succeed him on January 22, 1922.

Ratti chose the name Pius as "a name of peace." As if he could see what was coming, he dedicated his whole pontificate to peace, even secretly offering God his life for it. In the crowd in St. Peter's Square receiving the new Pope's first blessing was Benito Mussolini, soon to assume dictatorial power in Italy and to become the first exponent of totalitarianism, which he described succinctly as *la feroce volontà*—the ferocious will of a single leader. The two would become fierce antagonists, Peter and Caesar locked in perennial struggle. Indeed, the stubborn resolve of the scholar–priest from Milan would soon be pitted not only against Mussolini in Italy, but also against Hitler in Germany, and Stalin in the steadily expansionist Soviet empire. Taking as his motto "The Peace of Christ in the Kingdom of Christ," Pius XI, almost as if in defiance, established the universal feast day of Christ the King. He called for the Catholic laity to awaken, to organize themselves voluntarily, and to act for justice. In 1937, he warned the totalitarians (Hitler, in particular) that "The day will come when the *Te Deum* of liberation will succeed premature hymns of the enemies of Christ."

Pius XI died on February 10, 1939, shortly after the German occupation of Czechoslovakia and annexation of Austria, and only months before the outbreak of full hostilities. He was 82 years old. Gloom covered Europe like a pall, and the war he had tried to prevent soon overwhelmed Europe and Asia, at an unprecedented cost in human life.

When Pius XI wrote of social change, therefore, he knew the stakes. When he wrote of social justice, he sought an alternative to the mad principles on which Europe was then basing its social order. In large measure he blamed liberalism—not so much for its institutions as for its irreligious mores and ideology. In sweeping the house of Europe bare of the morals of its ancient and medieval past, liberalism in the Continental sense had invited into this "clean, well-lighted place" a nihilism inhabited by seven devils (as the biblical parable puts it) worse than the first. From his earliest years as Pope he had hearkened back to Leo XIII's plea for a sounder reconstruction of Europe's values—not in opposition to change, like Pius IX, but in search of a better alternative.

"There is an instability from which no single thing can escape, for that, precisely, is the essence of created things," Pius XI had written in 1926, for the thirty-fifth anniversary of *Rerum Novarum*. "Precisely in those social elements which seem fundamental, and most exempt from change, such as property, capital, labor, a constant change is not only possible, but is real, and an accomplished fact." He looked at each of these fundamental social elements in turn. Here is his discussion of labor:

From the primitive work of the man of the stone age,
to the great organization of production of our day,
how many transitions, ascensions, and complications,
diversities! . . . What an enormous difference! It is
therefore necessary to take such changes into account,
and to prepare oneself, by an enlightened foresight
and with complete resignation, to this instability of
things and of human institutions, which are not all
perfect, but necessarily imperfect and susceptible of
changes.[25]

This is the perspective in which, five years later, Pius XI took
up the term "social justice" as his solution to the moral problems
inherent in social change. The Pope used this new term ten times
in his encyclical "On the Reconstruction of the Social Order"
(*Quadragesimo Anno*, 1931). No single meaning is easy to derive
from these ten texts.[26] But where there had been considerable
confusion and vagueness about the three terms "legal justice,"
"general justice," and "social justice," Pius XI intended to establish a term for practical modern use. He thereby raised questions
no one had asked with such clarity before.

In most of the passages in which he uses this term in *Quadragesimo Anno*, the Pope begins with a concrete problem—in #71,
for example, the fact that fathers of families are not receiving wages
adequate to support their children. The Pope had already noted
that social systems are in flux and that social change is quite natural.
What he now adds is that free citizens have a responsibility to
shape these changes in a moral way. If fathers are not receiving
wages sufficient to support their families "under existing circumstances," he writes, "social justice demands that changes be introduced into the system as soon as possible, whereby such a wage
will be assured to every adult workingman." A society that would
allow children to starve, and individual fathers to be helpless in
improving their family's condition, is in his view neither a good
nor a stable nor a fully legitimate society. Humans must not simply
wring their hands about this. They should "introduce changes into
the system as soon as possible." To introduce such changes is the
object of the virtue of social justice.

Three points are worth stressing here: personal responsibility,
institutional change, and practicality. First, humans are required

by the morality written into their own nature to accept responsibility for the shape of the institutions of their society. This is because it is their nature both to be responsible and to live in society. Second, they should fix their eyes on changes in the *system*—that is, in those institutions and organizations that in their ensemble constitute society. Third, they should be realistic, fixing their aim on what is "possible," not on utopian visions. These three characteristics help to clarify the nature of the new virtue for whose development Pope Pius XI calls. During past ages, common people were relatively passive "subjects" rather than responsible "citizens." In the new circumstances of 1931, they needed to exercise new responsibilities whose object and methods are social and whose exercise requires prudence and practicality.

The way was open here for *Quadragesimo Anno* to set forth a full theory of social justice as a virtue. Pius XI did not do that. While it is true that the concept of social justice has undergone many changes since 1931, *Quadragesimo Anno* remains the *Urtext* to which all others refer. And according to Nell-Breuning's commentary:

> Social justice is a spiritual and intellectual *guiding rule*
> which does not act through itself, but assisted by a
> power. This power, according to Leo XIII and Pius
> XI, is the *state*. The right social and economic order is
> established by the *supreme* authority in society, which
> in turn is bound by the demands of social justice from
> which it draws all its legal authority to direct and to
> regulate. In a properly regulated community, social
> justice finds its *natural* realization in public institu-
> tions, and *acts* through public authorities or their rep-
> resentatives.[27]

Thus in the view of Pius XI, Nell-Breuning writes, social justice "is always an efficient principle in public authority." It looks "first of all to social legislation." Its aim is to "bring about a legal social order that will result in the proper economic order." Christian social philosophy "seeks to restore order which would lead economics back into firm and regulated channels and would ultimately exert its beneficial influence upon property." In this sense, social justice is "a spiritual and intellectual principle of the form of human society." Social justice "becomes an institution in the constitution and laws of society." Further, social justice "determines the structural form and shape as well as the functioniong of society and economics."[28]

Let me summarize. Looked at in this way, social justice is plainly not a virtue. It is an *institution* in the constitution and laws of society. It determines the structural *form* and *shape* of society. It is a spiritual and intellectual guiding *rule*. It is an efficient *principle* in public authority. It gives the state its legal (moral) *authority*. It looks first to social *legislation*. It brings about a legal social *order*. It results in the proper moral order for a sound *economy*.

To the Anglo–American ear, this program is not at first glance easy to distinguish from the heavy-handed political order which plans and directs the economy, and enforces the monistic cultural order enshrined in the corporatist states of socialism and fascism. But to see Pius XI's program in this way is a great mistake. To be sure, as Nell-Breuning admits, the Pope bent over backwards not to antagonize Mussolini and to be fair to the "aims" of fascism. From Mussolini's program, Pius XI tried to distinguish his own only by way of irony.[29] Nonetheless, his words did antagonize Mussolini, whose followers bellowed in sour rage against *Quadragesimo Anno*.[30] Furthermore, Pius XI was vehement in his denunciations of socialism, even going so far as to say that no Catholic could in good faith be a socialist.[31] But what exactly were the differences Pius XI saw between a Christian social order built around "the guiding rule" of social justice and a fascist or socialist order? (Fascism, it is important to recall, was a form of socialism—national socialism.)

There are, above all, differences in fundamental philosophy. "The Pope," Nell-Breuning writes, "contrasts this truly social idea with the mechanistic–individualist reform plans of socialism and its followers." Socialism may desire "a restoration of sound social order" over against liberal individualism, but it accepts all the materialism and individualism of the liberal order.[32] Besides, socialists (even when they try to appear moderate) seek the abolition of private property, and maintain both a dominant antireligious animosity and an anti-Christian morality of free love and the like. What socialism and social justice appear to have in common, however, is the above-mentioned drive "to restore order which could lead economics back into firm and regulated channels."

There can be no mistaking the animosity of Pius XI and Nell-

Breuning toward "the liberalist illusion." Nell-Breuning writes: "The Pope keenly attacks the erroneous belief that the market under competition regulates itself." Pius XI rejects the theory "that the human mind is capable of directing economic developments according to a definite plan." "We must admit," Nell-Breuning confesses, "that human endeavors to regulate economics are subject to the danger of error and false judgment, and that, indeed, not all experiments have led to the desired result." The conclusion that Nell-Breuning draws from these mistakes is only that "It is necessary to advance cautiously and to learn from our mistakes."[33] He emphasizes that economics is a social science, concerned with "the existence of economic society," and society is "far more than a non-cooperative mass of individuals." It is this, he writes, that obliges the Pope to conclude in #88 that it is "very necessary that economic affairs be once more subjected to and governed by a true and effective guiding principle." The Pope, in short, "looks for something that is above economic power, and can therefore direct it toward the right goals." Here "He conceives of two powers: *social justice and social charity.*" And in seeking how these can be "implanted into economic society as a regulating force," the Pope "attaches first importance to governmental and social institutions."[34]

Pius XI, Nell-Breuning comments, is here thinking of large institutional matters: of "institutions and government administration, something that can be attained by properly formed legal and national institutions."[35] Pius XI insists at this point on the principle of subsidiarity—a principle that can be traced to Abraham Lincoln.[36] The state is not an unlimited or totalitarian power. It is *limited.* The Pope "puts his greatest and highest expectations on the state—not a state that intends to take care of everything, but a state strictly following the principle of subsidiarity. Therefore, while demanding security and protection for proper social order based on social justice, he also appeals to state authority to abstain from interference with all matters of minor importance, in order the better to solve the one great task which it is called to take care of."[37] Nell-Breuning seems to mean by this "one great task" what the Preamble to the U.S. Constitution identifies as "to promote the General Welfare."

In these central passages on social justice in his commentary, it is painfully obvious that Nell-Breuning begins by speaking of social justice both as a virtue *and* as a principle, but ends by treating it solely as a principle. Thus, he falls neatly into Hayek's trap. If social justice is a regulative principle of social order, it is not a virtue. For if the subject of social justice is society, it is not a person, and only the latter can practice a moral virtue. Social justice appears at best to be an intellectual ideal—of indeterminate institutional shape—in the light of which concrete institutions are judged. For it seems to characterize no society that yet has been. Indeed, the use of the term seems uncommonly slippery.

Besides, free modern societies are so complex that no one authority can possibly control their manifold outcomes, whether regarding supply and demand, or prices, or the distribution of income. The failures of socialism (so visible after 1989) make all this plain. To attribute all social outcomes to someone's personal intention or capacity to control is, therefore, far too simple. Consequently, say Hayek and other objectors, to claim to be speaking for social justice can only be to advance one's own abstract preferences. Those who claim to speak for social justice prejudice arguments concerning means and ends by defining their opponents as "unjust." In brief, use of the term social justice is moral imperialism by the imposition of abstraction. How can Nell-Breuning escape this accusation?

A WAY OUT

It does not seem that Nell-Breuning *can* do so. His commentary, written during the early 1930s, lacks sufficient conceptual equipment. His animus against "liberal individualism" blinds him to the actual social texture of nations beyond those of continental Europe. The influence of Weimar Germany is tangible on every page of Nell-Breuning's commentary, in his references to cartelizations and the unchecked power of central banks, and in his underlying conceptual imagery—many of its terms having been forged in the German discussions led by Heinrich Pesch, S.J., and others of his school, in which Nell-Breuning had been formed.

Still, if we go back to the need for social reorganization announced by Pius XI, an approach to social justice overlooked by Nell-Breuning becomes apparent. In free societies, citizens need to use their capacity for association to exercise new responsibilities and to act for social purposes. Suppose that we define social justice in this way: *Social justice is a specific modern form of the ancient virtue of justice.* Men and women exercise this specific *social* habit when they (a) join with others (b) to change the institutions of society. The practice of social justice means activism; it means organizing; it means trying to make the system better. It does not necessarily mean enlarging the state; on the contrary, it means enlarging civil society. Father Ferree thinks that this is Pius XI's intention. I am less certain of that, but this specification does seem to follow from Pius XI's premises.

This formulation recovers Aristotle's sense of the impact of the ethos of the polity on the ethics of the individual. The Pope adds two things to Aristotle: First, an emphasis on the citizen's responsibility for the shape of the *polis*; and, second, a call for voluntary organizations to empower individuals by bringing them out of isolation. The Pope sees that free men and women in modern times can join together, organize, and make changes in the institutions of the societies in which they live. To fulfill this social potential requires of them vigilance, initiative, farsightedness, courage, realism, organizational skills, and perseverance (and probably the advice of lawyers). Furthermore, without the exercise of this virtue, the principle of subsidiarity would have no social groups lesser than the state to which to make appeal.

Since the uses of this virtue are plural, its definition must necessarily be very general. But the concept is far from empty. The easiest way to understand it is to encounter its opposite. Visit a housing project in East St. Louis where the apathetic, alienated, anomic residents seem unable or unwilling to organize themselves to meet the many problems that besiege them. Visit a Bolivian or Sicilian village in which family is the only recognized social reality, and outside the family no one is trusted, committees do not form, few organizations function, and men with armed force have a virtual free run of society. One can expect to see a capacity for social initiative only when citizens have a certain inner strength and a basic trust in others. Certain spontaneous sentences indicate the presence of the right stuff: "We've got to do something." "Let's do it." "Divide up the responsibilities." "Who'll volunteer?" We take such sentiments so for granted in America that we may not recognize a habit that many among us possess in abundance, and others at least a little. Children in playgrounds spontaneously "choose up" sides, arrange bases, establish boundaries. The art of association, Tocqueville wrote, is the first law of democracy.

In the absence of that art, the practice of modern citizenship is almost impossible. Without it, there is only the state, civil society has no vivacity, the public square is empty, and citizens huddle in solitary privacy. Well before 1776 the Americans were a people, knit together by habits of association, whereas the French were still a mob of solitary individuals unused to civil cooperation. "When the Revolution started, it would have been impossible to find, in most parts of France, even ten men," Tocqueville writes in *The Ancient Regime*, "who before the Revolution were used to acting in concert and defending their interests without appealing to the central power for aid."[38]

The virtue of social justice does not consist solely of the habit of association, though, since many forms of association are for *private* purposes. The habit of social justice has as its aim the improvement of some feature of the common good—possibly of the social system in whole or in part (the welfare system, say), but possibly as well of some nonofficial feature (putting up a statue in a public park, organizing a dramatic society in a college, etc.). To tutor a disadvantaged person in the inner city could be a work of social justice; to organize a referendum to prevent the building of a nightclub on a residential street might be another. To build a factory in a poor area; to organize to protect workers' rights; to organize a prolife or prochoice group—all these and other analogous activities are *prima facie* instances of the exercise of social justice.

Not all who claim to be acting for social justice, of course, may actually be furthering the work of justice. Their motives may be suspect, and so may their grasp of important facts, their moral analysis, or their methods. We would not count "skinheads" or neo-Nazis as those doing the work of social justice. So it is with all claims to be practicing a virtue: Those claims must be examined in greater detail. In order to be just, an act must be correct in every aspect—manner, timing, motive, accuracy of perception, and all the other qualities of action; otherwise, it is defective. Thus, to show someone that what he or she claims to be a virtue falls short of either some or all of the demands of virtue is to affirm the ideal of social justice as a standard of moral judgment. In a study of liberation theology, for example, it is legitimate to ask whether its diagnosis of reality is correct, and whether its recommendations are likely to bring about the desired results. One need not accept uncritically its *claim* to be practicing social justice.[39]

A different concrete grasp of current realities, and a different vision of the right ordering of the society, might therefore—under the very same name of social justice—lead people to diametrically opposite courses of action. The claim to be practicing social justice, then, does not close off further argument. On the contrary, it is a demand for further rigorous debate. Indeed, in a pluralistic society one would expect several alternative visions of the just society, many rival interpretations of the condition of society and what is to be done about it, and stiff public debate about matters of fact and moral analysis. Activists of both right and left may claim to have justice on their side—and thereby incur the responsibility to set forth their reasons for this claim.

It is no inconsiderable bonus that this way of understanding the matter justifies (against Hayek) the validity of the term "social justice."[40] This term does not automatically belong to statists or those in favor of big government. On the contrary, there is room in the free society for individuals to work in association for goals they deem enhancing of the common good, independent of government, particularly (but not only) to help the least fortunate. Indeed, both democracy and a dynamic economy need citizens to be civic-minded, to take the larger view, to apply their temporal energies to alleviating pressing social ills, and to remedy obvious social deficiencies. Hayek, too, wants citizens to practice the virtue of acting freely, and in concert with others, for the many social goods—political, economic, cultural—that, in a free society, individuals must have the enterprise both to imagine and to achieve for themselves.[41]

In many U.S. cities such as Newark and East St. Louis, social disorder scorches the terrain. Part of the meaning of "social disorder" is that where the virtue of social justice should be, apathy and inaction reign. Before dealing with such grievous disorders, we need some further distinctions.

THE CIVIL SOCIETY: FIVE FURTHER STEPS

The concept of social justice has greater explanatory power when its relations with several other concepts are set forth. The first step in rescuing the virtue of social justice is to recognize the role of *civil society*, a far richer and more variegated domain than the state. This is the sphere enlivened by the principle of subsidiarity.

The second step is to recognize that fully free societies—those that empower the full range of institutions proper to civil society—are divided into *three* (independent, yet interdependent) *systems of liberty*: political, economic, and moral–cultural.

The third step is to grasp the concept of *spontaneous order* and *catallaxy*. The fourth is to make the concept of the *common good* relevant for complex, dynamic, free societies. The fifth is to analyze the source of dynamism in modern societies, the *principle of change* (or "creative destruction," as Joseph Schumpeter called it), the principle of invention.

1. *Civil society.*   Nell-Breuning calls Leo XIII "the Pope of the principle of association" because of the emphasis the latter placed on free labor unions and other forms of voluntary social action.[42] Indeed, the more widespread and various the free associations in any society, the richer and more complex are its social life, its activism, and its well-being. When free citizens join together cooperatively through their mutual consent, whether to accomplish practical or immanent ends, they act according to their social nature. The full panoply of their social actions beyond their strictly defined duties of citizenship constitutes civil society. And the habitual exercise of these activities for the sake of the common good is an act of social justice. The building and enriching of civil society is in itself an act of social justice. It was clearly seen to be so by Civic Forum and People Against Violence in Czechoslovakia in that year of miracles, 1989. The reawakening of social justice—and of civil society—brought down communism.[43]

2. *The three systems of liberty.*   Social justice requires for its full exercise the institutional supports of three independent, yet interdependent systems. Without the protection of civil and political rights; without the institutions of private property, markets, incentives, and the social supports required for the exercise of personal initiative, enterprise, and discovery; and without the institutions of religious, intellectual, and cultural liberty—without all these, the exercise of social justice would be severely restricted. The preconditions for the full practice of social justice are systemic and institutional. They require a radical separation of powers among the three types of authority. This separation is usually implicit in the term "limited government," according to which government leaves room for other spheres of agency beyond itself.

3. *Spontaneous order and catallaxy.*   Since the exercise of

social justice arises out of free initiative and is freely deployed, it gives rise to a distinctive form of social order. To grasp the nature of this order, however, it is necessary to see that, as a fruit of human freedom, such an order is different from the order of a hive of bees, the order of the stars in the skies, the order by which an acorn becomes an oak, or any other order visible in nonhuman nature. Precisely as free, this order springs from citizens who are creative, adaptive, and alert to context—including social context. Precisely as free, this order inculcates in its citizens notions of responsibility and accountability. It is a specifically *human* order, attainable by no other creature. This does not mean that it "comes naturally," without effort; on the contrary, it is seldom achieved and difficult to sustain. Humans say they want liberty, but when they get it begin immediately to flee from its responsibilities. They say they want social justice, but resist putting in the effort. Spontaneous order is not "spontaneous" in the sense that it is automatic and universal, but only in the sense that it arises out of many free choices and, from any one point of view, contrary purposes.

When human order is shot through with intelligence and mutual adaptation, it is usually not preplanned, prescripted, or puppeteered. Not all forms of rational order must be preplanned from above. Among free citizens cooperating for the common good of all, great latitude is wisely left to individual agents and smaller associations. However, such liberty requires a special kind of order. To promote reasoned exchange, mutual adjustment, and the redress of grievances, for example, the "spontaneous order" requires a system of rules and procedures. While spontaneous or undirected from above, this order is neither anarchic nor without rules. This capacity of free agents to achieve forms of social order apart from constant direction from above, but not apart from those rules and procedures that appertain to "the constitution of liberty," produces what Hayek calls catallaxy. Catallaxy is the order achieved through the exercise of natural instincts for social adaptation and social cooperation. Hayek calls the ideal term of catallaxy the Great Society, the specific and uniquely human social order of liberty. To describe this insight further would take us too far afield.[44] Yet it opens up a vista of great importance to the ever broader exercise of social justice by free citizens.

4. *Common good.* As the French Jesuit Jean-Yves Calvez points out, the concept of the common good lies at the core of the concept of social justice. Social justice "concerns the dealing

of men with one another, inasmuch as they are related to the whole society and its common good, and also the dealings of rulers with ruled, inasmuch as the ruled receive from society their part of the common good. The concept of the common good is at the center of its definition."[45] Yet, in free societies, citizens are not merely "the ruled"; they are the sovereigns. As I have tried to point out in detail in *Free Persons and the Common Good*,[46] contemporary societies have need of a more complex concept of the common good than did ancient and medieval societies, precisely because of the greater scope that advanced societies today give to free persons and free associations.

Two steps toward acquiring this new and more complex concept of the common good must be stressed. First, the ancient and medieval concepts depended heavily on the authority of the state to discern the temporal common good of all and to direct the various elements of society in its pursuit. Hidden in this assertion is the epistemic claim that some group of officers of the state has the capacity to know all the factors that bring improvement in the common good of all, as well as the moral claim that officers of the state can be trusted to be benevolent. Both of these claims are difficult to defend. The contemporary state is far more powerful (and dangerous) than ancient and medieval states, and far more bureaucratic and cumbersome. Thus was born the profound desire for a "constitutional" state, with limited powers and functions. "Congress shall make no law . . ." reads the First Amendment to the U.S. Constitution, which thereby exempted from governmental control the spheres of religion and the free press. In an analogous way, the power of the state over the free economy was also limited, by comparison with the state-directed economies of the Holy Roman Empire and other earlier regimes.

This "division of fundamental social systems"—political, economic, and moral–cultural—effectively empowers other authorities besides the state with respect to countless spheres of the common good. Furthermore, to protect individual rights, minority rights, and rights of association, a large sphere of social action— called in Czechoslovakia after 1989 "the civic forum"—is exempted from governmental control. In short, many agencies and institutional actors are charged with promoting the common good, well beyond the reach of state authorities.

Accordingly, the contemporary concept of the common good has a far richer structure than the medieval concept. It opens up considerable "civic space" for the free exercise of many human capacities essential to the pursuit of the full common good. The modern concept of the common good, adapted to respect the freedom of persons and their associations according to the Lincolnian "principle of subsidiarity," is thus far more ample than the traditional and simpler concept.

Second, the resulting pluralism now built into the concept of the common good requires a far more careful distinction between two different aspects of the common good: its material and its formal content. Formally, the concept of the common good looks both to the social whole and to the dignity of each free person. (The full development of every one of its members individually is one aim of social life; such personal development is also one formal constituent of the whole common good.) This formal concept *does not* change with respect to different historical circumstances. But the material content *does* change dramatically from age to age and from place to place. Materially, for example, so many concrete goods, both spiritual and physical, are now required for the full development of every individual person, and of the human community as a whole, that enormous scope must be given to concrete prudential judgment in their ordering and in their realization. Today the common good includes highways, low-cost health care, low inflation, universal education, abundant employment, and balanced government budgets. Reconciling all these contrary demands is no mean feat.

It is, therefore, far easier to will the formal common good (of all persons together and of each singly) than to discern and to realize in harmonious order the whole material common good, in all its rich profusion and variety. Individual societies differ enormously in their institutional and cultural histories, in their material endowments, and in their capacity for flexible response to concrete needs. Societies labor under many constraints, limitations, and scarcities. A truly remarkable degree of practical wisdom is necessary for a nation's integral human development. As they approach the achievement of the material common good in discrete societies, theoreticians of the common good must, therefore, allow ample scope to the exercise of practical wisdom and prudential reasoning. For that matter, efforts to think globally and to pursue a new world order also require enormous reservoirs of practical wisdom, amid the contingencies and ironies to which social action is prey.

In brief, theoreticians who would truly respect human capacities for liberty and accountability require much fresh thinking about the systems, institutions, social rules, procedures, and concrete social decisions actually embodied in the common good, materially considered. To invoke the common good is to invoke no simple or draconian scheme. On the one hand, theoreticians wed to the ideal of practical wisdom must be on constant guard against utopianism. On the other hand, they should not hesitate to establish benchmarks of concrete social goods yet to be achieved.[47] The required combination of dream and practicality— of *mystique* and *politique*—is necessarily a quite rare human endowment, a gift, in the end, of the Holy Spirit Who "o'er the bent world broods" (G.M. Hopkins).

5. *The principle of change.* Advanced contemporary societies, as Pius XI discerned, are characterized by rapid social and technological change. Yet these changes, while they derive from many sources, are not entirely random. What distinguishes a capitalist society from all previous forms of economic order is its institutional base in processes of innovation, discovery, invention—or in a word, in *mind*.

It is worth dwelling on this point a moment. The decisive, defining characteristic of a capitalist economy is neither the free market nor private property nor incentives nor profit. All these are found in traditional precapitalist economies. All these are important preconditions for a capitalist economy. But capitalism, truly defined, does not come into existence until institutions are established that systematically support and nourish the creative capacities of human beings to invent, discover, and innovate, and to practice the fundamental human right of personal economic initiative.[48] The highlighting of this fundamental human right by Pope John Paul II, first in *Sollicitudo Rei Socialis*, then later and more fully in *Centesimus Annus*, is one of the enduring contributions of his papacy to Catholic social thought.[49]

This inalienable human endowment, springing from the image of the Creator impressed upon each human being, provides the essential dynamism of the free society—both of its economy and of its political and cultural life. The principal source of dynamism of the free society is the fecundity of the human mind, derived from the Creator. Not able to measure the height and depth of the Creator's mind, the human mind is nonetheless called to be as much like the former as it can be.

For this reason, theoreticians of the common good and of social justice need to build into their theories a dynamic (rather than an equilibrium) model of social change. For the human spirit is free, inventive, and creative. Institutions shaped by that spirit *must* be open to change. But this change is not, or need not be, random. For it springs from the workings of the human mind in its creative capacity. And the mind's inherent drive is toward communication, cooperative adaptation, and public as well as private choice. Although free, a human order is not of its nature anarchic. For works intended to serve the goods and interests of others, even if for reasons of profit, must be adapted to the consent of those others. In this way, even self-interest must be to some extent other-regarding—and the more so, the better. For civilization means appealing to reasoned choice within a framework of voluntary social cooperation.

Thus, as the study of public choice brings economists to focus more thoroughly on the laws and constraints of public (and private) choice, economics in a postsocialist era is likely to become ever more humanistic.[50] Social philosophers and theologians, in becoming more sophisticated about economic laws and dynamics, are likely to share common materials with economists who study public choice.[51]

FROM 1931 TO 1991

Insofar as humans are likely to misuse, squander, and abuse their freedoms, the free society is constantly at risk. For the free society, not all choices are equal. Some are self-destructive. Citizens will need to be vigilant about public choices, if the experiment of the free society is not to end in shipwreck. For the free society *is* an experiment, not a guarantee. Thus the widespread exercise of the virtue of social justice is indispensable for the preservation of liberty. By this virtue, citizens join together to do for themselves what in earlier systems they had to turn to the state to do.

Perhaps for this reason the American framers at first planned to use the word "virtue" on the Seal of the United States, where they ended by choosing instead "Novus Ordo Seclorum." There can be no free republic if its citizens do not act with the virtues proper to liberty. And the virtue most proper to citizens of free societies, precisely as such, is social justice. The full development

of the theology of social justice, however, awaited the fuller recognition, in a theological context, of the tripartite system of free
institutions, which creates breathing room for civil society.

Quadragesimo Anno (1931) appeared in the midst of the Great
Depression, which was particularly severe in Germany. It was
followed by the Second World War, which broke out just after
the death of Pope Pius XI, who had wanted to be known as the
Pope of peace. After the horrid travails of that war, Pius XII (1939–
58) led the Catholic Church, belatedly, to support the rebuilding
of democracies as the best defense of human rights. Christian
Democratic and Social Democratic parties rose up to defend those
rights against Communism. Leo XIII's pioneering effort to root
concepts of human rights in Christian soil was capped by Pope
John XXIII's proliferation of rights in Pacem in Terris (1963).
Paul VI (1963–78), while avoiding the term "socialism," began to
speak of a necessary process of "socialization," a euphemism that
many interpreted as an endorsement of social democracy and the
welfare state. Then, on October 16, 1978, the feast day of St.
Hedwig (patroness of reconciliation between neighboring states),
the College of Cardinals electrified the world with the selection
of the first non-Italian Pope in more than four centuries, the Polish
Cardinal–Archbishop of Krakow, Karol Wojtyla, who chose the
name Pope John Paul II.

The new Pope—dramatist, poet, athlete, polylinguist—took
as his mission the reconciliation not only of neighboring states but
of neighboring blocs, which from the first he insisted on calling
"the two great branches of the one tree of Christian Europe." The
first Slavic Pope designated as copatrons of all Europe, together
with its traditionally recognized patron, St. Benedict (480–547),
the founders of Slavic Christianity, Sts. Cyril and Methodius. (A
thousand years earlier, these two brothers first codified the Sla-
vonic tongue at Nitra, in present-day Slovakia, at the very center
of Europe "from the Atlantic to the Urals.")

A philosopher by training (who received an honorary degree
from Harvard for his work The Acting Person), the vigorous Pope
John Paul II early made clear that he wished to impart to the
Catholic body a deep and original philosophic stamp. "Ordered
liberty" is the key concept with which he chose to begin, a liberty
practiced by the human person at his or her best as a free and
creative agent of his or her own destiny. The Pope's emphasis on
ordered liberty had special resonance behind the Iron Curtain, as

well as among all those struggling under military dictatorships and "national security states" in the Third World. Helping to shape the Declaration of Vatican Council II (1963) on religious liberty, Pope John Paul II continued over the years to articulate his vision of religious liberty, the "first liberty."[52] Gradually, he built up the foundations of a fresh theory of the "second liberty," economic liberty. Here he stressed the "creative subjectivity" of the free man and woman at work. This was fresh material, indeed—and to it we must now turn.

PART TWO

A NEW BIRTH OF FREEDOM

John Paul II (1978–   )

CHAPTER 4

THE SECOND LIBERTY

Less than seventy-five years after it officially began,
the contest between capitalism and socialism is over:
capitalism has won.

ROBERT HEILBRONER

Definition: Liberty is the reign of conscience.

LORD ACTON

FROM LEO XIII TO PIUS XI ONLY 40 YEARS ELAPSED, but between
Quadragesimo Anno and *Centesimus Annus* a full 60 years—and
what a 60 years! The rise of Hitler; World War II and the death
camps; the clanging down of the Iron Curtain in 1948; the spread
of communism far beyond the Soviet Union; the amassing of nu-
clear weapons; the sprouting of Soviet SS-20s in a ring around
Western Europe: There was a lot of history packed into those 60
years.

By the hundredth anniversary of *Rerum Novarum* (in 1991)
the totalitarian dictators of the twentieth century (Mussolini, Stalin, Hitler) had long since passed from the world's stage, their
ambitions in ruins, their crimes the subject of the world's revul-
sion. But the papcy seemed in 1991 stronger than it had been in
many generations. When the Polish Pope John Paul II summoned
leaders from all the world's religions (rabbis, swamis, imams,
Buddhist monks, patriarchs, archbishops, presbyters, and rever-
ends) to come together with him to pray at Assisi in 1989, it did
not seem unfitting that he should do so—indeed, it seemed like
an open and magnanimous and imaginative gesture, of a sort no
other religious leader on earch could have credibly carried off.

By 1991 the predictions that Leo XIII had made about the

"futility" of actual socialism, predictions made when so many intelligent philosophers were giving socialism their hearts, had been dramatically vindicated by the great crowds cheering the demolition of the Berlin Wall and the fall of socialism. The appeals that Pius XI had made for social justice had encircled the globe, and advanced societies after World War II had reshaped themselves by democratic checks and balances, enterprise economics, and welfare systems barely imagined in 1931. The world in 1991 faced a very different prospect than it did in 1891, when the bloodiest hundred years in history lay just ahead.

Not only did civil society and social justice enjoy a new lease on life; so also did the "first and second liberties." Religious liberty and economic liberty, as intimately connected as two branches of the same root, are inalienably endowed in humans by their Creator. Looking ahead to the twenty-first century, we can expect to see the disciplines of economics and theology (and philosophy) come closer together in the study of many common materials— especially those of human choice.

Three important intellectual streams brought us to this point. After the collapse of "real existing socialism" in 1989, Eastern Europeans emerging from the ruins began rediscovering—and with fresh appreciation—the moral practices of the free society. Second, distinguished economists such as Nobel Prize winner James M. Buchanan began foreseeing new directions in economic science which will render that science more humanistic than it has been in recent decades.[1] Further evidence is given by the 15 economists who met for a colloquium at the Vatican on November 5, 1990, to discuss the ethical dimensions of economics.[2] Third, while remaining highly critical of many aspects of Western economies, Pope John Paul II took two important steps to bring Catholic social thought into closer contact with the genius of modern economic practice: He recognized the human right to personal economic initiative, and emphasized the role of human creativity in overcoming poverty and producing wealth.

In thinking through these problems in a spirit of international solidarity, however, we must overcome a serious gap between the cultural traditions of Latin Catholic Europe (France, Italy, and Spain) and those of England and America. David Martin links this divide, metaphorically at least, to the war between England and Spain, settled by the tragic fate of the brilliantly rigged and gleaming Spanish Armada.[3] Had the Spaniards won, the history of liberty (not only in the Americas) would have been very different. The continental tradition of *liberté* implied a different conception of social order than that of the Anglo–American tradition. Many Anglo–Americans are barely, if at all, aware of this difference, and many continental and Latin American intellectuals read into the Anglo–American experience their own interpretations of *liberté*. A great deal of mutual incomprehension needs straightening out. So we will need to proceed slowly through brief discussions of the two different concepts of liberty, the two different concepts of order, and the coming convergence of theology and economics in questions of human choice.

TWO CONCEPTS OF LIBERTY

Liberty is not the easiest concept to understand. In particular, the traditions of Roman law (and the Napoleonic code) give rise to a different view of liberty than that implicit in the common law. In the popular speech of continental Europe, liberty—the French *liberté*, the Italian *libertà*, the Spanish *liberdad*, and perhaps even the Latin *libertas*—seems to embrace the realm of "whatever is not forbidden." Within this horizon, liberty and law are conceived of as opposites: on one side, those things commanded or forbidden; on the other side, those things not covered in the law, concerning which one is free. The Anglo–American conception (the Whig conception) is quite different. Here liberty is conceived of as the inner form of the law. The intelligibility of the free act derives from reason, law, duty, and a well-ordered conscience.

We need to examine this notion further, for it brings religious reflection closer to the economists' notion of "rational choice," while at the same time enriching the economists' notion. It makes plain that "rational" does not mean only "utilitarian" or only "materialistic." Empirically, this enriched notion seems to have a basis in fact. Human beings do sometimes act from more than materialistic motives and from motives in no narrow sense utilitarian.

My favorite author on the theme of liberty is the great English historian, Lord Acton. For Acton, the design of Providence for human history is the expansion of human liberty. And, following on Judaism, Christianity is the chief historical force imparting this design to history. "Liberty has not subsisted outside of Christianity," he concludes, after showing painstakingly how the development of institutions of liberty awaited the awakening of personal conscience, beyond all bond of blood or belonging.[4] Judaism is normally imparted through genealogy, Christianity through conscience. He adds:

> The Christian notion of conscience imperatively demands a corresponding measure of personal liberty. The feeling of duty and responsibility to God is the only arbiter of a Christian's actions. With this no human authority can be permitted to interfere. We are bound to extend to the utmost, and to guard from every encroachment, the sphere in which we can act in obedience to the sole voice of conscience, regardless of any other consideration.[5]

"The center and supreme object of liberty," Acton said, "is the reign of conscience."[6] And conscience, as Acton understood it, is not free-floating or arbitrary, but responsible to reason. He means a *rightly ordered* conscience.

Among other "definitions of liberty" given by Acton, we read: "reason reigning over reason, not will over will." And again: "reason before will."[7] Before rushing onward, let us linger over several more of Acton's reflections on liberty, to make sure we get his concept:

> Religious liberty is not the negative right of being without any particular religion, just as self-government is not anarchy. It is the right of religious communities to the practice of their own duties, the enjoyment of their own constitution, and the protection of the law, which equally secures to all the possession of their own independence.[8]

> The center and supreme object of liberty is the reign of conscience. Religion produced this force only in the seventeenth century—just as it redeemed slavery only in the nineteenth century, in the 30 years from 1833 to 1864.[9]

> If happiness is the end of society, then liberty is superfluous. It does not make men happy. It depends on

the other world. It is the sphere of duty—not of
rights. Suffering, sacrifice for an end beyond this life.
If there is none, then there is no object to sacrifice
to.[10]

It will be clear from these quotations that the Anglo–American
definition of liberty is distinctive. It means liberty *under* law, not
liberty *from* law. It means the liberty to do what we *ought* to do,
not the liberty to do what we *wish* to do. In this respect, liberty
in the Anglo–American sense is like the definition of practical
wisdom in Aristotle. In Aristotle, prudence is *recta ratio, ordered*
understanding (*recta* here means directed by a good will). In American terms, liberty is *ordered* liberty. This is illustrated in the classic
and popular American anthem:

> *Confirm thy soul in self control;*
> *Thy liberty in law.*

Consider four concrete cases. Is it really enough in the current
debate over abortion to be "prochoice"? (Those who say "choose
life" are also prochoice.) The real question is: Which choice is the
rightly ordered choice? Which better meets the tests of inquiring
intellect, an intellect willing to strip away evasions and euphe-
misms, to describe exactly what that choice entails (what the procedure is like), and to count carefully its personal and social
consequences? This is not the place to give my own account of the
most reasonable answer to these questions. But it does seem significant that many who announce in favor of "prochoice" shrink
from saying that this makes them "proabortion." Abortion strikes
them as an ugly thing. What they hope for, they say, is that
individual citizens should make this choice in private, rather than
that the society at large should make it through public law.

But has the public no interest in the legal definition of the
boundaries of life? Of course it does. Every one of us has an
interest in establishing in stable law who will have the power to
let us die and thus, as well, in the legal definition of life. Principles
of law, even settled practices of the law, have a logic that normally
carries them far beyond the passions and interests of one generation. A nation must protect that logic with vigilance. Thus the
"prochoice" position earns respect only when its implications for
setting the boundaries of life are submitted to the searching light

of reason. By itself, the meaning of the cry "prochoice" is not self-evident. Of life and death, one cannot say "I am prochoice" as one would say "I prefer vanilla." The issue is one for measured reflection, not one for taste. *De gustibus non disputandum.*

To favor abortion, it is necessary to have very good reasons—and not only personal reasons, but reasons that uphold the public interest. It may be (I doubt it) that, drawing up a list of these reasons, someone can make a sound argument for abortion. Mostly, one encounters evasions, purposeful ignorance, and assertions of naked domination: "It's my body, and I will control whatever is in it"; even if it is different from me, human in form, and individual in its genetic code.

Even if (perhaps especially if) the reader reasons differently about abortion than I do, perhaps I have said enough to show the great difference between merely doing what one wishes and doing what reason commands.

Consider a second case. A 14-year-old male in Washington, DC, in possession of a .38 revolver, shoots to death another boy in a schoolyard ("wastes him") "because he looked at me funny." The killer expresses no feeling of wrongdoing or regret. The murder of innocent young life is horrible, of course; but even more horrible is the killer's lack of moral perception. This juvenile, it turns out, is by no means insane or even (in the ordinary sense) emotionally disturbed; he is simply deaf to certain moral appeals, as some people are tone-deaf or color-blind. *This* moral blindness is far more incapacitating than color-blindness. Humans without moral perception are a menace to other human beings. There is virtually universal loathing for Central American "death squads," for example, since to be able to kill for no reason and without remorse is almost without exception considered monstrous. "Choice" without moral perception is inhuman.

A third case. Although we sometimes use expressions like "free as a bird" or "born free," the freedom of the creatures of the animal kingdom bears no real comparison with human freedom. For one thing, humans feel the sting of conscience and the bitter lash of remorse. For another, even to mount one truly free act, a human being needs to gather his or her best powers. Much of the time we drift, act from routine, and follow well-worn paths of little resistance, much as other animals do. We do not often in one day manage to exercise our full capacities for reflective and deliberate choice. When on occasion we *are* shocked by a challenge that forces us to take full responsibility for what we are doing, we often hedge and draw back and, at the very least, begin to work out a line of retreat. (Dostoevsky invited us to watch ourselves clamor for freedom and then, once given it, try desperately to hand it back, dreading responsibility.) Leaders get to become leaders because they seize responsibilities that others surrender. To live up to the potential inherent in being a human being requires all-out effort.

A fourth case. A liberal activist I know admires committed people—people of principle who are true, resolute, and sound in judgment (not kooky). Yet when he talks about liberty, despite the fact that he himself is conspicuous for his habits of equanimity, moral purpose, fidelity, fortitude, justice, and prudence, my friend leaves all these admirable qualities of character out of the picture. He talks as if liberty means to him doing whatever he pleases. For instance, if an adult couple were to make love openly on the public stage, for him the only moral issue at stake would be whether they were being paid the minimum wage. This admirable liberal friend is strictly laissez-faire in sexual matters, even though he is strongly in favor of tight state regulation over economic transactions, even between consenting adults. In this, he is the direct reverse of a conservative friend who is laissez-faire in economics but strict about sex.

My liberal friend is so busy defending liberty of expression that he never gets around to defending the admirable virtues that make true liberty possible, and make him the reliable and responsible man that he is. He never mentions how many virtues liberals need to practice every day before lunch, although he exercises them. Liberalism in the United States is nothing if not a movement for moral athletes whose consciences are well-honed and whose commitments are strong enough to withstand losing elections. More virtue is involved in the practice of liberty than my liberal friend's philosophy speaks of.

What my friend fails further to see is that citizens with little capacity to govern their passions in the private sphere are not likely to meet the heavy demands of self-government in the public forum. For great passions—of envy, fear, desire, anger, greed, and ambition—sweep over the body politic on a regular basis, like waves breaking upon a beach. As a beach prey to erosion is soon no beach at all, a republic vulnerable to the accumulated force of uncontrolled passions is soon torn to tatters. Without those specific habits of the soul that keep safe the harbors of calm reflection, confidence in republican government is chimerical.

I also have a paleoconservative friend who, like my liberal friend, consistently interprets the word "liberty" as "license." He draws support for this interpretation from watching the behavior of some liberals. Authority is his anchor against license. He speaks of "obedience to truth" rather than "religious liberty." He concedes (sometimes grudgingly) that the latter may be necessary in the political order, as a codicil to an armistice, but that it has no "moral status." Humans are *obligated* to seek, find, and obey God; they are not "free" not to do so, except in the technical sense that of their own volition they may indeed (and often do) turn away from God. He thinks it necessary to insist on putting things in this almost intolerant and inquisitorial way, out of the rage he feels against licentiousness.

My paleo friend conveniently forgets that there are (at least) two traditions within Anglo–American liberalism whose outlooks may be contrasted through the following three oppositions:

- The tradition of license (liberty to do whatever one wishes) vs. the tradition of ordered liberty (liberty to do what one ought).
- Liberty *from* the law vs. liberty *under* the law.
- The liberty of "letting go" vs. the liberty of self-control.

The possibility of republican self-government is based on the second part of each of these oppositions. Together, these contrasts adumbrate a sober concept of liberty, weighty with responsibility, and yet a liberty that lightens the heart by the sweet dignity it imparts. In one part of each of these contrasts, obedience to truth—as best a lively sense of reality (and God's grace) draws one *to* the truth—is part of liberty's definition. To speak here of "obedience to truth" would be redundant.

In sum, certain specific virtues are necessary to the life of the republic, just as "the fundamentals" of blocking, tackling, and concentration are necessary to a football team. Liberal activists too often neglect to praise in public the very virtues on which their own behavior (and the republic itself) depends. Their lives are sometimes more admirable than their theories. Morally, they talk a better game of laissez-faire than they practice. They talk *liberté* but practice ordered liberty.

ORDER IN THE ANCIEN RÉGIME

In those parts of the world whose traditions descend from the ancien régime (the political and social system of Europe as it existed before the French Revolution), countries in which the Anglo–American style of liberal order is not a matter of experience, the concept of ordered liberty is especially hard to grasp. Indeed, the four cases just mentioned suggest that our Anglo–American habits of speech contribute to international confusion. We are scarcely good exponents of the tradition we inherit.

To begin with, those who live in Latin countries in particular are accustomed to thinking of *liberté* as lawless. In Latin countries, many early leaders of the liberal party prided themselves on being anticlerical, atheistic, not infrequently amoral, and metaphysical skeptics. They didn't believe in God; they scarcely believed in *anything*. Thus religious traditionalists in Latin nations (especially clergymen) grew accustomed to associating liberalism with libertinism. They do not share the experience of Anglo–American "liberal" countries, in which laws are framed by the consent of the governed, and respect for the law is high. They do not conceive of liberty as ordered by law, reason, and conscience, or recognize that, without law, liberty (in the Anglo–American sense) cannot be achieved.

Second, clerical traditionalists in Latin countries tend to imagine that liberty *must* lead to chaos. Where there is liberty, they think, each person will go off in a different direction, at whim, or in pursuit of crass self-interest without order. Only the law, they imagine, or only a strong leader (a *caudillo*) can hold other wills in check, channel them—and make the trains run on time.

In traditional cultures, this may be so. But in cultures based upon free and dynamic markets, purely *centrifugal* activities would be self-defeating. For there is one secret to the free society that traditionalists do not grasp: The free market is a *centripetal* force. Where it is truly dynamic, based upon invention and innovation, and where it is animated by a culture that believes in fair play and obeying the rules, the free market obliges those who would succeed in it to pay attention to others—even to the unexpressed wants and desires of others; even to their right to basic respect and dignity. For they are obliged to approach others only through the latter's freely given consent.

Unlike an aristocratic order, a market order begins on the assumption that all who enter the market are equal under the law, that each has dignity, and that each deserves respect. Where these are lacking, participants in the market will loudly and properly complain. The market's ideal is that every exchange should be based on the full consent of those who take part. In the ideal situation, not only should both parties to an exchange be satisfied, but each should think that, in a way, each has got the better of the deal (given the different immediate needs and concrete situations of the two). And each should be glad to do business with the other again. This is the meaning behind the common policy, "The customer is always right." If you want your customers to return, they must leave your presence with a certain sense not only of satisfaction generally obtained, but also of dignity fully intact.

Thus the insight most lacking to traditionalists is that intelligent and practical persons, acting freely and on behalf of their own practical wisdom, can in their free exchanges generate a spontaneous order, a form of catallaxy superior in its reasonableness to any order that might be planned, directed, or enforced from above. Traditionalists seem to believe that the only possible order is order enforced from on high. Order, in the traditionalist view, is first an intellectual construct conceived in the mind of the leader, then promulgated, then enforced. In a free society the conception of order is quite different. When free persons try to be cooperative, and attempt to enter into reasonable contracts with their fellows, these very efforts give rise to a social order more alive with intelligence, and more subtly and gracefully ordered, than all the planned and top-down orders on earth.

That free markets, under certain cultural and political conditions, will produce a superior social order should be treated as an empirical hypothesis. Such a statement would be true only if, under extended social experiments, the predicted consequences did in fact occur. The prediction of the *traditionalists* is that a free society will lack all order. The prediction of those who believe in the power of *free markets* to encourage reasonable and cooperative behavior is that such markets will give rise to a more dynamic order, shot through with greater intelligence and a wider and deeper intelligibility, than any known alternative. Try out these two hypotheses and see for yourself.

A GREAT YEAR, 1989

Quite impressively, Pope John Paul II titles one of the chapters of *Centesimus Annus* "The Year 1989." (Usually, popes are concerned with eternity; it is unusual to focus on a single year, but this one seemed especially providential.) The collapse of socialism, although predicted by Leo XIII, surprised the whole world by its suddenness. Before one could quite absorb it all the Berlin Wall came down, the Iron Curtain disintegrated, and the Soviet Empire began to implode. The prestige of "real existing socialism" vanished like fog in sunlight. It will be written that at the start of the last decade of the twentieth century, the world finally entered a post-socialist era—one in which disillusioned socialists in the Third World, as well as leftist parties of the United Kingdom, France, and Germany also had to reconstruct their moral foundations.

Michael Ignatieff has written in *The New Republic* that the startling defeat of Labour in 1992 (for the fourth time in a row) was due to the fact that Margaret Thatcher's capitalist revolution of 1979 had come to have greater *moral* appeal:

> Labour always tells people what it is going to do for
> them. It never encourages them to do it for them-
> selves. In other words, Labour's language of rights
> and entitlements lost the battle of values to the lan-
> guage of personal initiative. Its core value—redistribu-
> tive justice—was decisively rejected.[11]

In a word, Labour too had to back away from a socialist psychology, as well as from socialist economics. A post-socialist era had dawned even for the left.

As Nobel laureate James M. Buchanan wrote in a recent issue of *The Economic Journal*: "The post-socialist century will be marked by a convergence of scientific understanding among those who profess to be economists."[12] We are all capitalist now, even the Pope.[13] Both traditionalist (Third World) and socialist methods have failed; for the whole world there is now only one form of economics.

In a curious way, then, the citizens of the formerly socialist world are awakening, like Rip van Winkle, from a long slumber—as if rubbing their eyes with wonder at the world of ordinary human experience. For example, in April 1991 a young woman in what was then still called Leningrad, Nataliya Yeromeeva, legally opened a small housewares shop, and thus became one of the first private shopkeepers in the Soviet Union in 70 years. "It's in people's nature that if something is theirs, it's theirs," she says, "and a person works with a totally different mind set if he [sic] has property."[14]

Through such eyes, the foundations of capitalism have looked quite different than they have to elites in the jaded West. Whereas our aristocratic forebears looked down upon commerical activities, those who have experienced the controlled economy saw capitalist activities as a moral advance. Thus the East is discovering the moral case for capitalism in the humble events of daily life, as in Mrs. Yeromeeva's discovery of private property.

Former socialists praise the moral advantages of capitalism and emphasize its humanistic qualities; for example, the simple experience of acting as a free consumer. As a text crucial for those who too glibly denigrate "consumerism," recall the Bulgarian citizen who wrote:

> Several German intellectuals and politicians had hard
> words for the fellow citizens who flung themselves on
> the West German shops as soon as they could. . . .
> These could only be the words of people who have
> forgotten, or never knew, the personal humiliation in-
> flicted by the permanent lack of the most elementary
> consumer goods: the humiliation of silent and hostile
> lines, the humiliation inflicted upon you by salespeo-
> ple who seem angry to see you standing there, the hu-
> miliation of always having to buy what there is, not
> what you need. The systematic penury of material
> goods strikes a blow at the moral dignity of the indi-
> vidual.[15]

Simple access to material things conveys a moral lesson to those who under socialism stood in lines for four to six hours every day.

The *overall* lesson of the events in Eastern Europe since 1989 is that there is now no "socialist economics." In the words of many Eastern Europeans, socialism does not work; there is no "third way."[16] There is only one form of economics, and it includes (1) markets, (2) private property, (3) incentives, and (4) invention, initiative, and enterprise. Haven't Western economists known this all along? Yes and no.

In Chapter 2 we noted Robert Heilbroner's plaint that the only economists who actually predicted the downfall of socialism were those such as Friedrich Hayek and Ludwig von Mises, both of whom were treated dismissively by mainline economists in the United States and elsewhere. On the other hand, mainline economists have for decades been persuaded of the virtues of markets, choice, and incentives; and they have effectively marginalized the social democrats (such as Heilbroner, Galbraith, Bowles, Lekachman, and others) who minimize the dynamics of markets and enterprise. This is as true at MIT as the University of Chicago, and in virtually every department of economics across the country. Most of the best economists consider themselves scientists. Writing mainly *for* scientists, they are less eager to communicate their convictions to the public than to their peers. Only in the media of the literate public, from *The New Yorker* and *Harper's* to *The New York Times Book Review* and the *New York Review of Books*, does the social democratic voice appear to be the mainstream.

Thus, as far as the public knows, most economists did not openly insist that "socialist economics" is an oxymoron, or confidently predict that the Soviet economy would inevitably fail. There are thousands of books on the transition from capitalism to socialism, but not a single one by a Western economist on the transition from socialism to capitalism. In this way did "the best lack all conviction."

Professor Buchanan asks:

> Why did economists fail to recognize that incentives remain relevant in all choice settings? Why did economists forget so completely the simple Aristotelian defense of private property? Why did so many economists overlook the psychology of value, which locates evaluation in persons, not in goods? Why did so many professionals in choice analysis fail to recognize the informational requirements of a centrally controlled economy in both the logical and empirical dimensions?

Why was there the near-total failure to incorporate the creative potential of human choice in models of human interaction?[17]

To philosophers and theologians, these questions from Prof. Buchanan are quite stimulating. To a remarkable extent, they bring economists into a territory that philosophers and theologians alike are also obliged to explore. Incentives? Private property? A psychology of value? Persons rather than goods? Creative potential? Human choice? These subjects of economic inquiry are in fact concepts that *excite* philosophers and theologians. (Indeed, these are concepts that philosophers and theologians were the *first* to draw from the mists of human experience.) For some decades now, these concepts have slowly been leading mainstream economists (with various theories of value) not only to a deeper and broader philosophical investigation of human action, but also to inquiries of considerable theological moment.

THE ANTICAPITALIST BIAS OF INTELLECTUALS

Professor Heilbroner's questions remind us of the anticapitalist bias of the intellectuals—and not only of social scientists, but also of theologians.[18] Why were intellectuals (both secular and religious), Marxists, Keynesians, and modernists, so opposed to liberal capitalism? Mostly, they stressed its negative features. They feared such dangers as "excessive individualism," "materialism," "acquisitiveness," and, whether in monopolies or in narrow financial circles, "excessive concentrations of economic power." They were not wrong to fear such dangers and to denounce abuses. Rather systematically, however, they underestimated the spiritual resources of existing capitalist countries, and especially those in which counterweights came into play: where, namely, democratic institutions were powerful, the law was held in high respect, and the religious traditions of Judaism, Christianity, and a certain ethical humanism remained strong. Over the decades, the original capitalist countries of the Anglo–American world, and others on the continent, undertook many forms of social reorganization. In his encyclical of 1991, indeed, Pope John Paul II recognized these internal transformations—and encouraged yet more of them.[19]

One reason why intellectuals overlooked the self-reforming

capacities of capitalism when the latter is embedded in powerful democratic and moral–religious traditions may have to do with the aristocratic biases of modern intellectual life. For modern economics was born not in an era altogether neutral regarding commerce, trade, and industry. As the economic historian Jacob Viner has written:

> Among the Greek and Roman philosophers hostile or contemptuous attitudes towards trade and the merchant were common, based in the main on aristocratic and snobbish prejudice, and with no or naive underpinning of economic argument. Thus Aristotle maintained that trade was an unseemly activity for nobles or gentlemen, a "blameable" activity. He insisted that wealth was essential for nobility, but it must be inherited wealth. Wealth was also an essential need of the state, but it should be obtained by piracy or brigandage, and by war for the conquest of slaves, and should be maintained by slave workers. . . .
>
> The early Christian fathers on the whole took a suspicious if not definitely hostile attitude towards the trade of the merchant or middleman, as being sinful or conducive to sin.[20]

The reader will recall that Adam Smith, the eighteenth-century inventor of economic science, was a student of theology in his youth and was occupied professionally throughout his life in the teaching of moral philosophy. Nonetheless, theology in his time was deeply embedded in the habits, images, and practices of preceding centuries. Its viewpoint, rooted in the land, was that of landholders and rural peasants. It was adversarial to both commerce and manufacturing. It was aristocratic. The viewpoint of this earlier theology was, on the whole, favorable to inherited wealth (or wealth conferred by royal endowment); but it was quite dismissive of earned wealth, and particularly of wealth earned through commerce and manufacturing. ("Wealth is morally all right if you inherited it," it seemed to hold, "but if you earned it by your own sweat, it is grubby.") It celebrated the arts of statecraft and war, of entertaining and dining, of magnificence and lavish giving, of ceremony and play. It did not look with equal esteem upon the vulgar arts of providing goods and services, of

buying and selling, and of pioneering in invention and manufac-
ture. It loved the nobility (and implied leisure) of the liberal arts,
and looked down upon the "servile" industrial and commerical
arts. It called the liberal arts "noble" and the commerical arts
"merely useful." The first it commended as a way of "being,"
while it dismissed the second as crassly "utilitarian."[21] Resenting
this rebuff, economists for their part regarded religious reflection
as unrealistic and irrelevant, if not positively harmful to honest
empirical inquiry and to the condition of the poor.

RECONCILING ECONOMICS AND RELIGION

The encyclical of Pope John Paul II, *Centesimus Annus*, issued
on May 1, 1991, indicated a strong desire to end the divorce
between religion and economics once and for all. Noting the collapse of Marxism, the Pope completed the efforts begun by Leo
XIII a century before to point to necessary reforms of a democratic, law-abiding, anthropologically sound form of capitalism.[22]
    As Leo XIII won the name "pope of associations" for himself
because he made free associations central to his social teaching, so
100 years from now, John Paul II may be accorded fame as "the
pope of economic enterprise," because he made "personal economic initiative" central to his social teaching. In *Sollicitudo Rei
Socialis* (1987), the latter declared the right of personal economic
initiative to be a fundamental human right, second only to the
right of religious liberty, rooted (like religious liberty) in the image
of the Creator endowed in every human being.[23] Like their Maker,
he suggested, men and women are called to be co-creators in the
economic realm.
    Perhaps those who have been trained in the disciplines of busi-
ness life and economics will immediately discern the significance
of this theological insight. Schumpeter, Hayek, and Kirzner have
taught that the cause of the wealth of nations is invention, discovery, enterprise. In important ways, therefore, human capital
is prior to physical capital. Thus, in turning to the Creation story
of Genesis as a guide to his reflections on economics, John Paul
II found a way to heal the breach between religion and economics
from which the West has suffered for 200 years. This move allowed
him to emphasize the creativity of the human person—in a sense,
the priority of human capital over material capital.

All these moves allow us to look again at the history of the last two centuries, especially the rise of inventiveness. The new order of the eighteenth century—the "commercial republic"—first commended itself to Western civilization by its moral superiority to the old order.[24] In place of brigandage and war, it offered law and consensual contracts. "Commerce and Peace" was the motto of commercial Amsterdam. To have grasped that the path to wealth is blazed by innovation, industry, and exchange, rather than by plunder, brigandage, and conquest, was a great moral gain for the West.

To be sure, a new economy was not—is not—enough; it must be checked and balanced by a *democratic* polity, since a fully humane free economy requires a sound juridical system rooted in the consent of the governed, and also requires the guidance of disciplined, compassionate, and realistic cultural institutions. But here the classical liberal economists made a mistake. They tried to describe economic reality (and particularly the new institutions they were recommending) in objective *scientific* terms, while neglecting to state explicitly the sort of *moral* habits required to make those institutions work. They simply took for granted the moral heritage of Western civilization, in which Judaism and Christianity had been teaching peoples two crucial points: that every person has a vocation to bring "this earthly kingdom" more into accord with the pattern of the City of God, and that even the most lowly citizens are precious in the eyes of God and made in His image.

In such a culture, even the poorest had a right to try "to better their condition," and were given a vocation of personal initiative and creativity. All were taught that one of the names God cherishes is Truth, and that this name implies both moral duties of strict honesty (before the gaze of an undeceivable Judge) and intellectual duties beyond the temptations of skepticism and relativism—a vocation of rigorous intellectual inquiry into the intelligibility of all things. Moreover, Judaism and Christianity hold that history has a point, direction, and purpose; human existence is more than an endless cycle of repetitions, even though the human being is fallible and weak and prone to falling into the same pitfalls again and again.

In brief, Judaism and Christianity broke through the constraints of "nature" (conceived of via pagan myths of repetition) and inspired the West with a vision of progress and an acute sense of "history." This philosophy of being—historical and existential without being historicist—laid the groundwork for a civilization of high morale, strong moral habits, and a taste for making critical judgments about what meets the tests of daily reality and what does not.

Max Weber rightly thought it necessary to make this moral dimension of the culture of capitalism explicit. He may have erred in calling it only the Protestant ethic, and in limiting it chiefly to certain branches of Calvinism, at that. But he is quite right in discerning that without a certain moral ethos—that is, without the daily practice and conscious legitimation of certain moral habits— the objective institutions of capitalism would be hollow sepulchers. This perception has been borne out in the most striking way since the events of 1989. After 40 (or 70) years of Communist morality in Central and Eastern Europe, the sudden appearance of capitalist institutions is by no means sufficient to bring economic dynamism. When the Polish *Sejm* (parliament) passes legislation permitting market exchange, recognizing private property rights, and allowing private profits, nothing much changes so long as the people of Poland continue behaving as they have been taught to behave for 40 years: remaining passive, waiting for the state to do something else. The birth of a capitalist system requires a *moral* revolution. The *moral* habits of the Polish people must change. They must cease thinking of themselves as objects of the state and begin thinking of themselves (in Pope John Paul II's words) as "creative subjects." They must begin to practice "personal economic initiative." They must become creators. (Observers are happy to note that this is what Poles did begin to do, starting over 400,000 new small enterprises in the first year after the revolution of 1989.) Many individuals must choose to live in a new way, and by a more demanding regimen of choice. Capitalism is a moral revolution, or not at all.

For a people satisfied with dependency on the state, who show little or no initiative, whose work habits are deplorable, and whose basic honesty (whether as managers or statisticians or workers) is suspect are not likely to be wealth-producers. Choice runs through every aspect of economic activity. People must learn the habits (temperance, reflectiveness, discernment, steadiness) that allow them to choose swiftly, truly, and well. Similarly, economic activity depends on a sound political order, the rule of law, and a recognition of basic rights. In such a political order, choice is also central.

In its politics, in its morals, and in its economic activities, a free society makes constant and regular use of one fundamental reality: choice. It takes no daring, then, to predict that economics will increasingly come to be seen as the study of human choice. To cite Buchanan again: "The political economy is already *arti-factual*; it has been constructed by human choices."[25] Choice will become ever more central in economic analysis. This means that the human being (and human morality) will become more central. Now that the world is turning rather more unanimously to forms of political economy which enlarge the scope of choice in the political, economic, and moral–cultural fields, economics will necessarily become more focused on the human capacity both to reflect and to choose. It will become a humanistic discipline. It is in exactly these two activities, reflection and choice, that the human creature is properly said to be made in the image of God.[26]

CONVERGENCE ON CHOICE

Down the ages, many metaphors have been used of God: God is like the mountains, or like the boundless seas, or like the constant stars, or like the hen taking her chicks under her wing. But the most compelling analogies for God have come from the most complicated form of life found on earth, the human being. No one has seen God, but whatever God is like, He is imagined to be more like the activities of reflecting and choosing—of understanding and loving—than like anything else in the world. Within the human being, since at least the time of Plato and Aristotle, nothing has been found more godlike than the human capacity for insight and choice: that fire of light, and passionate longing for the good, which have so animated Western civilization.

Buchanan is shaping a new economic vision around the concept of choice—public choice *and* private choice. Theologically, choice based on understanding is the human activity held to be most godlike; it is also the activity in which religious liberty (the first liberty) and economic liberty (the second liberty) are most closely linked. Both, according to Pope John Paul II, have the same root, in the image of the Creator endowed in every human being: "Religious freedom . . . is the basis of all other freedoms and is inseparably tied to them all by reason of that very dignity which is the human person."[27] And again, in *Sollicitudo Rei Socialis*:

> On the *internal level* of every nation, respect for all rights takes on great importance, especially . . . the rights based on the *transcendent vocation* of the human being, beginning with the right of freedom to profess and practice one's own religious belief.[28]

Add to this the human right of economic enterprise, of which the Pope also writes in the same letter:

> In today's world, among other rights, *the right of economic initiative* is often suppressed. Yet it is a right which is important not only for the individual but also for the common good. Experience shows us that the denial of this right, or its limitation in the name of an alleged "equality" of everyone in society, diminishes, or in practice absolutely destroys the spirit of initiative, that is to say *the creative subjectivity of the citizen.*[29]

Already in *Laborem Exercens* (1981), Pope John Paul II had written that the Book of Genesis "teaches that man ought to imitate God, his Creator, in working, because man alone has the unique characteristic of the likeness to God."[30] And in *Sollicitudo Rei Socialis* he insists that the denial of religious and economic liberty and other core liberties impoverishes humans:

> The denial or the limitation of human rights—as for example the right to religious freedom, the right to share in the building of society, the freedom to organize and to form unions, or to take initiative in economic matters—do these not impoverish the human person as much as, if not more than, the deprivation of material goods?[31]

This vision of fundamental personal liberties implies a certain kind of world order. Such an order, open to "the acting person," the "creative subject," must be a dynamic order; and it will likely tend in the direction of mind.

DYNAMIC ORDER

The democratic order is not a static order; it is subject to the whims (or steadiness) of a free people. But neither is a capitalist order a static order. New inventions continually disrupt it. Before there was an automobile culture, there was a culture of horses and carriages. Before there were word processors, there were only typewriters—but typewriters were already a great advance over quill pens. Before there was an electronic revolution, there was an industrial revolution (characterized by pulleys and pistons, gears, and grease). The amazing thing about a civilization built upon choice is that it is a civilization of the most remarkable dynamism. Its order is not the order of static equilibrium, but the order of continual change.

Moreover, this principle of change appears to have a fascinating characteristic: The direction of change does not seem to be random. On the contrary, change fairly regularly occurs in the direction of a purer and more immediate expression of the human mind. If the typewriter seemed obedient to the human mind, the electronic display of the word processor seems to reflect the human mind ever more translucently. Before the computer screen, the human mind has hardly to think before it sees an expression of itself. The logic built into the computer encourages the human mind to take flight and to imagine yet more docile machines.

The creativity of the human mind is at the origin of a humane democratic and capitalist order. To nourish that creative mind in its efforts to reflect the full beauty of the Creator from Whom it derives (and from Whom the beauties of creation derive) is also its end.

IN THE DIRECTION OF MIND

If the precapitalist, traditionalist philosophers and theologians of Latin America and elsewhere are to comprehend the reality of a free society, they will need to give much thought to this issue: Is a "spontaneous order" really possible? Since it is obvious that such orders already exist, how do they come to pass? What are their constituent parts? What is the dynamism that allows such orders to happen as they do? The hypothesis of catallaxy will have to be thoroughly explored.

For if catallaxy is not possible, then a free society is not possible. If individuals of practical wisdom (a.k.a. prudence or providence) cannot achieve reasonable and cooperative outcomes in pursuing their own desires for community, then any hope for the free society is in vain.

But there really *are* free societies—none perfectly so, but many rather remarkably so. And thus, our task is to understand more clearly and in greater detail what we already see around us, rather than to invent some figment of imagination, or to say that what has happened cannot happen. For who can doubt that in many free societies today, without an Office of Planners and without dictatorship, the telephones do work, daily newspapers appear, the trains run and the airplanes fly, offices open, and daily life is remarkably well-ordered? In such societies, many citizens earn their living by looking for niches in which useful services are not yet being supplied, or in which existing procedures are not yet efficient, striving to remedy these defects. Thus is a free order slowly perfected by trial-and-error, voluntarily, without orders from above.

In a free society, ironically, the most dissatisfied citizens are those romantics and restless ones who despise the regularity and order that they see all around them. Recall that early critics of the market order feared that it would give rise to anarchy. Then note that their progeny fear excessive regimentation, "the organization man," the routine of working "nine-to-five," "the iron cage," and "the treadmill." Nobody directs such an order. Nobody preplans it. Yet that order is quite marvelous just the same.

THE THREE SPHERES OF LIBERTY

We have not come to the end of history, the terminus of a long series of social experiments to build a social order worthy of the human mind and soul.[32] But we have so far discovered that there are three fundamental orders of liberty: political liberty, economic liberty, and cultural liberty. The document of Vatican II on the Church and the world, *Gaudium et Spes*, devoted one section to each of these three spheres of liberty.

Yet, curiously enough, modern attempts to develop institutions that more fully express the human capacity for liberty *in all three spheres* have resulted in a world more interdependent than before.

One must again conclude that ordered liberty is a centripetal force. Far from leading to anarchy, ordered liberty leads to interdependence. Far from leading to uniformity, it nourishes cultural variety.[33] Indeed (as we shall see in Chapter 6), seldom in history have movements of ethnic, religious, cultural, and linguistic differentiation been stronger. These forces of differentiation are normally expressed within, and balanced by, powerful centripetal forces of interdependence. In an important way, the motto of such a world could be: *E pluribus unum*.

ONE ROOT, TWO LIBERTIES

One may thus imagine that in the twenty-first century philosophers and theologians will acquire a great deal more economic sophistication than they now have. One may also imagine that economists will become ever more skillful in developing humanistic categories—philosophical *and* theological—adequate to the complex phenomena of human choice with which they must grapple.

More than they have so far spelled out in their theories, economists already dimly recognize that a free economy cannot function unless its participants have mastered certain moral virtues. Important ethical assumptions are built into the free economy. These assumptions need to be articulated. Otherwise, peoples who wish to develop free economies will not focus on developing the necessary moral skills.[34] And peoples who have them, in losing the necessary virtues, will lose them.

Fundamentally, the material subject of both economics and theology (philosophy) is the human person and community, in their creativity and mutual sustenance. This subject matter includes character, choice, and action. International experience is forcing economists to turn in this direction. That is why, in the twenty-first century, the disciplines of economics and religious reflection are likely to overlap more than in the past. No religious figure has contributed more initiatives to this potential reconciliation than Pope John Paul II. And nowhere did he set forth so many of these initiatives as in his encyclical, *Centesimus Annus*, the "hundredth year," to which we now turn.

CHAPTER 5

CAPITALISM RIGHTLY UNDERSTOOD

> Whereas at one time the decisive factor of production
> was *the land*, and later capital—understood as a total
> complex of the instruments of production—today the
> decisive factor is increasingly *man himself*, that is, his
> knowledge, especially his scientific knowledge, his
> capacity for interrelated and compact organization, as
> well as his ability *to perceive the needs of others* and to
> satisfy them.
>
> *Centesimus Annus*, #32

Centesimus Annus EXPLODED ACROSS THE ROMAN SKY ON MAY 1,
1991, LIKE A SONIC BOOM. Even the first fleeting sight of this new
encyclical of Pope John Paul II led commentators around the world
to predict that it would lift the worldwide terms of debate on
political economy to a new level. Immediately evoking praise from
both left and right, this encyclical seemed to some to be the greatest
in the series of which it is a part.[1] In reply to questions raised
about political economy and free social institutions by the events
of 1989, it is a classic restatement of Christian anthropology.

As Karol Wojtyla, Pope John Paul II had already done significant work in phenomenology, particularly in his book *The
Acting Person*.[2] The title of that book furnishes us a key to the
nuanced approval that the Pope now gives to capitalism rightly
understood—a capitalism he recommends to his native Poland,
other formerly socialist nations, and the Third World. This approval surprised many commentators. The London *Financial*

Times, probably basing its story on leaks from one faction among those preparing the document, had predicted the ringing endorsement of a socialism more advanced than that of Neil Kinnock, Willy Brandt, and Felipé Gonzalez.[3] The Christian anthropology of Pope John Paul II, plus his acute observation of the way the world works, led him to other conclusions.[4]

The success of *Centesimus Annus* is due, in any case, to its philosophical profundity. From the beginning of his pontificate, the Pope has thought in a worldwide framework, appealing to the bond of human "solidarity"—a contemporary (and powerfully Polish) expression for the *caritas* (charity) of God that binds all men together. But he has also thought deeply, not only broadly. He has rooted his social proposals in his anthropology of "the acting person" and "creative subjectivity." This enables him to criticize every existing ideology, including democratic capitalism. Of the three great ideologies that put their mark upon this bloodiest of centuries, first national socialism failed, then communist socialism. From Eastern Europe, from the Third World, many were asking the Pope: What next?

Pope John Paul II proposed a tripartite social structure composed of a free political system, a free economy, and a culture of liberty.[5] After living through the great political debate of this century, he is in favor of democracy; after living through the great economic debate, he is in favor of capitalism rightly understood (that is, not *all* forms of capitalism). He is not satisfied with the way things are. He warns that a formidable struggle awaits us, in building a culture worthy of freedom. If we have the politics and the economics roughly (but only roughly) straight, how should we live? How should we shape our culture? These questions are now front-and-center.

BACKGROUND REFLECTIONS

Soon after his election to the papacy in 1979, his countrymen in Poland began to recognize that Karol Wojtyla was their international tribune. Lech Walesa, an electrician in Gdansk, inspired the labor union *Solidarnosc* (Solidarity), which soon became the greatest civic association of the Polish nation, committed to social justice, democracy, nonviolence, and a profound moral transformation of Polish society. Meanwile, as long as a son of Poland sat on the chair of Peter, the Communist rulers of Poland found themselves in a glaring international light. The Iron Curtain no longer hid their movements. Although they attempted to crush Solidarity, they could not.

For the ten long years until 1989, a certain space for civic activity—intense, intellectual, practical—opened up within the bosom of totalitarian society. Citizens in other Eastern European nations took heart. Poland was the first to nurture an independent people, spiritually free of Communism, able to negotiate with the Communist leaders as equals—even more than equals. Once Solidarity broke the mask of totalitarian conformity, democratic movements began to grow in boldness throughout that Empire which many now dared to call evil.

In the days when he was a young Archbishop of Krakow attending the Second Vatican Council in Rome (1961–65), Wojtyla first came to international attention for a speech he gave before the Council on Religious Liberty. The American echoes of that speech were widely noted, for at the time high among the priorities of the American bishops was a strong statement on religious liberty. Then, from his first days as Pope, John Paul II spoke often about liberty of conscience, going so far as to call it "the first liberty." Gradually, too, he came to understand that the American meaning of liberty—"ordered liberty," as he came to call it (liberty under law, liberty under reason)—does not mean libertinism, laissez-faire, the devil take the hindmost. At least one American bishop played an important role in drawing the Pope's attention to the vital difference in this respect between the American Revolution and the French Revolution.

In his many years as Archbishop of Krakow and professor at the Catholic University of Lublin, Karol Wojtyla provided intellectual leadership for the people who gave rise to Solidarity. When he became Pope, but before the imposition of martial law in Poland in 1980, he announced to the world that all of Europe was a single tree with two branches, East and West. Europe's destiny, he said, is to be rejoined as one, drawing life from its common roots in Judaism and Christianity. As Pope, he could on any day broadcast the pain of Poland and give every Communist abuse a reverberating echo around the world. Perhaps unhappy with this role, someone sent one or more assassins to slay him on May 13, 1981. Although the Pope nearly died, he recovered. Within a few days, he had planned to issue an encyclical celebrating the ninetieth anniversary of Leo XIII's *Rerum Novarum*; it had to be released nearly a year later, in early 1982, under the title *Laborem Exercens*. Here John Paul II appealed to the anthropology implicit in the Creation story of Genesis, the single best starting place for religious inquiry into the nature and causes of the creation of wealth.[6]

The underlying principle of the Polish Pope's anthropology is the "creative subjectivity" of the human person, together with the resulting "subjectivity of society." From his earliest work on, including his phenomenological inquiry *The Acting Person*, the Pope had been struck by the human being's most arresting characteristic: his or her capacity to originate action; that is, to imagine and to conceive of new things and then to do them. He found in creative acts the clue to human identity. Humans, he held, cannot take refuge from this responsibility by hiding behind "society"— there, too, they are responsible for their acts. Being in society does not absolve them of the burdens of subjectivity.

An unbeliever may achieve this insight with no benefit of religious belief. Karol Wojtyla approached it from two different directions—first in a philosophical way, second in a Jewish–Christian way. For him, philosophy and theology meet in the anthropology of the "real existing" human person. The philosopher sees *homo creator*; the theologian sees *imago Dei*. Man the creator (philosophy) is made in the image of the divine Creator (theology), and is endowed by Him with an inalienable right to creative initiative.

From this principle John Paul II derives a corollary for social systems: It is an affront to human dignity for a social system to repress the human capacity to create, to invent, and to be enterprising. In human "creative subjectivity" Wojtyla sees the principle of liberty, and for him this liberty naturally deploys itself in the three fields of conscience, inquiry, and action. It would be fair to say that John Paul II is a philosopher of liberty. Deeper in his eyes than liberty, however, is creativity. No end in itself, freedom is *for* something and must be *ordered by* something. Of these two notions, liberty is less satisfying; it raises further questions. Creativity is the deeper and more substantive notion. So it is more accurate to think of John Paul II as the philosopher of creativity. From this starting point in creativity, the Pope has over the years slowly approached that much-disputed beast, capitalism.

At the beginning of his pontificate, John Paul II used the word "capitalism" in a pejorative sense—as it is often used in European countries, the more so wherever the Marxist tradition has been strong. In his first social encyclical, *Laborem Exercens* (1982), he used "capital" to mean *things*, objects, instruments of production. He reserved for the word "labor" all humane and virtuous attributes, including creative subjectivity.[7]

Some years later, in *Sollicitudo Rei Socialis* (1987), the Pope moved from the "acting person" and "creative subjectivity" to "the fundamental human right of personal economic initiative."[8] This was the strongest recognition of enterprise in Catholic social thought. He saw enterprise as a vocation, a virtue, and a right.

By May of 1991, in *Centesimus Annus*, Wojtyla had moved beyond enterprise as a vocation, a virtue, and a right to a theory of the institutions necessary for its flowering. From this he moved to a theory of the business firm, and to a critique of the welfare state.[9] At the heart of each of these positions lies his fundamental insight: Every woman and every man has been created in the image of the Creator, in order to help co-create the future of the world.

The Pope emphasized how noble it is, and how many complex talents are required, to gain insight into the economic needs of the human race, to organize available resources, to invent new resources and methods, and to lead a cooperative, voluntary community to achieve real results.[10] In the whole of section 32, the Pope was eloquent about the lessons of creativity and community found in a modern economy. By contrast, the fundamental flaw in socialism, John Paul II wrote, was its faulty anthropology.[11] It misconceived the active, creative nature of the individual; it misconceived both human misery and human grandeur.

John Paul II rooted the capitalist ethos in the positive thrust of Judaism and Christianity, in their capacity for inspiring new visions and creative actions, rather than in the negative "this-worldly asceticism" that Max Weber found in the Protestant ethic. Common to the Jewish, Catholic, and Protestant views of the human economic agent is the "calling" or "vocation," which Weber erroneously thought to be distinctively Protestant. Every Jew and every Christian is called to be like God, since each is made in the image of God and called to be active and creative. Thence arises the visible dynamism of the Jewish and the Christian peoples in human history.

OUTLINE OF *CENTESIMUS ANNUS*

Before plunging too far into the particulars, it may be well to fix in mind an outline of the six chapters of *Centesimus Annus*. First, John Paul II undertook a "re-reading" of *Rerum Novarum*, thus handing down an authoritative reinterpretation of that document, much as in the case of the commentary of the U.S. Supreme Court on an earlier decision of that Court.

In Chapter 2, the Pope took up the "new things" that have happened since 1891 and that still affect us today. He analyzed the shortcomings of socialist anthropology, and described the reforms that transformed the "real existing capitalism" of the advanced countries from what it had been in 1891.[12]

Next the Pope lingered reflectively on the great events of "The Year 1989," one of the watershed years of human history. He laid out several reasons for the collapse of socialism, and a few lessons of worldwide importance to be drawn from it.

In Chapter 4, John Paul II addressed the classic Christian theme of "the universal destination of material goods." There is some affinity between this tradition and Locke's liberal doctrine of private property.[13] In this, the longest part of the encyclical, the Pope examined existing political economies for their compatibility with the dignity of the human person. Here he developed his new approach to initiative, enterprise, profit, and capitalism itself. He criticized severely abuses that still exist, particularly of the poor in the Third World, in whose name he eloquently urged inclusion in property ownership, the active worldwide market, and the spread of knowledge and skill.

Chapter 5 discussed the state and culture. Here the Pope stressed the limited state, democratic checks and balances, human rights, and constraints upon the state regarding welfare rights.[14] He criticized rather harshly the present excesses of the welfare state in economically advanced countries. He turned as well to the moral and cultural sphere, which is too often ignored: "People lose sight of the fact that life in society has neither the market nor the state as its final purpose."[15] Here, too, are found the Pope's comments on the formation of a "culture of peace."

Chapter 6, concluding on a theological note, looked to the future. We are, the Pope thinks, "ever more aware that solving serious national or international problems is not just a matter of economic production or of juridical or social organization."

Rather, most problems call for "specific ethical and religious values as well as changes of mentality, behavior, and structures."[16] The most perfect structures will not function if citizens do not have the relevant attitudes, habits, and behaviors. Among these is the habit of effective concern for one's fellow human beings around the world (the habit of "solidarity," as the Pope calls it), a new term for the old virtue of charity, calling attention to its international dimension.

In sum, *Centesimus Annus* called for serious reform of the moral and cultural institutions of democratic and capitalist societies—including the institutions of the mass media, cinema, universities, and families—in order to make democracy and capitalism fulfill their best promises. Neither the preservation of free political space achieved by democracy nor the achievement of liberation from oppressive poverty wrought by capitalism are sufficient (alone *or* together) to meet the human desire for truth and justice. Only a vital cultural life, at its heights infused by God's grace, can do that. Meanwhile, some 2 billion poor persons on this planet are not yet included within free and dynamic economies,[17] and their condition cannot be forgotten. Practical reforms of the international economic order are desperately needed.

A CHRISTIAN SOCIAL ANTHROPOLOGY

This overview of the whole terrain fixed in our minds, it should now be easier to grasp the inner logic of *Centesimus Annus*. This logic begins with concrete inspection of the human being:

> We are not dealing here with man in the "abstract,"
> but with the real, "concrete," "historical" man. We
> are dealing with each individual. . . . The horizon of
> the Church's whole wealth of doctrine is man in his
> concrete reality as sinful and righteous.[18]

When the young Wojtyla as a student first wrestled with modern Western thinkers such as Scheler and Heidegger, he fully expected that he would be living the rest of his life under real existing socialism. In that ideology, the individual counted for very little. In actual practice, socialist work was wholly oriented toward the piling-up of objects, products, *things*, with no real regard for the subjectivity of the worker. After toiling for days on the freezing seas at the risk of their lives, fishermen would discover that the refrigeration unit of the storehouse in which their catch had been deposited was defective and that the entire fruit of their labors had spoiled. Steelworkers would see the steel beams on which they had labored pile up in huge lots and rust, because distribution systems (such as they were) had broken down. Under Marxism, it was in no one's interest to see a product all the way through from conception to execution to delivery to satisfying use. Every person felt like a cog in *someone else's* machine. A new type of alienation was experienced which John Paul II described in *Sollicitudo Rei Socialis* (1987), his second social encyclical, precisely in contrast to a sense of personal action and initiative:

> In the place of creative initiative there appear passivity, dependence and submission to the bureaucratic apparatus which, as the only "ordering" and "decision-making" body—if not also the "owner"—of the entire totality of goods and the means of production, puts everyone in a position of almost absolute dependence, which is similar to the traditional dependence of the worker–proletarian in capitalism. This provokes a sense of frustration or desperation and predisposes people to opt out of national life, impelling many to emigrate and also favoring a form of "psychological" emigration.[19]

Amid such sour alienation, Wojtyla's emphasis on "the acting person" was entirely convincing. His emphasis on the creative subjectivity of the worker unsettled those Marxists who were assigned to do ideological battle with him. He turned the tables on them: He forced them to argue on Christian terrain. Thus he accepted their emphasis upon work, but then asked about the meaning of work to the worker—obliging them to confront, on the one hand, the alienation inherent in socialist organizations, and, on the other, a deeper and richer humanism, Christian in lineage. While he was the Archbishop of Krakow, the Pope had noted that the front between Catholicism and Marxism (or, more broadly, between humanism and socialism) had become a contestation over the meaning of man. In *Centesimus Annus* he hit the mark exactly:

> The fundamental error of socialism is anthropological
> in nature. Socialism considers the individual person
> simply as an element, a molecule within the social or-
> ganism, so that the good of the individual is com-
> pletely subordinated to the functioning of the socio-
> economic mechanism. Socialism likewise maintains
> that the good of the individual can be realized without
> reference to his free choice, to the unique and exclu-
> sive responsibility he exercises in the face of good or
> evil. Man is thus reduced to a series of social relation-
> ships, and the concept of the person as the autono-
> mous subject of moral decision disappears, the very
> subject whose decisions build the social order.[20]

"Reduced to a series of social relationships"—that was the
fatal flaw: the loss of "the autonomous subject of moral decision." In other words, the loss of a healthy respect for the individual—the acting, deciding person—and the loss of society's subjectivity too.

This point-blank thrust into the erroneous anthropology of
socialism allows Pope John Paul II to begin with the human individual and move to the larger context of social relations and
social systems: "Today, the church's social doctrine focuses especially on man as he is involved in a complex network of relationships within modern societies."[21] The individual is not *merely*
the sum of social relationships, but is socially engaged. As we have
already seen, the Pope's emphasis on invention and choice obliges
Western economists, too, to deepen their understanding of work,
the worker, and creative activity.

Thus the main lines of *Centesimus Annus* are clean and clear:
the human as an acting, creative person, capable of initiative and
responsibility, seeking institutions in the three main spheres of life
(political, economic, and cultural) worthy of his or her capacities—
institutions that do not stifle or distort human liberty. For God
Himself made human beings free:

> Not only is it wrong from the ethical point of view to
> disregard human nature, which is made for freedom,
> but in practice it is impossible to do so. Where society
> is so organized as to reduce arbitrarily or even sup-

press the sphere in which freedom is legitimately exercised, the result is that the life of society becomes progressively disorganized and goes into decline.[22]

This is the lesson the Pope draws from the self-destruction of socialism.

There is a further lesson about human capacities for evil. A good Calvinist joke roughly expresses the Pope's views: "The man who said that man is totally depraved couldn't be all bad." Analogously, the Pope: "Man tends toward good, but he is also capable of evil. He can transcend his immediate interest and still remain bound to it."[23]

Thus, respecting man's limited but genuine goodness, the Pope urges us not to stress an opposition between "self-interest" and "the common good." He urges us, rather, to seek a "harmony" between "self-interest" and "the interests of society as a whole," wherever this may be possible: "The social order will be all the more stable, the more it takes this fact [man's two-sided nature] into account and does not place in opposition personal interest and the interests of society as a whole, but rather seeks ways to bring them into fruitful harmony."[24]

One of the cautions of James Madison and Alexander Hamilton in *The Federalist* is that the perfect should not be the enemy of the good.[25] They resisted "utopic theorists" and appealed to a basic realism about human beings rooted in a sober consideration of historical experience. In a spirit not altogether dissimilar, the Pope recognizes the claims of legitimate self-interest:

> In fact, where self-interest is violently suppressed, it is replaced by a burdensome system of bureaucratic control which dries up the wellsprings of initiative and creativity. When people think they possess the secret of a perfect social organization which makes evil impossible, they also think that they can use any means, including violence and deceit, in order to bring that organization into being. Politics then becomes a "secular religion" which operates under the illusion of creating paradise in this world. But no political society—which possesses its own autonomy and laws—can ever be confused with the kingdom of God.[26]

In politics, Aristotle wrote, it is necessary to be satisfied with a "tincture of virtue." The Pope displays a similar sobriety.

In this direct way, Pope John Paul II grasps the horns of the contemporary problem of "free persons and the common good." It was relatively easy to determine what the common good was when, as of old, a single chief was charged with pointing it out. It is far more difficult when the freedom of each person to discern the common good is respected. Moreover, many aspects of the good of a whole people are not achieved in concert or by single-minded direction from above; on the contrary, they are achieved by a large number of persons and groups independently performing their own tasks with excellence. A sound family life is not achieved throughout society by *diktat* from above, for example, but by each set of parents independently doing their best. And individual small businesses do not await commands from planning boards, but achieve their purposes within their own markets and in their own particular niches in their own various ways. Thus, in asserting the principle that the coincidence of private interest and public good, as often as it can occur, achieves an outcome not at all bad for society, the Pope is being more than worldly-wise. He is not only taking account of both the good in humans and its ordinary limits. He is also assuming a more subtle view of the common good than was possible in the less pluralistic past.[27]

There is a difficulty here, of course. Many societies today are riven by "culture wars." Large and important factions hold radically different views about which way the society as a whole ought to go. What one faction finds good, another finds evil. In the last chapter of his encyclical, the Pope points out that cultural issues are the most important of all—and perhaps the most neglected by thinkers and doers. So much energy has gone into earlier conflicts over which political and economic order is most suited to human nature, that for more than two centuries the West has been living off of cultural capital. Concern over the physical climate has not yet been matched by concern over the moral climate. The ecology of liberty needs as much attention as the ecology of air, water, sea, and flame.[28] We are entering a period of cultural crisis.

Since personal action always entails risk, fault, and possible failure, the universe of freedom must be open, indeterminate, contingent. Some new things appear in it; some old things disappear. Pope John Paul II regularly stresses the new things that happen; for example, the new ideas that emerged in the years before *Rerum*

Novarum,[29] and how much the world changed between 1891 and 1991.[30] For him, history is a realm of trial and error, of costly mistakes and lessons hard-earned.[31] Moreover, the human person seldom experiences societies worthy of his or her capacities for freedom, for love, for truth, for justice—and it is these that the human race seeks.

At this point, the Pope passes from the analysis of personal action to the analysis of social structures—and, in particular, of economic systems.

CAPITALISM, YES

Papal social thought was once said to lack sophistication in the social sciences and to be too focused on the individual. *Centesimus Annus* intends to expand its analytic apparatus broadly enough to contrast not just ideologies, but actual systems of political economy such as real existing socialism and real existing examples of democracy and capitalist economies.[32]

With some sophistication, the Pope distinguished the sphere of the social from that of the state, the civil society from government. He emphasized the importance of free labor unions, citizens' initiatives, and free associations.[33] In a passage reminiscent of Tocqueville's worries about the "new soft despotism" of democracies, he launched a systemic critique of "the social assistance state," contrasting local "neighborly" work among the poor with the sterility of bureaucratic relationships.[34] Whereas for centuries the Catholic tradition has maintained a positive view of the role of the state in social life, John Paul II was especially careful and detailed in setting limits to the overly ambitious states of the late twentieth century.[35]

There has never been any question in this Pope's mind that democratic institutions, whatever their faults, are the best available protection for human rights. He now added that capitalist virtues and institutions, whatever *their* faults, are the best available protection for democracy.

To be sure, it was the famous "paragraph 42" that drew most of the attention in the world's press. Until that point, the Pope had been dealing with the events that have changed the world since 1891, and especially the events of 1989, preparatory to offering his practical advice for today. Then in #42 the Pope was at last ready to return to the underlying question being pressed upon him from Poland, Czechoslovakia, Hungary, the Third World, and many other quarters: After the collapse of socialism, what do you propose? It is worth giving his answer in full, since the only sensible answer to the question requires some care with the highly disputed term "capitalism."

> Returning now [for the third time] to the initial question: Can it perhaps be said that after the failure of communism capitalism is the victorious social system and that capitalism should be the goal of the countries now making efforts to rebuild their economy and society? Is this the model which ought to be proposed to the countries of the Third World, which are searching for the path to true economic and civil progress?
>
> The answer is obviously complex. If by *capitalism* is meant an economic system which recognizes the fundamental and positive role of business, the market, private property and the resulting responsibility for the means of production as well as free human creativity in the economic sector, then the answer is certainly in the affirmative even though it would perhaps be more appropriate to speak of a *business economy, market economy* or simply *free economy*. But if by *capitalism* is meant a system in which freedom in the economic sector is not circumscribed within a strong juridical framework which places it at the service of human freedom in its totality and which sees it as a particular aspect of that freedom, the core of which is ethical and religious, then the reply is certainly negative.[36]

Point by point, this reply reflects the experience of those nations that since World War II have experienced both political liberty and economic prosperity. For example, recovering from the experience of Nazism, Germany after World War II had to undergo a major transformation which was not economic only, but also political and moral.[37] In the formerly communist nations, the situation today is similar. So also in the Anglo–American nations a structure of law has evolved over centuries, from which slowly emerged the political, economic, and cultural institutions that, together, frame "the free society." In fact, such neoliberal thinkers as Friedrich von Hayek in *The Constitution of Liberty* and Bruno Leoni in *Freedom and Law* particularly stress these noneconomic factors.[38]

In *The Spirit of Democratic Capitalism* (1982), I called the resulting *Gestalt* a "tripartite system":

> Democratic capitalism is not a "free enterprise system" alone. It cannot thrive apart from the moral culture that nourishes the virtues and values on which its existence depends. It cannot thrive apart from a democratic polity committed, on the one hand, to limited government and, on the other hand, to many legitimate activities without which a prosperous economy is impossible. The inarticulate practical wisdom embedded in the political system and in the moral–cultural system has profoundly affected the workings of the economic system. Both political decisions and the moral climate encouraged this development. At various times in American history, both the political system and the moral–cultural system have seriously intervened, positively and negatively, in the economic system. Each of the three systems has modified the others.[39]

In the second part of #42, cited above, Pope John Paul II carefully orders the roles of all three systems—economic, juridical, and moral.[40]

As one part of the tripartite structure, capitalism rightly understood flows from the Pope's anthropology: "Man's principal resource is man himself. His intelligence enables him to discover the earth's productive potential and the many different ways in which human needs can be satisfied."[41] "Man," he writes again, "discovers his capacity to transform and in a certain sense create the world through his own work . . . carrying out his role as cooperator with God in the work of creation."[42] And yet again, "Man fulfills himself by using his intelligence and freedom. In so doing he utilizes the things of this world as objects and instruments and makes them his own. The foundation of the right of private initiative and ownership is to be found in this activity."[43]

Moreover, the expression of personal creativity through work entails a social dimension: "By means of his work man commits himself not only for his own sake, but also for others and with others. Each person collaborates in the work of others and for their own good. Man works in order to provide for the needs of his family, his community, his nation, and ultimately all humanity."[44]

In these texts we see the elemental form of the Pope's logic: from the image of the Creator endowed in each person to the work that flows from that source. Or again, from the fecund mind of the creative God to the exercise of human intelligence and choice in invention, initiative, and enterprise.

Already in *Sollicitudo Rei Socialis*, the Pope had seen that "the right to personal economic initiative" is a fundamental human right, second only to the right to religious liberty.[45] Like religious freedom, economic initiative also flows from the "creative subjectivity" of the human person.[46] This line of thought led the Pope to discern the role of enterprise in economic activity. As we have seen, Israel Kirzner defines enterprise as an act of discovery, an act of discerning either a new product or service to be supplied for the utility of others, or a new way of providing the same.[47] The Pope sees creativity at work in such acts of discovery and discernment. He even sees in them a new form of "capital." As pastor and theologian, of course, he goes beyond the purely economic evaluation of innovation to make ethical judgments about its impact on individual persons and the common good.

Although the origins of the word "capital" lie in a more primitive economic era, when *capita* referred to heads of cattle, and the major form of economic capital lay in the ownership of land, the same word also suggests the Latin *caput* (head), the human seat of that very creativity, invention, initiative the Pope sees in "creative subjectivity." Indeed, the Pope himself alludes to the crucial shift from the primitive meaning of capital as land to its modern meaning as human capital, as we must now examine.

The Pope's thinking on this point parallels that of Abraham Lincoln. In *Laborem Exercens*, the Pope had asserted "the principle of the priority of labor over capital" (where by "labor" he meant all sorts of work, even intellectual work, and by "capital" he meant material things).[48] Similarly, in his First Annual Message to Congress on December 3, 1861, rephrasing some of the very words he had used at the Wisconsin State Fair in 1859, Lincoln also wrote:

Labor is prior to, and independent of, capital. Capital
is only the fruit of labor, and could never have existed
if labor had not first existed. Labor is the superior of
capital, and deserves much the higher consideration.
Capital has its rights, which are as worthy of protection as any other rights. Nor is it denied that there is,
and probably always will be, a relation between labor
and capital, producing mutual benefits. The error is in
assuming that the whole labor of community exists
within that relation.[49]

Yet Lincoln also saw that the great cause of wealth is human
wit, and grew quite eloquent in praising the role of invention in
drawing wealth from the hidden bounty of creation.[50] Similarly,
he saw in the Patent and Copyright Clause of the U.S. Constitution a remarkable incentive for inventors and creators (and thus
one of history's great boons to human freedom), since the prospect
of the temporary ownership of ideas (as property) "added the fuel
of *interest* to the *fire* of genius."[51] The Pope writes:

The earth, by reason of its fruitfulness and its capacity
to satisfy human needs, is God's first gift for the
sustenance of human life. But the earth does not yield
its fruits without a particular human response to
God's gift, that is to say, without work. It is through
work that man, using his intelligence and exercising
his freedom, succeeds in dominating the earth and
making it a fitting home.
    In history, these two factors—work and the
land—are to be found at the beginning of every
human society. However, they do not always stand in
the same relationship to each other. At one time the
natural fruitfulness of the earth appeared to be and
was in fact the primary factor of wealth, while work
was, as it were, the help and support for his fruitfulness. In our time, the role of human work is becoming increasingly important as the productive factor
both of non-material and of material wealth.
    Work becomes ever more fruitful and productive
to the extent that people become more knowledgeable
of the productive potentialities of the earth and more

profoundly cognizant of the needs of those for whom their work is done.[52]

In a way different from that of Ludwig von Mises and Friedrich Hayek, but with an analogous concern, the Pope sees work as building up the tacit, experiential, evolving network of a "Great Society."[53] "It is becoming clearer how a person's work is naturally interrelated with the work of others. More than ever, work is work with others and work for others: It is a matter of doing something for someone else."[54]

In an odd way, then, modern capitalism centers more and more attention on *caput*, on factors such as knowledge, insight, discovery, enterprise, and inquiry. "Human capital" becomes the major cause of the wealth of nations, more important even than natural resources. A country without natural resources can in fact become wealthy; another country quite rich in natural resources can remain very poor. The reader can think of his or her own examples, but for me—all due complexities added—Japan and Brazil offer a potent contrast.[55] Such considerations lead the Pope to a new meaning of "capital."

> In our time in particular there exists another form of ownership which is becoming no less important than land: the possession of know-how, technology and skill. The wealth of the industrialized nations is based much more on this kind of ownership than on natural resources.[56]

The Pope's emphasis on the "community of work" also leads him to appreciate "entrepreneurial ability." It is not so easy to discern just how to put together human needs and human resources in a productive and efficient way; in many nations today economic failure, not success, seems to be the rule. The Pope discovers in a kind of foresight a key to avoiding failure:

> A person who produces something other than for his own use generally does so in order that others may use it after they have paid a just price mutually agreed upon through free bargaining. It is precisely the ability to foresee both the needs of others and the combinations of productive factors most adapted to satisfying

those needs that constitutes another important source
of wealth in modern society.[57]

In particular, the Pope stresses the social aspects of entrepreneurship. A free economic system is nothing if not a social system of
exchange, based upon voluntary agreement. The Pope follows this
logic closely:

> Many goods cannot be adequately produced through
> the work of an isolated individual; they require the
> cooperation of many people in working toward a
> common goal. Organizing such a productive effort,
> planning its duration in time, making sure that it cor-
> responds in a positive way to the demands which it
> must satisfy and taking the necessary risks—all this
> too is a source of wealth in today's society. In this
> way the role of disciplined and creative human work
> and, as an essential part of that work, initiative and
> entrepreneurial ability becomes increasingly evident
> and decisive.[58]

At this point, everything that the Pope has heretofore written
about the acting person, about creative subjectivity, and about the
fundamental right to personal economic initiative falls into place.
He is in a position to render a systemic judgment:

> This [modern economic] process, which throws practi-
> cal light on a truth about the person which Christian-
> ity has constantly affirmed, should be viewed carefully
> and favorably.[59]

This is an astonishing statement. The Pope suggests that the free
and cooperative economy sheds light on Christian teaching in a
new way. Nor does the Pope neglect the virtues required to accomplish this task:

> Important virtues are involved in this process such as
> diligence, industriousness, prudence in undertaking
> reasonable risks, reliability and fidelity in interpersonal
> relationships as well as courage in carrying out deci-
> sions which are difficult and painful, but necessary

both for the overall working of a business and in
meeting possible setbacks.[60]

The basis of the modern business economy, the Pope writes,
"is human freedom exercised in the economic field."[61] This is a
very important recognition. To papal approval for the free political
life of democracy, it adds approval for a free economic life; and
in both cases freedom implies accountability.

The Pope even finds it useful to say a good word for profit as
"a regulator of the life of a business": "The Church acknowledges
the legitimate role of profit as an indication that a business is
functioning well. When a firm makes a profit, this means that
productive factors have been properly employed and correspond-
ing human needs have been satisfied."[62] Like many good business
writers today, the Pope also stresses that profit is not the only
regulator of the life of a business: "Human and moral factors must
also be considered, which in the long term are at least equally
important for the life of a business."[63] Business writers such as
Peter Drucker stress the crucial role of various types of human
relations within firms;[64] the Pope speaks of a firm as "a community
of persons . . . who form a particular group at the service of the
whole of society."[65]

THE LIMITS OF CAPITALISM

Nevertheless, Pope John Paul II does not forget the costs of a
new modern capitalism, based upon human creativity, whose other
face is necessarily what Joseph A. Schumpeter called "creative
destruction."[66] The Pope writes that "The constant transformation
of the methods of production and consumption devalues certain
acquired skills and professional expertise, and thus requires a continual effort of retraining and updating."[67] He particularly worries
about the elderly, the young who cannot find jobs, and "in general
those who are weakest." He refers to the vulnerable in advanced
societies as "the Fourth World." Meeting their needs is the unfinished work of *Rerum Novarum*, including "a sufficient wage
for the support of the family, social insurance for old age and
unemployment, and adequate protections for the conditions of
employment."[68] All such deficiencies of a market system need to
be redressed with practical wisdom. In some cases government

will have to take a leading role; in other cases various sectors of civil society. The Pope is no libertarian—but neither is he a statist. Christian ends leave a great deal of room within these boundaries for rival approaches to means, programs, and policies.

The Pope is also eager to distinguish capitalism rightly understood from the "primitive" or "early" type of capitalism of which he does not approve. The latter is characterized by (1) systems of "domination of things over people"; (2) systems "in which the rules of the earliest period of capitalism still flourish in conditions of 'ruthlessness' in no way inferior to the darkest moments of the first phase of industrialization"; and (3) systems in which "land is still the central element in the economic process, while those who cultivate it are excluded from ownership and are reduced to a position of quasi-servitude."[69] In the Third World (quite visibly so in parts of Latin America), landless multitudes suffer cruelly and stream toward the great megalopolis where pitifully little work (or housing) is available to them. Like Hernando de Soto, the Pope sees in such propertylessness and exclusion the conditions in which "the great majority of the people in the Third World still live."[70]

By contrast, the Pope approves of "a society of free work, of enterprise, and of participation."[71] He adds:

> Such a society is not directed against the market, but
> demands that the market be appropriately controlled
> by the forces of society and by the state so as to guar-
> antee that the basic needs of the whole of society are
> satisfied.[72]

The words "appropriately controlled" exclude a pure version of laissez-faire, but are in line with the concept of the tripartite society envisaged in #42. "Society" is distinguished from "state"; the moral and cultural institutions of civil society are distinguished from the political organs of the government. *Both* the society *and* the state check, balance, and regulate the economy. That the Pope does not mean a socialist method of "control" is obvious from the preceding sentence, wherein the Pope is crystal clear: "What is being proposed as an alternative is not the socialist system."

In the same spirit, the Pope repeats three times that "It is unacceptable to say that the defeat of so-called 'real socialism' leaves capitalism as the only model of economic organization."[73]

But here as elsewhere his cure for unbridled capitalism is capitalism of a more balanced, well-ordered kind. For he immediately proposes as a remedy:

> It is necessary to break down the barriers and monopolies which leave so many countries on the margins of development and to provide all individuals and nations with the basic conditions which will enable them to share in development. This goal calls for programmed and responsible efforts on the part of the entire international community. Stronger nations must offer weaker ones opportunities for taking their place in international life, and the latter must learn how to use these opportunities by making the necessary efforts and sacrifices and by ensuring political and economic stability, the certainty of better prospects for the future, the improvement of workers' skills and the training of competent business leaders who are conscious of their responsibilities.[74]

Similarly, in #42, after having introduced capitalism rightly understood, the Pope again attacks "a radical capitalistic ideology":

> Vast multitudes are still living in conditions of great material and moral poverty. The collapse of the communist system in so many countries certainly removes an obstacle to facing these problems in an appropriate and realistic way, but it is not enough to bring about their solution. Indeed, there is a risk that a radical capitalistic ideology could spread which refuses even to consider these problems in the *a priori* belief that any attempt to solve them is doomed to failure, and which blindly entrusts their solution to the free development of market forces.[75]

By "radical capitalistic ideology," the Pope seems to mean total reliance on market mechanisms and economic reasoning alone. In the United States, we usually call such a view "libertarianism"; it is the view of a small (but influential) minority. United States libertarians do not "refuse to consider" the poverty of multitudes; they offer their own sustained analyses and practical remedies, and with some success. The economy of Chile has become one of the leading economies of Latin America, in part through the sustained advice of libertarians from "the Chicago school," who were once much maligned.[76]

Ironically, nonetheless, the Pope prefers to call the capitalism of which he approves the *"business economy, market economy*, or simply *free economy."* This is probably because of European emotional resistance to the word "capitalism."[77] My own reasoning in preferring to speak of "democratic capitalism," rather than "the market economy," is to avoid sounding libertarian—that is, narrowly focused on the economic system alone. For in reality, in advanced societies the institutions of both the juridical order and the cultural order do impinge greatly on, modify, and "control" the economic system. Indeed, any religious leftist or traditionalist who still believes that the United States is an example of unrestrained capitalism has not inspected the whole thirty-foot-long shelf of volumes containing the Federal Register of legally binding commercial regulations. One might more plausibly argue that the economies of the capitalist nations today are too heavily regulated (and too unwisely) than too lightly.

In the real world of fact, the business economy is restrained by law, custom, moral codes, and public opinion, as anyone can see who counts the socially imposed costs they are obliged to meet—and the number of employees they must hire (lawyers, affirmative-action officers, public-affairs officers, inspectors, community-relations specialists, pension-plan supervisors, health-plan specialists, child-care custodians, etc.). The term "democratic capitalism" is an attempt to capture these political and cultural restraints upon any humane economic system. It is defined in a way broad enough to include political parties from the conservative to the social democratic, and systems as diverse as Sweden and the United States.[78]

In a similar vein, the Pope notes three clear moral limits to the writ of the free market: (1) many human needs are not met by the market but lie beyond it; (2) some goods "cannot and must not be bought and sold"; and (3) whole groups of people are without the resources to enter the market and need nonmarket assistance. The market principle is a good one, but it is neither universal in its competence nor perfectly unconditioned. It is not an idol.

In addition, the Pope thinks in terms of international solidarity. The whole world is his parish. The Pope's frequent travels by jet to the Third World are meant to dramatize the primary human (and Christian) responsibility to attend to the needs of the poor everywhere. Economic interdependence and the communications revolution have brought the Catholic people (and indeed all people) closer together than ever. This fact brings to his attention many moral and social imperatives surrounding and suffusing economic activities. For example: Care must be taken not to injure the environment.[79] States and societies need to establish a framework favorable to creativity, full employment, a decent family wage, and social insurance for various contingencies.[80] The common good of all should be served, not violated by a few. Individuals should be treated as ends, not as means—and their dignity should be respected.[81]

The tasks to be met by the good society are many. No system is as likely to achieve all these goods as is a market system,[82] but in order to be counted as fully good, the market system must in fact achieve them. The Pope explicitly commends the successes registered in these respects by mixed economies after World War II.[83] But he also stresses how much needs yet to be done. *Finding good systems is a step forward; but after that comes the hard part.*[84]

On matters of population growth, the Pope's claim that human capital is the chief resource of nations may lead to a new approach to population control. Those who say dogmatically that a large population causes poverty have not thought carefully about highly successful societies of dense population such as Japan, Hong Kong, and the Netherlands. Although he does not himself develop this point as Julian Simon does,[85] the Pope's emphasis on the creative capacity of every human being offers one reason why densely populated countries can become wealthy. *The principle behind economic progress is the fact that most people can create more in one lifetime than they consume.* The cause of poverty is not "overpopulation." It is, on the contrary, a system of political economy that represses the economic creativity that God has endowed in every woman and man. Nations ought not to repress that creative capacity.

TOWARD A MORE CIVIL DEBATE

Centesimus Annus is so balanced a document that, even while neoconservatives such as myself took it up with enthusiasm, many

on the left too (quietly shedding their more extreme socialist economics, and pointing out that even the left these days is in favor
of markets, enterprise, economic growth, and personal initiative)
quickly embraced it. Only in America did the Catholic left react
grudgingly, perhaps because of the intense emotional commitment
of many to "liberation theology."

Thus the first response of the American Catholic left to *Centesimus Annus* was shocked silence, followed less by an exposition
of its themes than by an attack on "neoconservatives" for "hi-
jacking" the encyclical. For example, a leading American Catholic
progressive columnist, Fr. Richard P. McBrien, warned: "Neoconservatives who seem to exalt democratic capitalism as if it were
the moral as well as the economic norm for the rest of the world
cannot, on the basis of this encyclical, enlist the Pope in their
cause. Pope John Paul II is more cautious and more critical." As
evidence, McBrien cites #42: "Is this [capitalism] the model which
ought to be proposed to the countries of the Third World?"
McBrien replies: "If I understand the neoconservatives' position
correctly, their answer would be, 'obviously yes.' For John Paul
II, the answer is 'obviously complex.' "[86] This passage reveals that
McBrien confuses neoconservatives with libertarians. In fact, it is
the neoconservatives who introduced the idea of political and
moral–cultural counterbalances to capitalism into Catholic social
thought. That is why without hesitation or cavil they endorsed
the precise words the Pope used, as an echo of their own. Even
the sentence: "The answer is complex."

The editors of the lay Catholic journal *Commonweal* also
shared McBrien's confusions. As if it were a counter to the encyclical's "praise for the freedom and efficiency of market economies," they quoted another line from the encyclical: "Even the
decision to invest in one place rather than another is always a
moral and cultural choice." Then, they added in their own voice:
"So much for the magic altruism of the Invisible Hand."[87] That
is precisely the reason why some of us have long emphasized, with
Pope John Paul II, the legitimate roles of the political system and
the moral–cultural system in supplementing and correcting the
market economy.

In the not-so-centrist *Center Focus*, newsletter of the radical
Center of Concern, Fr. Jim Hug, S.J., fastened on a sentence from
#56: "Western countries, in turn, run the risk of seeing this col-
lapse [of Eastern European socialism] as a one-sided victory of

their own economic system, and thereby failing to make corrections in that system."[88] He also liked #34: "There are many human needs which find no place in the market. It is a strict duty of justice and truth not to allow fundamental human needs to remain unsatisfied, and not to allow those burdened by such needs to perish." (Such a sentiment, said Samuel Johnson, is the test of any good society.[89]) Astutely, Fr. Hug concedes that "some of the language and emphasis of *Centesimus Annus* suggests that U.S. neoconservatives helped to shape its content." He urges the left to outdo the neocons next time: "We in the progressive segment of the Church justice community need to become 'wise as serpents' to the ways of influencing Vatican teaching."[90] One suspects that popes pay more attention to real-world experience.

Most assuredly, *Centesimus Annus* is no libertarian document—and precisely that, to many of us, is its beauty. Quite as *The Commonweal* asserted, "What the encyclical grants to market mechanisms it does not take away from its witness to injustice or defense of the poor." It denounced conditions of "inhuman exploitation."[91] Quite truly, as Fr. Hug writes: "*Centesimus Annus* does not, then, anoint any existing system." The Pope saw a great many faults in the economic, political, and moral–cultural systems of even the most highly developed societies today. His conclusion was as pointed as the obelisk in the center of St. Peter's Square. He made a nuanced, complex, but entirely forthright judgment about "which model ought to be proposed to the countries of the Third World, which are searching for the path to economic and civil progress." His considered judgment? "The business economy, market economy, or simply free economy." What could be plainer?

I want to stress that *Centesimus Annus* gives encouragement to social democrats and others of the moderate left, *as well as* to persons who share my own proclivities, *and* to those further to my right. It is not a party document. Part of its brilliance lies in its discernment of *several* constellations in the vast night sky of social goods. John Paul II sees, as it were, the stars that those on the reasonable left are following, but also the stars that attract those on the reasonable right. Some reasonable persons, if they are also partisans, tend to glance past the stars that others follow, to focus with passion on their own. Pope John Paul II has had the largeness of mind to keep *all* the stars in view, and with remarkable equanimity and balance. Indeed, I had the happy experience in London in April 1992 of hearing a leftist church worker describe *Centesimus Annus* as virtually a Labour Party manifesto, in the conference room of an Institute sometimes described as a Thatcherite think-tank, among conservatives delighted with the fair play that *Centesimus Annus* had shown toward enterprise, and the nobility it saw in civil society. The Tories liked its praise of creative subjectivity and its criticism of the welfare state (#48), while the Labourites were pleased to note the limits it set to market principles, and its various appeals to state assistance.

Nonetheless, it took nearly a whole year for a serious essay to be offered from the American Catholic left, gingerly requesting room in the conversation for a chastened socialist vision from Latin America[92] and the liberal agenda of the American bishops. Here is how that plea (by David Hollenbach, S.J., in *Theological Studies*) poignantly concludes:

> Those who have been led to believe that *Centesimus Annus* endorses "really existing capitalism" should take a hard look at the text. I hope that this modest "note" will encourage both such careful reading and subsequent talking in the spirit of solidarity and commitment to the common good that permeates the encyclical.[93]

When Fr. Hollenbach cites sources for his own discussion of poverty in the United States, however, he uses the Democratic Senator from New York, Daniel Patrick Moynihan, as his opponent on the *right*, and cites as his own "careful and balanced" mentors three figures to Moynihan's left (David Ellwood, William Julius Wilson, and Alan Wolfe). He leaves entirely out of the discussion other figures quite concerned about the poor—such as Charles Murray, Lawrence Mead,[94] Stuart Butler, and Secretary of Housing and Urban Development Jack Kemp. Such exclusion leads him to unnecessary factual errors, such as that "many of the poor in the United States work full time." In actual fact, a majority of the poor who receive social assistance are over 65 and under 18, ill, or disabled. Among the able-bodied of working age, the actual percentage of the householders of poor families who worked full-time year-round in 1988 was 16.4.[95] More depressing still, among poor female householders with no husband present the percentage who worked full-time year-round was only 9.5. (But

56 percent of *non*poor women in the same category, with no husband present, worked full-time year-round.)

Hollenbach quotes (but only in part) one of my favorite passages from *Centesimus Annus*, as follows:

> The fact is that many people, perhaps the majority today, do not have the means which would enable them to take their place in an effective and humanly dignified way within a productive system in which work is truly central. . . . Thus, if not actually exploited, they are to a great extent marginalized; economic development takes place over their heads.[96]

But the two sentences that Hollenbach leaves out in his ellipsis are central to the Pope's argument, since they put the stress on human capital:

> They have no possibility of acquiring the basic knowledge which would enable them to express their creativity and develop their potential. They have no way of entering the network of knowledge and intercommunication which would enable them to see their qualities appreciated and utilized.[97]

In other words, the communication of knowledge and the opening of markets and trade are among the best services the advanced societies can offer to the poor of the Third World.

Further, the Pope insists that the poor of the Third World must be allowed to become more economically active. But this will require basic structural reform, including changes in the laws of those Third World nations (particularly in Latin America) that hold most enterprise by the common people to be illegal.[98] Skipping this radical critique of precapitalist states, Hollenbach interprets the Pope as merely restating the formulation used by the U.S. Catholic bishops, which seems to picture the people as passive: "Basic justice demands the establishment of minimum levels of participation in the life of the human community for all persons."[99] In the Pope's view, by contrast, governments must support the fundamental right of all persons to personal economic initiative. The Pope stresses the creativity and activism of the poor and criticizes the barriers (often imposed by states) to the full exercise of their potential.

In summarizing the Pope's proposed remedy for Third World ills, Hollenbach cites its promarket beginning: "The chief problem [for poor countries] is that of gaining fair access to the international market. . . ." But he leaves off its even more significant ending: ". . . based not on the unilateral principle of the exploitation of the natural resources of these countries but on the proper use of *human* resources."[100] Here again the Pope focuses on human knowledge and creativity. These need to be developed to their full potential. These need proper institutional support. These are the source of wealth. Repressing them is a very great evil. Most Third World states cruelly punish and neglect the human creativity of their citizens. More strikingly still, the two sentences the Pope supplies that lead into this passage are quite stunning:

> Even in recent years it was thought that the poorest
> countries would develop by isolating themselves from
> the world market and by depending only on their own
> resources. Recent experience has shown that countries
> which did this have suffered stagnation and recession,
> while the countries which experienced development
> were those which succeeded in taking part in the gen-
> eral interrelated economic activities at the international
> level.

"In my judgment," Hollenbach writes, "the principles [of *Centesimus Annus*] call for major changes both in the domestic arrangements presently in place in the United States as well as in the global marketplace." On that point, Hollenbach and I read the encyclical the same way. On what those "major changes" should be, however, Hollenbach and I are in different camps. The Pope systematically recommends changes that open up and extend the benefits of market systems and the domestic development of human resources. But Hollenbach has nowhere yet considered the concrete steps necessary to bring about "the proper use of human resources" in the Third World, particularly in the institutions that make personal economic creativity possible.[101] One needs to ask him: How does one raise the human skills of ordinary people, their knowledge, know-how, and capacities for enterprise (i.e., human capital)? What institutional changes are necessary in Bo-livia, Brazil, Colombia—and south central Los Angeles?

Recall again Michael Ignatieff's description of the moral flaw in the British Labour Party, as shown by the loss of four straight elections, including that of 1992: "Labour always tells people what it is going to do for them. It never encourages them to do it for themselves."[102] Far better is it to build up institutions of enterprise and creativity, the social supports for that personal exercise of creativity and self-determination in which human dignity consists. This is Pope John Paul II's point: a clear call for creative new approaches to replace tired "progressive" remedies, while giving the latter due credit for what they did indeed achieve. There is room in John Paul's house for many arguments among different tendencies and parties. But it is also important for those who disagree to include each other in the discussion, and to conduct that discussion forthrightly, openly, and civilly.

The Catholic left (in the United States, at least) has expressed substantive agreement with *Centesimus Annus* even while showing considerable annoyance that the neoconservatives like it more than they. The left sees the poor and the vulnerable as passive, awaiting the ministrations of the state. The right and the center see the poor as capable, creative, and active. The left clings to its appeals to action by the state; it has become conservative in rhetoric, looking backward. The center and the right long for a new beginning, and sound positively radical in their demand for "civil society" rather than "state" as their main hope for the future. Those in the center and on the right tend to emphasize all the encyclical's appeals to civil society; those on the left (but not so much as before) tend to emphasize the state. This debate among left, center, and right—besides being unavoidably built into the tripartite system—is al-together healthy.

Having always resented such moral imperialism as Paul Til-lich's "Every serious Christian must be a socialist," and the British left's "Christianity is the religion of which socialism is the prac-tice," I would by no means support the sentiment that "Every serious Christian must be a democratic capitalist," or that "Chris-tianity is the religion of which democratic capitalism is the prac-tice." As *Centesimus Annus* insists, the Catholic Church "has no models to offer"[103]—and, indeed, has powerful reasons to criticize many abuses and wrongs in democratic capitalist societies. The Pope rightly insists that no worldly system can ever claim to be the Kingdom of God. What good would a Church be if it didn't constantly criticize the City of Man in the light of the City of God, *sub specie aeternitatis*? Indeed, as Thomas Pangle reports in his study of Tocqueville's *Democracy in America*, this emphasis on immortality and eternal life is the indispensable contribution of religion to the democratic experiment.[104]

The dread menace of communism, which in the Soviet Union alone took millions more lives than Hitler took in all Europe, and which blighted so many hundreds of millions of other lives, has now been defeated. The ideology of socialism (at least as an economic idea) has been discredited, except among those whose investment in it has been too heavy to surrender quickly, such as Leonardo Boff. In the long run of history, socialist economics will appear to have been a distraction; our descendants will wonder how so many of us, at least for a part of our lives, could have been taken in by it. The death of socialism gives us an opportunity to think in fresh ways and to begin again with a new burst of social creativity. To have established that perspective is the true achievement of *Centesimus Annus*.

Meanwhile, we have a lot of hard work to do to bring the poor billions of the Third World within the system of liberty and creativity. And a good deal to do to assist the poor in advanced countries, too.

We now turn to a whole host of concrete perplexities and serious needs for social reform in the West, first in the area of poverty and race, then in the area of moral and intellectual life. One thing that Jews and Christians know well: Our resting place is not where we are, not here, not yet. The question proper to pilgrim peoples is always: What's next?

PART THREE

NEXT?

*Poverty, Race, Ethnicity, and
Other Perplexities of the
21st Century*

Chapter 6

WAR ON POVERTY

"Created Goods Should Abound"

SINCE LEO XIII condemned socialism and criticized capitalism, many concluded that the Catholic Church must be propounding a "middle way." A great deal of effort went into the search for this elusive middle way. This was a futile search, however, for it overlooked the asymmetry between capitalism and socialism. Socialism is a moral, economic, and political system all in one. But capitalism is the name only of an economic system which, for its full and free development, requires a democratic polity and a humanistic and pluralist culture. Indeed, the threefold *combination* of democracy, capitalism, and religious liberty *is* the "middle way" between socialism and capitalism. In Part Three of this book, however, we must address the serious political problems of poverty and ethnicity, and the even deeper problems of culture and moral ecology. The *culture* of democracy and capitalism is now in question.

THE UNIVERSAL DESTINATION AND THE WAY

In Central Europe these days, the term "middle way" is spoken of disdainfully. Thus Leszek Balcerowicz, Finance Minister of Poland, in 1989: "We don't want to try out a third way. We will leave it to the richer countries to try out a third way and if they succeed maybe we will follow."[1] The future president of Bulgaria went further: "To speak of any future for socialism in this country is nonsense. . . . Our goal now is to lead Bulgaria to a modern, democratic capitalism."[2] As if with this in mind, Pope John Paul II said emphatically in *Sollicitudo Rei Socialis* (1989) that the Catholic Church is *not* seeking a middle way.[3]

Some persons in the Church, particularly in Latin countries, reluctantly accept the fact that papal social thinking proposes neither a socialist way nor a middle way; but they hesitate to draw the conclusion that one must begin with the best human materials available, however poor these are—and that that leaves only one alternative: the combination of democracy and capitalism. "Democratic capitalism is a poor system," one might say, "but the known alternatives are worse." For Catholic social thought, the perfect is not the enemy of the good—and the ethic proper to political economy is an ethic of prudence, suffused with charity;[4] of justice, tempered with mercy.[5] A sound political economy encourages virtue, but must be designed to cope with the fact that citizens sometimes sin.

Nonetheless, Catholic social thought does insist on one principle that some regard as contrary to the spirit of democracy and capitalism. In a single sentence in *Sollicitudo Rei Socialis*, the Pope stated this "characteristic principle of Christian social doctrine" quite simply: "The goods of this world are *originally meant for all*."[6] This principle is formally known as "the universal destination of created goods." Vatican II states it in these words: "God intended the earth and all that it contains for the use of every human being and people. Thus, as men follow justice and unite in charity, created goods should abound for them on a reasonable basis."[7]

"*Created goods should abound*"—this new version of the ancient principle includes two modern assumptions: first, that the goods of creation do abound in support of human life; second, that human economic creativity can keep ahead of population growth. Quite different were premodern assumptions concerning scarcity, hardship, poverty, and the persistent threat of famine, plague, and demographic decline. At a time when the earth supported only 735 million persons, the predictions of Thomas Malthus (1766–1834) that population growth would outrun food supply terrified many sober people. Yet, after experiencing the inventiveness of capitalism in free societies (especially in medicine and agriculture), the earth by 1990 supported 5.3 billion persons.

Thus the assumption that human inventiveness and economic creativity can keep ahead of population to provide abundance "on a reasonable basis" turns out to have been a sound assumption, but only on one condition: the smooth functioning of open capitalist institutions. In the noncapitalist countries of the world, poverty and scarcity still prevail. Nearly a billion people still live under systems that repress their creative capacities and leave them in a poverty so biting that they are deprived of normal daily caloric intake. The continued existence of such repressive regimes is a moral scandal.

Abundance may be taken for granted only where (among other things) rights to private property are respected by law. Yet here some modern papal documents take a curious turn. Since ancient times—in Aristotle, in Cicero, in St. Augustine, and consistently in the Catholic tradition—this universal destination as final *end* has led to the selection of private property as its necessary *means*. But during the high tide of Eurosocialism in 1967, Pope Paul VI's *Populorum Progressio* took the opposite tack: "Private property does not constitute for anyone an absolute and unconditional right. No one is justified in keeping for his exclusive use what he does not need, when others lack necessities."[8] This affirmation can be found in St. Thomas Aquinas, it is true, but his main argument ran in exactly the *opposite* direction. St. Thomas argued *against* communitarians; *Populorum Progressio* seemed to lean in their direction.

The issue that confronted Aquinas was this: "Whether it is lawful for a man to possess a thing as his own?" On Aquinas's view, natural law leaves the issue of possession open; so the inquirer must study experience. The argument for private property arose from seeking by trial-and-error the practical laws by which the world actually works. Aquinas addresses three objections against the legitimacy of private property which had been raised by traditional communitarians. The first objection was this: "According to the natural law all things are common property." The second was a criticism by St. Basil of "the rich who deem as their own property the goods that they have seized." The third was from St. Ambrose, who had written "Let no man call his own that which is common property."

St. Thomas replies to these objections by distinguishing between two powers of humans over material goods: the power to procure and distribute material goods, and the power to use them.

Regarding the second, the *use* of material goods, he says that a human being "ought to possess external things, not as his own, but as common, so that he is ready to communicate them to others in their need." Aquinas seems to hold this principle as a matter of Christian belief. In support of it, he quotes from 1 Timothy 6:17–18; St. Basil; and St. Ambrose.

Regarding the *production* and *distribution* of material goods, however, Aquinas gives four reasons why a regime of private property is "necessary." He cites one argument from faith (from St. Augustine), then three based on natural reason. Arguing from reason alone, a regime of private property

> is necessary to human life for three reasons. First because every man is more careful to procure what is for himself alone than that which is common to many or to all: since each one would shirk the labor and leave to another that which concerns the community, as happens where there is a great number of servants. Secondly, because human affairs are conducted in more orderly fashion if each man is charged with taking care of some particular thing himself, whereas there would be confusion if everyone had to look after any one thing indeterminately. Thirdly, because a more peaceful state is ensured to man if each one is contented with his own. Hence it is to be observed that quarrels arise more frequently where there is no division of the things possessed.[9]

If men were angels, the common ownership of the means of production might work, but human experience has taught us that private property is a practical necessity. Having learned these lessons again under "real existing socialism," Pope John Paul II has taken pains to spell out St. Thomas's reasoning anew.[10]

A regime of private property is taken for granted by the Ten Commandments. Neither "Thou shall not steal" nor "Thou shall not covet" makes sense apart from the right to personal property. Beyond this, the arguments of Aquinas underline the social functions of private property. A regime of private property serves social peace, good order, and positive personal incentives. Without these, the raw goods of creation would almost certainly not be transmuted by human labor into usable goods and services. Creation left to itself does not supply for human needs. If a man wants to eat, he must work "by the sweat of his brow."

Nowadays, the resource-rich Soviet Union is a living lesson in the fate of a nation that abandons private property. So, too, is most of the Third World. In Latin America, even where in principle respected, property rights are insecure in practice. The property of the wealthiest has often been arbitrarily confiscated, nationalized, or illicitly seized; the property of the lowliest is still less secure. Title to property often is unverifiable; and huge majorities of the population are propertyless.[11] Wherever rights to property are not protected across the generations, stagnation (or even decline) must be expected. The long-term incentive to improve property is its permanence as a family heritage.

This traditional Catholic reasoning on the universal destination of created goods as the end, and property rights as the means, is not exactly identical to that of John Locke and the Anglo–American tradition; but neither is it wholly different. Locke, too, held that by nature all earthly goods belong to the entire human race.[12] Abandoned to itself and without human labor, the earth would hardly support human life—thus the use of human wit and human labor is indispensable for its cultivation and improvement. Left to nature alone, a field might yield a harvest only one-tenth to one-hundredth as large as the same field under human care and cultivation.[13]

Locke concluded that the most practical means of drawing usable wealth out of nature (of improving the land, for example) is a system of laws which would secure man's "natural right" to private property across the generations. Locke's conception of "natural right" may be modern, but the underlying argument for private property is not. Human creativity needs many social supports, including limited government, the rule of law, monogamous marriage and the family, systems of transport and markets—and a regime of private property. A regime of private property is a social institution designed for social purposes whose benefits redound to all. Indeed, John Stuart Mill even allowed that an owner of land who did not improve property by his labor would lose his claim to private ownership, since the justification for private property is its service to the common good.[14] This principle cuts two ways: A society that arbitrarily abridges private property will destroy incentives; but individuals who do not use private property to improve the public good undercut their claim to ownership.

A serious Jewish or Christian conscience (even the conscience of a serious humanist) feels the bite of the principle that the material goods of this world are intended to benefit all human beings. A human society is judged morally, even in secular thought, by how well it cares for the most vulnerable in its midst.[15] But how best to secure this? By outright grants? By loans? By the transmission of basic skills and assistance? By training in the practices of a sound and growing economy? By good counsel regarding how to establish the basic institutions of a productive system? It is not enough to say that citizens of the commercially successful nations have an obligation to help their less fortunate brothers and sisters. It is crucial to begin to say *how* this obligation can be fruitfully acquitted. Few tasks in life are more difficult than giving truly useful help to the needy, without reducing the latter to servile dependence on their donors.

RECONSTRUCTING THE WORLD ORDER

Ever since the decree of Vatican II, *Gaudium et Spes* (1965), papal statements on "the universal destination of goods" have been directed toward persuading the rich to give of their abundance to the poor. They have done less well in persuading the citizens of precapitalist states to reconstruct their inadequate social systems. To secure this reconstruction, several different arguments have been in play.

Self-reliance—*within* nations and *among* nations—is a crucial concept for Catholic social thought, as the Vatican Institute for Justice and Peace has emphasized for many years.[16] Dependency is not healthy.

Again, papal social teaching has also spoken metaphorically of a "gap" between the affluent nations and the noncapitalist nations. This "gap" is not to be understood arithmetically. Even though a poor country should grow by 10 percent while a wealthy one grew by only 1 percent, the base on which the 1 percent is calculated might be so much larger than the base on which the 10 percent is calculated that at the end the absolute difference between the two GDPs might be larger, not smaller. Ten percent of a $50 billion economy is only $5 billion, for example, but one percent of a $5 trillion economy is $50 billion. Thus the situation of poorer countries might be improving at a faster rate even though the "gap" did not seem to be diminishing. This "gap" is not the moral point, but the need for rapid improvement in the lot of the poor.

Third, the inability of some Third World nations to pay their debts indicates that their economies do not use borrowed money creatively enough to make a profit on it from which interest could be paid. Instead, the money seems simply to vanish, sometimes with little to show for it. This fact indicates that even massive infusions of grants from other countries might also be of little lasting benefit. Moneys paid into the coffers of governments, bankers, industrialists, and other members of local power elites do not always find their way into use for the benefit of ordinary people, or even into productive investments at home. On the contrary, amounts equal to half or more of the total debt of Latin America have actually been reinvested in Switzerland, North America, and elsewhere, in the phenomenon known as "capital flight."[17]

No wonder many scholars are opposed to foreign aid, on the grounds that it encourages an irresponsible use of the money of others for which those who receive it feel little obligation.[18] They are particularly opposed to foreign aid granted by one government to another, on the grounds that the corruption of political elites in Third World countries is virtually uncontrollable. Even the international lending agencies often make this mistake: In recent years the World Bank made only two of 197 loans in Brazil to the private sector. By contrast, much more aid should be given directly to ordinary people—not in the form of welfare benefits but in the form of education, training, and small amounts of carefully supervised credit for the launching of small local businesses.

A few writers on the Catholic left still believe that *Centesimus Annus* demands large "structural" changes in existing democratic societies, and in this they are correct; but they are wrong about the direction of those changes. Pope John Paul II does not propose more socialism or more dependency-creating welfare. He sees that markets, private property, profits, and (above all) the institutions that support personal economic creativity, contribute mightily to the common good. What he insists on is the inclusion of the currently excluded within the beneficent circle of fruitful practices and institutions. He recommends the expansion of this circle, not its abandonment or contraction. In particular, he emphasizes the need to bring Third World nations into the international system of free trade, technological transfer, and education in skills and investment.[19] This means opening the markets of Europe, Japan,

North America, and other centers of dynamic economic growth to the products and services of the poorer nations.

Finally, when we speak of "created goods" or "material things," we need to see that many of God's precious gifts to the human race are not being developed for the benefit of humankind, but are lying neglected or abused for want of creative, productive systems of political economy. Some nations with enormous material resources—Brazil and Russia, for example—are in this way violating the principle of the universal destination of created goods, by failing to develop (for the good of the whole race) the great resources they have. Further, it is particularly sad that the United States and the countries of Western Europe are not yet opening their markets sufficiently to the goods of Eastern Europe in the latter's desperate struggle for survival. If we fail in this task, we shall stand accused for generations to come.

It does the poor no good if "reformers" entrap them further into defective, illiberal, and inhumane systems. As the failure of socialism teaches us, reforms must be well-designed. Furthermore, being saddled with a defective system frustrates even a virtuous people, whereas getting the system right helps them mightily. Sound theory, well-rooted in human nature, is pivotal. The most obvious problem, but not the deepest or most difficult, concerns what to do in practice to alleviate poverty, both in the Third World and at home.

In what follows in Part Three, the rhetorical strategy of this book must change. To this point we have examined the new ethic for democracy and markets set forth by the Catholic encyclical tradition. From here on, each lively conscience must begin to address the concrete perplexities of the world's many and dissimilar societies. Here I would not want my own poor opinions to be mistaken for the voice of "Catholic social thought." If heretofore I have tried in this book to understand the Catholic ethic fairly and truly, henceforth in this book I am on my own, as are my readers. We each do our best to understand reality truly, to take its full measure, and to act with biblical creativity. But no one of us (even the Pope) is in such practical matters infallible. We work as in a darkness, doing the best we can, knowing that some explorations into uncharted territory will be successful, others not. All, including this one, deserve to be submitted to rigorous criticism in the lively and active "public square" of civil society.

There follow, then, my own explorations into the darkness of the near future. These pages represent one man's controversial attempt to apply "the Catholic ethic." Their errors are my own.

INTERNATIONAL POVERTY

Liberation theology in Latin America deserves credit for directing the eyes of the world to the attention of the world's poor, especially in Latin America and Africa. But liberation theologians made a faulty analysis of the dynamics of poverty. In relying on outmoded and dysfunctional Marxist categories, and in attaching their dream of liberation to "socialism," they seriously miscalculated. They tied their hopes to mistaken nineteenth-century economic theories concerning the abolition of private property, class struggle, the labor theory of value, and the zero-sum logic of "oppressors vs. oppressed." Events in Eastern Europe during 1989–91 undermined that method of analysis, however.

Eastern Europeans by the millions have risen up against the strategy of fulfilling the "basic needs" of the people. The socialist strategy of "basic needs" may be sufficient for animals, or even prisoners in jail, but it is intolerable to free human beings. One can feed a cow, give it shelter, milk it, and leave it content; but human beings demand more than sustenance by way of provision—they demand, for example, responsibility, and government formed by their own consent. Since 1989, liberation theologians who once attributed Latin America's poverty to excessive "dependency" on Europe and North America have been worried that Europe and North America will turn to the needs of Eastern Europe and leave Latin America in excessive "independence."[20]

In short, liberation theologians called attention to the problem. But they did little to solve it—and perhaps even delayed its solution for a generation. The bitter condition of the poor must now be addressed in *practical* terms.

Among the 165 or so nations of the world, the nations most conspicuous for their poverty lie either in the precapitalist, traditionalist parts of the world (Africa, Latin America, and South Asia) or in the socialist world. We have learned recently, indeed, that the "Second World" did not even exist, except as a more heavily armed part of the Third World. The crumbling economy of the former USSR, now visibly revealed, resembles the economy of India or China more than that of Western Europe. Even in the newly united Germany, the economic inferiority of its Eastern portion was a shock. Thus the promise of economic development, which originated in Adam Smith's *Inquiry into the Nature and Causes of the Wealth of Nations*, seems to have been realized almost exclusively among the relatively few capitalist nations of the world. The standard of living of the poor is higher in capitalist economies than in either of the latter. Capitalism, for all its faults, is a better system for the poor than any other existing system.

In Latin America, what is called "capitalism" is actually a form of the precapitalist, state-sponsored, patrimonial mercantilism that Adam Smith was writing *against*. It needs to be changed decisively. To be specific, there are in Latin America today some 90 million youngsters under the age of 15 who will be entering the work force each year for the next 15 years. But scores of millions of older adults in Latin America are also unemployed or underemployed. Moreover, since the flight from farm to city is virtually universal, by the year 2000 fewer Latin Americans than today will be working in agriculture. It is nearly as certain that fewer will be working for transnational corporations. This vast pool of the unemployed contrasts vividly with the enormous amounts of work that need to be done to improve the conditions of daily life among the poor. By what mechanism shall these two factors—work to be done and workers needing employment—be brought together, if not by the rapid generation of tens of millions of small businesses engaged in manufacturing and services?

Moreover, large proportions of the poor of Latin America are not only excluded from participation in employment; they are also excluded from access to the legal incorporation of small businesses. Notwithstanding this disability, 43 percent of the houses in Peru have been constructed by *illegals*, and 93 percent of public transport is provided by them.[21] Indeed, two-thirds of all the poor in Peru are neither peasants nor factory workers (proletarians); they are entrepreneurs. Yet their work is treated by the traditonal authorities as illegal, and is often criminalized. No legitimate institutions exist to extend credit (the mother's milk of enterprise) to the poor.

All these exclusions—from employment, from incorporation, and from credit—are unjust. So also is the exclusion of the poor from property ownership, whether in land or home or business. Property titles in Peru are in extreme disarray and exceedingly unstable.[22] As truly in Peru as anywhere else in the world do the words of *Centesimus Annus* ring in the air: "In these cases it is still possible today, as in the days of *Rerum Novarum*, to speak of inhumane exploitation."[23] But such exploitation today often comes instead from oppressive laws.

Much the same situation, *mutatis mutandis*, obtains throughout Latin America: *There is no capitalism for the poor of Latin America.* Nearly all the economies of Latin America are in the grip of the state, and the state in turn is typically bent to the service of a relatively few elite families. This situation is only marginally better—because more open to reform—than the socialist "alternative." Neither in Cuba nor in Nicaragua, nor in any other socialist experiment, has socialism proved to be an answer to the longings of the poor for material progress, creative opportunity, and civic liberty.

The reason for the moral and practical superiority of capitalism (surprising to so many) appears to be twofold. First, as a system capitalism is constituted by a set of institutions nourishing invention, innovation, and enterprise. These are the primary cause of economic development. Second, market systems better recognize the dignity of individuals and respect their choices, better reward cooperation and mutual adjustment, and better precipitate reform, experiment, and steady progress. Both in creativity and in cooperative voluntary activities the capitalist order attains a progressively higher standard of the common good.[24]

Nonetheless, two great tasks remain: In the Third World, the scores of millions of the poor, currently kept by law outside the dynamism of invention, markets, and enterprise, must be brought into the system.[25] The tight grip of small elites on the levers of state power, and of state power on nearly all creative economic activity, must be broken.

Within capitalist nations, secondly, the good of the poor needs to be much better served than it has been by dependency-creating welfare programs.

DOMESTIC POVERTY

In commending the welfare programs of the advanced nations, the document of Vatican II, *Gaudium et Spes*, also included a prescient warning about problems that would become apparent in all welfare states three decades later:

In highly developed nations a body of social institutions dealing with insurance and security can, for its
part, make the common purpose of earthly goods effective. Family and social services, especially those
which provide for culture and education, should be
further promoted. Still, care must be taken lest, as a
result of all these provisions, the citizenry fall into a
kind of sluggishness toward society, and reject the
burdens of office and of public service.[26]

Analogously, the Working Seminar on Family and American
Welfare Policy examined both the successes and the failures of the
so-called War on Poverty launched within the United States by
President Lyndon Johnson in 1964.[27] It found that after 20 years,
the welfare of the elderly had been dramatically improved, and
both medical and other noncash benefits had substantially bettered
the economic plight of the elderly. By contrast with this success,
however, considerable evidence showed that the condition of
younger cohorts among the poor, particularly children and single
parents, had seriously deteriorated. There were far more births
out of wedlock in 1985 than there had been in 1965, and far more
single parents (especially young parents). In urban areas crime,
family dysfunction, and morale among the poor seemed to be
considerably worse in 1985 than in 1965.

Undeniably, there was more money in poor areas of the inner
city than ever before, but also far more social dysfunction. Material
circumstances in 1985 were at far higher levels than in 1965. By
many measures, the American poor were living at higher material
standards than many in the European middle class.[28] Indeed, beyond their relatively high levels of reported income, the poor (in
a separate survey) admitted to spending three times as much money
as they reported in income.[29]

Despite all these favorable developments, levels of behavioral
dysfunction were higher in 1985 than in 1965. Drug use and crime
rates were higher than ever; a certain pall of despondency had
become visible. Many households seemed trapped in a cycle of
welfare, unmarried pregnancy, unemployment (or even unemployability), and inability to cope. Even though schooling through
high school is free, many drop out. Even though books are more
widely available than ever, many do not learn to read. Even though

jobs are so plentiful that immigrants from abroad flock to them, many remain out of the work force, neither finding nor even seeking gainful employment.

In the United States, condition-free grants of material benefits trap a significant proportion of able-bodied adults between the ages of 18 and 64 in more-or-less permanent dependency upon the public purse. Financially, many (not all) recipients remain on-and-off, if not continuous, wards of the welfare state.[30] These adults are supposed to be of an age at which others—older and younger—could depend on them. Sadly, these adults cannot be depended on to support their children or their parents; they themselves are dependent on the state. Worse, the behaviors of substantial numbers of them, and others affected by them, trap them in dependencies weightier than financial dependency: drugs, alcohol, illiteracy, unemployability, having children out of wedlock. The results of their behaviors on their children are not difficult to trace. Having children out of wedlock dramatically increases the chances of infant mortality, and children of such unions have a higher likelihood of poor health, difficulties in school, truancy, unemployment, crime, and involvement in drugs.

By 1991, on the hundredth anniversary of *Rerum Novarum*, Pope John Paul II described such new developments in these words:

> In recent years the range of [state] intervention has vastly expanded, to the point of creating a new type of State, the so-called "Welfare State." This has happened in some countries in order to respond better to many needs and demands by remedying forms of poverty and deprivation unworthy of the human person. However, excesses and abuses, especially in recent years, have provoked very harsh criticisms of the Welfare State dubbed the "Social Assistance State." Malfunctions and defects in the Social Assistance State are the result of an inadequate understanding of the tasks proper to the State. Here again *the principle of subsidiarity* must be respected: a community of a higher order should not interfere in the internal life of a community of a lower order, depriving the latter of its functions, but rather should support it in case of need and help to coordinate its activity with the activities of

the rest of society, always with a view to the common good.[31]

This passage recalls Edmund Burke's stress on the importance of the institutions of civil society, and especially those of neighborly community life—"the little platoons" that make life human, teach the required social virtues, and supply the necessary moral inspirations and constraints.[32] Immediately, the Pope resumes:

> By intervening directly and depriving society of its responsibility, the Social Assistance State leads to a loss of human energies and an inordinate increase of public agencies, which are dominated more by bureaucratic ways of thinking than by concern for serving their clients, and which are accompanied by an enormous increase in spending. In fact, it would appear that needs are best understood and satisfied by people who are closest to them and who act as neighbors to those in need. It should be added that certain kinds of demands often call for a response which is not simply material but which is capable of perceiving the deeper human need.[33]

One can hear in these words the fear of a great impersonal Leviathan, without neighborly feeling or respect for individual vulnerability or strength. Indeed, Alexis de Tocqueville predicted that a misuse of the American ideal of equality would lead to a "new soft despotism":

> I am trying to imagine under what novel features despotism may appear in the world. In the first place, I see an innumerable multitude of men, alike and equal, constantly circling around in pursuit of the petty and banal pleasures with which they glut their souls. Each one of them, withdrawn into himself, is almost unaware of the fate of the rest. Mankind, for him, consists in his children and his personal friends. As for the rest of his fellow citizens, they are near enough, but he does not notice them. He touches them but feels nothing. He exists in and for himself, and though

he still may have a family, one can at least say that he
has not got a fatherland.

Over this kind of men stands an immense, protective power which is alone responsible for securing
their enjoyment and watching over their fate. That
power is absolute, thoughtful of detail, orderly, provident, and gentle. It would resemble parental authority
if, fatherlike, it tried to prepare its charges for a man's
life, but on the contrary, it only tries to keep them in
perpetual childhood. It likes to see the citizens enjoy
themselves, provided that they think of nothing but
enjoyment. It gladly works for their happiness but
wants to be sole agent and judge of it. It provides for
their security, foresees and supplies their necessities,
facilitates their pleasures, manages their principal concerns, directs their industry, makes rules for their testaments, and divides their inheritances. Why should it
not entirely relieve them from the trouble of thinking
and all the cares of living?[34]

From a year's study of the evidence, the Working Seminar,
with the warnings of Alexis de Tocqueville in mind, decided from
abundant evidence that the radical problem of the poor in the
United States is no longer merely monetary. The urban poor often
have considerably more disposable income than did the immigrant
poor of preceding generations (or today). The radical problem (as
the Pope saw clearly) has a thicker human dimension and requires
solutions more humane than can be reached by monetary grants
alone. Civic life has broken down among some of the poor, and
needs to be rebuilt from within, with the assistance of sympathetic
helping hands. Many suffer from self-destruction via drugs, alcohol, rampant violence, and daily dissolution.

The rest of the human community has to reach out to the most
injured among these vulnerable ones, helping them to restore behaviors, motivations, outlooks, and habits to healthier modes and
to bring back to life the small and vital "little platoons" of a healthy
civil society. Perhaps the Christian community will respond, as it
has historically, by inspiring new religious congregations to undertake this immense and delicate task. While in America that task
has an interracial dimension, the root problems of dependency

seem to be appearing in many welfare states independent of race, and also in rural and largely white areas of the United States.

The urban core of this problem has come to be identified under the regrettable name "underclass," a term that in the U.S. has been applied to some 4 million poor persons concentrated in poverty areas of the nation's 100 largest cities.[35] Unlike the large majority of the poor, whose poverty is primarily monetary and temporary, the "underclass" exhibits many self-destructive habits that keep them in perpetual dependency on others. Instead of living as free and independent citizens in a free society, they live almost as serfs, dependent on the state. Instead of contributing to the common good, they take from it and, in some cases, prey upon it. Moreover, it is the quasi-permanency of their dependent condition and the probability of their passing it on to their children that most inspires in observers dread and horror. This condition is not a result of the values of the poor; the fault lies in the system that cruelly enforces their dependency.

In fairly sharp contrast, those poor Americans who perform three traditional and relatively simple accomplishments well have almost no probability of remaining long in poverty: Some 97 percent of those who complete high school, stay married (even if not on the first try), and work full-time year-round (even at the minimum wage) are *not* poor. Nearly *all* poverty in the United States is associated with the absence of one or more of these three basic accomplishments.[36] Indeed, the vast majority of the more than 12 million immigrants, mostly nonwhite, who entered the U.S. in the 1970s and 1980s swiftly moved out of poverty, chiefly by means of strong family life and diligent work; not even inadequacy in the English language held them back. Lacking a high-school education or its equivalent, they made up for this by reliable work, commending themselves to employers (or starting their own businesses) by the soundness of their moral habits.

For two reasons it is important to stress how small the underclass is: less than 15 percent of all the poor, barely one out of every 55 U.S. citizens. First, by noting these small numbers we gain confidence in our ability to provide assistance. Second, we save the reputation of those other 85 percent of the poor who are able, law-abiding, and either moving out of poverty or living in retirement on past savings, many (40 percent) in homes they own and with goods long since acquired.[37] Any U.S. taxpayer whose gross adjusted income fell below $13,359 in 1990 (for a nonfarm family of four) was classified as poor, even if that year's annual income was the result of capital losses or other write-offs against salary or other earnings. Most graduate students were probably so classified. Some retired persons who owned two homes, but had only small pensions, also qualified. Those the Census Bureau coldly describes as "poor" do not always fit one's mental image of what "the poor" ought to look like.

Within capitalist countries, however, the residual poverty left behind by the generally rapid *embourgeoisement* of the "proletariat" seems resistant to traditional antipoverty techniques. Even under conditions of unprecedented job creation and the highest percentage of adult employment in history, many afflicted with this form of poverty worked not at all, or only for brief stints, even while immigrants streamed into the country to take "unwanted" jobs.[38] Some percentage of persons in every society will of course suffer from physical, emotional, or moral disabilities which prevent them from achieving the levels of independence and self-reliance that others do. (Indeed, this radical inequality of endowment and "starting places" has always been one of the main arguments of traditionalists against "liberalism": Liberals tend to imagine that all individuals are equal in nature, while overlooking existing inequalities of chances.) Too, in all societies some important fraction of the citizenry is bound to be without income because of age (too old or too young), illness, or ill fortune. With the right sort of assistance, some of these less fortunate persons may earn their way into the mainstream.

However, care must be taken lest ill-designed programs of assistance seduce even the able-bodied into self-destructive dependency. That this often happens is a powerful accusation against the present practice of democratic capitalist (and social democratic) societies. Preferably, as the Pope notes, care for the needy should be provided according to the principle of subsidiarity, with an emphasis on local and "neighborly" assistance, through family, neighbors, churches, unions, fraternal societies, or other associations.[39] The more human (immediate, concrete, neighborly) the scale of this assistance, the better. Few writers have provided more fresh thinking on how to do this in various areas of social life than Charles Murray; some passages of whose *In Pursuit of Happiness*[40] uncannily echo *Centesimus Annus*.

Then Secretary of Housing and Urban Development Jack Kemp once pointed out that 60 percent of East Harlem is owned by the federal government:

> Nearly two-thirds of the residents live in public housing. Almost a third are totally dependent upon government. East Harlem is not a part of America's mainstream economy, but the people want to be. It's an island of Third World socialism amid our sea of democratic capitalism. It's not the people's fault, it's the system's fault.[41]

The welfare system often prevents the people who receive it from meaningful savings. For example, Grace Capetillo, a welfare mother in Milwaukee who saved $3,000 so her daughter could go to college, was prosecuted for welfare fraud, and fined $15,000— and thus the system *took* her needed $3,000, *plus* $12,000 more, from her. This was in effect her condemnation to servitude.

Persons on welfare need to be *allowed* to accumulate assets. They need to be *allowed, encouraged,* even *helped* to gain their own independence. Social assistance should encourage the building-up of assets, not the prolongation of dependency. One way to do this is through privatizing public housing. Another is to help the willing poor to start their own businesses. From 1982 to 1987, the number of black-owned businesses in the United States jumped by 38 percent (compared to a national average of 14 percent), from 308,000 to 424,000. But 424,000 firms for a population of 29 million is many too few; 424,000 firms out of the nation's 14 million small firms is too few. Blacks, as the publisher of *Black Enterprise* says, "must not only collect paychecks; they must issue paychecks." They must not only be employees; "They must become employers."[42]

The poor should be approached as creators of wealth. They should be assisted in their efforts to make themselves asset-producers rather than mere consumers. The revolution needed in the welfare system—now a dependency-maintaining socialism— is to transform it into an asset-building system. Instead of issuing welfare checks, the government might issue matching grants to IRA funds begun by poor persons, by matching one-for-one every dollar saved. These funds would grow tax-free until put to use for capital investments in new businesses, home purchases, and education or training programs. In this way, government programs would be aimed at strengthening civil society rather than eroding it. For the poor and the vulnerable, government assistance is no doubt necessary; but *how* this assistance is designed is more important than either its existence or its size. The first maxim of medicine, *"Do no harm,"* should also be the first maxim of government assistance. A profound revolution in the conception of welfare is needed: to view the poor as creative, not as dependents; as agents of their own destiny, not as serfs.

Widespread skepticism about the effectiveness of many large-scale government-operated poverty programs has thrown experimental, limited, and local programs into the spotlight. Often surprisingly successful, the poor are able to take risks on unusual ventures. Even a cynic is forced to conclude: "In some instances, their success may consist only of failing less stupendously than [in the case of their] similar efforts elsewhere."[43] But often they *do* succeed. The Women's Economic Development Corporation (WEDCO) is a nonprofit corporation in St. Paul, Minnesota, that assists women with every step of entrepreneurship from marketing and management to finance and (crucial intangible) self-confidence. It is run by professionals and funded by private, for-profit banks and foundations. In four years of operation, WEDCO has helped 3,500 women by creating 644 new businesses and expanding 400 existing businesses, with a failure rate below 5 percent. Sixty-seven percent of the women starting or expanding businesses had incomes below $15,000, and 63 percent were single heads of households.[44]

Eugene Lang, a technology tycoon, found a way to break through an ethos of defeat in his old Harlem neighborhood: By guaranteeing success for effort, and offering many demonstrations of personal interest. He promised to send the kids in the local grammar school to college if they were accepted. This was the first "sure thing," other than failure, that most of these underclass kids had been offered: "If the kids did their part, they'd be rewarded. He proved his sincerity by staying in touch with the kids, bringing them to his office and to shows in New York. The certainty of his promise unlocked a torrent of dormant ambition."[45] Lang promised scholarships in a neighborhood where about three-fourths of the students were not high-school graduates, and where virtually no one went on to college. Seven years later, almost three-fourths of the students had graduated from high school. More than half are now college freshmen, a third in private institutions. By September 1991, two-thirds were enrolled.

The Twelfth Street Baptist Church of Detroit has done wonders to rebuild its community's civic life:

> The church used $300,000 in assets to form a company called Reach Inc. As the company bought former crack houses, one by one, the dealers were forced to evacuate. And, as those properties were renovated, job opportunities became available for community residents. Reach then sold the renovated properties to members of the congregation who needed housing.

Reach granted mortgages to the new owners because church leaders understood that, despite poor credit ratings, they were responsible people. Once their mortgage applications were accepted, the loan recipients were able to begin establishing a track record of making payments. This in turn enabled Reach to sell such mortgages to local banks and purchase more crack houses with its return. After nine years of Reach Inc.'s resourcefulness, crime had been reduced by 37 percent and the community was regaining a healthy civic life.[46]

In large, continental, highly mobile societies such as the United States (and perhaps in all truly modern societies), such local assistance will need to be backed up by a national safety net. This is not without risks of impersonality, exorbitant costs, and the unintended effects upon behavior mentioned above by the Pope. But those who are healthy and between the ages of (let us say) 18 and 64 are capable of remarkable initiative, self-development, and creativity; their capacities must not be stunted.

Since frictional unemployment (that is, unemployment caused by the pressures of international competition and rapid technological change) accompanies a free-market system, attention to the plight of the temporarily unemployed is especially necessary—to make certain that the unemployment is both temporary and as little damaging to families as possible.[47] Much more foresight is now needed concerning technological obsolescence and change-over than in the past.

SOCIAL INVENTION

The creativity that lies at the heart of true capitalism should not be checked at the door of public policy. Those who launched the Great Society in the United States and the "social market economies" of Western Europe tried to be inventive. If their best efforts in part failed, or led to unforeseen evils, such is the normal fate of earthly creativity. For the Catholic Whig tradition, accordingly, an ironic turn of mind is a useful habit. Human freedom often goes awry; the best-laid incentives can be turned to perverse purposes. For this reason, difficulty and inevitable partial failure are no excuses for inactivity. Our neighbor's needs must be met, even when our neighbor is partly or wholly responsible for being in need. If the leaders of an earlier generation could be creative, so can we. The age of social invention is not past. No doubt, as the Working Seminar found, there is no one single bullet that will put an end to the miseries preying upon the urban underclass. That did not, however, stop the Seminar from making some 70 practical proposals,[48] each small enough in itself, which cumulatively might undo the damage wrought by preceding decades.

Among politicians, Jack Kemp in early 1990s was at the forefront of those who advocated a new poverty agenda. Kemp emphasized giving the inhabitants of the inner cities a stake in their communities, fostering a sense of responsibility. With jobs and property ownership as incentives, community residents would begin to mobilize their energies to empower themselves. Among the government initiatives proposed by Kemp were: Eliminate the capital gains tax for those who work, save, and invest in the inner cities; reduce taxes on the wages of the poor by increasing the earned-income tax credit; reward, not penalize, poor people who take jobs to work their way off welfare; repeal the law that prohibits poor people from saving their way out of poverty; stop subsidizing family breakup, and reward families that stay together; expand homesteading in urban areas; and provide educational choice for all Americans, especially in the inner cities.[49] Stuart Butler has also called for a new war on poverty, to begin by removing regulations that stymie black economic improvement.[50]

To return to the worldwide perspective: There is much to be done in the noncapitalist world in order to construct institutions favorable to economic development from the bottom up. Among these desperately needed institutions are the following: universal education; institutions of credit and venture capital designed especially for the aspiring poor; easy access by the poor to the speedy and inexpensive legal incorporation of small businesses; and broad public support (in the schools, churches, and media) of an ethos of enterprise. Guy Sorman calls movement in this direction "barefoot capitalism,"[51] and others call it "popular" or "people's capitalism." Even those who grant that among imperfect alternatives a capitalist order is the best (perhaps the only) hope of the poor recognize clearly that hundreds of millions are not now *included* in that order. Laws, traditions, habits, and sometimes closed-minded elites keep them out. *The poor must be allowed in*!

Neither on the international nor on the national level will problems of poverty entirely disappear under capitalism. But poverty will certainly be far less extensive in scale than in socialist or Third World societies. The combination of democracy and capitalism will not bring about heaven on earth. But it will do more to free the poor from poverty and tyranny, and to release their creativity, than any known alternative. This is especially true when the welfare state is redesigned so as to open up the sphere of civil society—that is, free associations and "little platoons" that express the social side of human nature better than the state does. Put another way, the combination of democracy and capitalism may be an inadequate system, but the alternatives surely are worse. This is hardly a ringing endorsement—but then the real world itself is no utopia, and in this century dreams of utopia have already had a very bloody history.

Questions of poverty are sometimes complicated by questions of ethnicity and race. And it is to these yet more difficult questions that we now turn, attempting to approach them in the light of the new conception of social justice set forth in Chapter 3, "Social Justice Redefined."

CHAPTER 7
ETHNICITY, RACE, AND SOCIAL JUSTICE

POPE JOHN PAUL II'S FAVORITE JOKE, it is said, runs as follows: "There are only two solutions to the Eastern European crisis: the realistic solution and the miraculous solution. The realistic solution is that our Lady of Czestochowa will suddenly appear with all the angels and the saints and solve the Eastern European crisis. . . . The miraculous solution is—all the nationalities will cooperate."

An important virtue of the Catholic ethic is explicit in the word "catholic" (universal). The Christian faith is intended for all human beings of all races and cultural histories, but its aim is unity, not uniformity. It should act as yeast in different kinds of dough, assuming the world's many different shapes, sizes, colors, and forms. One can be Nigerian and Catholic, Polish and Catholic, Indian and Catholic, Japanese and Catholic, Bolivian and Catholic, a citizen of the United States (of any ethnic background) and Catholic. In this sense, Catholicism has been called "Judaism for the gentiles"—open to all the races and ethnicities of the planet. For a thousand years this model unified Europe, forging *E pluribus unum*, a unity of faith and in common law, under a common Creator of all, a unity remarkable for its diversity. Its inner drive aimed (far beyond Europe) at all humanity, diverse and yet one.

This unity of the human race is also explicit in the Jewish Covenant. For the God of Abraham, Isaac, and Jacob is the Biblical Creator of all, spoken of both in the story of creation and in the story of the universal flood. The Jewish emphasis on monotheism ensures human unity. One and yet many—it has been a great struggle for the human race in the long ages of its existence to come to terms with both these poles of the human reality. The picture of the blue-green earth against the vastness of space beamed from far-off rocket ships has sharpened the modern world's sense of oneness, but has not solved the perplexities of diversity felt acutely below.

The bloody wars in the former Yugoslavia, the violence between Armenians and Azerbaijanis in Azerbaijan, and other ethnic conflicts in Eastern Europe sprang both from remembered grievances and from social systems of political allocation that evoked tribal competition. From the bloody struggles in Northern Ireland and the "necklacings" of the black-on-black violence in South Africa to the reduction of once-beautiful Lebanon to rubble, the world has come to know a great deal about ethnic and racial violence.

Some 30 years ago, Daniel Patrick Moynihan and Nathan Glazer predicted that the last part of the twentieth century would be characterized by a heightened resurgence of ethnicity and race; few took them seriously.[1] In *The Rise of the Unmeltable Ethnics* (1972) I myself predicted that the 1970s would be the decade of growing ethnic awareness in the United States.[2] A little later, Alex Haley's *Roots* widened the discussion most helpfully. Such works as these stressed the positive possibilities of enhancing ethnicity and cultural memory. Now the breakup of the former Soviet Union, the awful shelling of cities and villages in Croatia and Bosnia–Herzegovina, ethnic conflict in Malaysia and Sri Lanka, and domestic clashes among immigrant cultures in nearly all advanced societies (and some not so advanced) have made all the world aware of a new potential for ethnic disorder.

A thorough analysis of these problems would require book-length treatment. But a few brief remarks may show how the concept of social justice, newly articulated in the context of the Catholic ethic, offers a fresh approach to ethnicity and race—or, as it is said today, multiculturalism. Let us begin with the dimension of international order and then move to racial discord in U.S. cities.

INTERNATIONAL PERSPECTIVES

Every human person has both a universal dimension and a concrete, particular, angular, unique dimension. There are some characteristics that all human beings share: a common Creator, destiny, and nature; a common struggle to become what is in each to become; and a common liability to crises of birth, suffering, love, sickness, accident, pain, and death. To emphasize these universals that mark us as members of one human family is practical as well as true: It helps build up a sense of human solidarity.

At the same time, each human being is born from the womb of an individual woman, within a particular culture and tradition, at a concrete place and moment; and each has a personal identity shared with no other human being, a singular vocation, a unique destiny. Each represents, in the beautiful metaphor of St. Thomas Aquinas, a distinctive reflection of the Creator—as if it takes a virtual infinity of human beings for the human race to begin to mirror, all together, the infinite Personality of God. To destroy even one human being, therefore, is to destroy a part of God's presence in the world.

The concrete uniqueness of each person, moreover, is far richer than the uniqueness of each animal of the other species in the animal kingdom. In our home, for example, we have two cats, each different in color and manner and temperament from the other—one orange, the other black and white; one fat, one thin; one extremely intelligent, the other notably slow; one unusually affectionate, the other much less so. Each cat is an individual. But each human being is more than an individual in that sense; each also has the further capacity to acquire insight, to choose, to make commitments—in short, to be an *Imago Dei* in sharing God's capacity to understand and to love.

To emphasize this added dimension, the Catholic tradition makes use of the word *person*, rather than merely *individual*. Every cat is an individual, but every human being, in addition, is a creature capable of reflection and choice, understanding and love. In this added capacity to create, to invent, and to work out a highly personal destiny lies the human being's distinctive vocation. This added distinctiveness grounds a kind of individuality that goes all the way to the unique, the irrepeatable, and the inexhaustible self-determination of the free woman and free man.[3]

This individualized side of the human person, however, also

has a *social* dimension that falls short of the *universality* mentioned above—namely, ethnic or cultural or linguistic particularity. The God of Judaism and Christianity highlighted this dimension by choosing one small and not very powerful people, the Jewish people, as his "chosen people," and in a paradoxical way. On the one hand, through this choice the Creator of all human beings (and of the world and all that is in it) communicated a universal message intended for all human beings everywhere. On the other hand, He chose to communicate by and through a particular people and, in the fullness of time, and without in any way withdrawing His eternal love from his chosen people, to communicate through one son of that people, the Son of Man, Jesus. The God of Judaism and Christianity is the God both of universality and of particularity—of every single human individual but also of all human peoples in their variety.

To detail the ways in which the personality of each of us is shaped and conditioned by the ethnic heritages of which we are a part would here require too much space. The answer is obvious, of course, to Poles or Italians or Danes in Europe; in America, among the descendants of immigrants, the answer is rather more complex. Still, even in America, it would be odd if coming from an Irish, Italian, Jewish, African, English, or other heritage made no difference in one's life whatever, even if unconscious or seldom alluded to. At the very least there tends to be an emotional response to the homeland of one's ancestors different from that of others to other homelands. Typically, too, there are inherited traits of gesture, gait, manner, humor, emotion, and memory. Sometimes outside observers notice these traits in us more clearly than we do in ourselves. Most important of all, diverse cultures carry with them particular skills transferable to their children, such as studiousness, entrepreneurship, wit, and delight in words.

The main point is that to be a human being is to be both universal and particular. Each of us is as human as every other, and at the same time distinctive, both in a highly personal and in a social dimension of our being. Given this two-sidedness of human nature, one should not be surprised to find in the contemporary world two complementary tendencies—one centripetal, one centrifugal. It really is not ironic (it fits human nature) that, just as the human race is gaining a clearer sense of itself as one, all portions of it having seen spacecraft photos of mother Earth, there is a heightened sensitivity to cultural differences.

As technology moves us toward homogeneity, something within us seeks more intense differentiation. As federations and commonwealths grow in size and number and scope, smaller units thereof clamor for greater autonomy, notice, status, and independence. As a single market economy has encircled more of the world, it has seemed both safer and more practical (without withdrawing from unprecedented economic interdependence) for the Scots to demand greater independence from England, the Slovaks from Bohemia–Moravia, the Croatians and Slovenians from Yugoslavia, and the various republics of the former USSR from one another. (The USSR was never truly a union, anyway, but a conglomeration of peoples conquered by Russia; and they were not really republics, either.)

Thus, it is as natural and good and necessary for human beings to have a kind of *pietas* toward, gratitude for, and loyalty to a local polity as it is for them to uphold universal standards and a sense of solidarity with humankind as a whole. Many Western intellectuals of both right and left have forgotten how local and special are the circumstances within which their own traditions of liberty took root. Some too glibly assume the discourse of universal rationality, as when leftists speak (or at least used to speak) of the bleaching of nationalism into international socialism, or when liberal sentimentalists used to assert that the era of the nation–state and national identity has passed, such that true liberals ought to think of themselves as internationalists, world federalists, citizens of Planet Earth. (There may be a lesson in the fact that it was precisely in the land of such extreme universalizing philosophers as Kant and Hegel that, under Nazism, the dreadful exaggeration of blood, race, and nationalism took hold.)

Meanwhile, other developments continue apace—relativism, for instance. Many American intellectuals today can no longer affirm with intellectual honesty, "We hold these truths to be self-evident: that all men are . . . endowed by their Creator . . . ," since they do not believe that there exist any objective truths, let alone self-evident truths; and they do not hold that any Creator exists, let alone one who endows rights. They do not find any "objective foundation" for American rights, institutions, or habits. The best they can do is say that they "prefer" the American way, not merely for reasons of taste or convenience but for "pragmatic" reasons. It works, and they like it. But this is a weak defense against totalitarian power. It is also an intellectually weak defense.

(To this question we shall return in Chapter 8, in considering the role of intellect in culture.)

Since human beings are animals, they naturally love more what is closer to them, and more familiar, and of their own blood and history and sense of belonging, than what is to them remote, foreign, and different. Since they are spirited animals, they are also capable of rising to a larger sense of universal solidarity. Both these sides of human nature are valid—and each is subject to its own special corruption: nationalism to exclusion, universalism to enforced homogenization.

Nationalism is not inherently evil; universal homogenization is not inherently good; neither one alone is fully human. As it happens, and in part due to the errors of Communist universalism, the republics of the former USSR at first nourished an unusually potent combination of democratic and nationalist fervor. Democracy meant to them no more totalitarianism. Nationalism meant to them no more enforced homogenization. Freedom meant the possibility, at last, of being oneself—not only as an individual but as a social being. Democracy and nationalism are in this way not foes, but companions.

Similarly, in becoming Catholic peoples do not give up their own culture. Poles remain Poles; Germans, Germans; the French, French. Catholicity and distinctive national identities are not mutually exclusive terms. As God in assuming human flesh had to enter among a particular people and to speak in one language among many, so in a similar way each human being as *Imago Dei* should properly be what she or he is—a child of a particular heritage, as well as a child of God in one universal human family. Here is a catholicity in which differences are cherished.

Analogously, one of the evolutionary advantages of the three-fold social system of democracy, capitalism, and pluralism is that it serves both human universality and human particularity. Neither high religious ideals nor preachments on moral virtue suffice to end tribal violence or inherited patterns of preference. For this, systems of political allocation must be abandoned, in favor of rules of law that apply to all individuals equally. Indeed, one of the faults that Marxists most commonly attributed to market systems is actually a virtue: viz., that markets are impersonal; that they are no respecter of persons. In circumstances of ethnic strife, this quality is no vice. Whereas systems of political and patrimonial allocation are by nature lost in mazes of preference and favoritism, markets respond directly to talent, service, and inherent value. Furthermore, free and open democratic governments allow individuals of all backgrounds to compete on a fair basis and to bring grievances to impartial adjudication.

Let us admit it: From the beginning, the human being has also been a *murderous* animal. No social system, no matter how benign, can exorcise Cain from human possibilities. The mere presence of a capitalist economy, an open democratic government, and a tradition of pluralist institutions will not suffice to quell enmities and retaliations remembered for generations. Still, no systems have more effectively generated alternatives to killing, or found more successful means for taming destructive passions. Ethnic violence tends to thrive where economic horizons are narrow and opportunity foreclosed; under such conditions meanness of life breeds resentments as humidity breeds fungus. Neither Northern Ireland, nor the Middle East, nor Yugoslavia have been places of full and free economic opportunity. By contrast, the prosperity that inventive, open, and enterprising systems have generated is the single best solvent for ethnic and racial hostility. When government is on the whole open and fair, and when all citizens experience improvement in their own economic standing, they are less inclined to resent others.

For any republic to survive, envy needs to be defeated, and the best systemic way to defeat it is via economic growth and open access. A system of open opportunity takes allocation, favoritism, and preference out of politics. Economic growth allows individuals expansive room to pursue their uniquely personal ideals. When persons are free to pursue their own happiness, they stop comparing themselves with the Joneses—whose idea of happiness is probably not theirs. That is why systems that produce economic growth and foster personal accountability are more likely to diminish ethnic and nationalistic hostilities than any other. To work toward such systems is a major task of social justice.

But this, it will be noted, is to turn the conventional statist conception of social justice inside out. Most leftists who use the term social justice wish (unwisely) to employ the power of the state to allocate goods and positions to selected groups. They should have learned long since that history knows no surer way to heighten inter-group antagonisms. By contrast, true social justice begins by removing systems of political allocation and group favoritism, so that the rule of law may be applicable to every individual equally: "the rule of law, not of men." Individuals differ so in personality, ability, character, talent, effort, family background, and even luck that no just system can predetermine or enforce equal outcomes. Therefore, true social justice inspires the just to design general rules and procedures, rooted in experience, that (1) apply to all impersonally; and (2) produce economic growth, from whose benefits none are excluded. The first condition defeats envy, summoning personal accountability to center stage. The second furthers the common good of all and raises the hope of all.

Nonetheless, the most abiding work of social justice, even in peaceable societies, is to form effective associations to meet continuing needs that markets alone cannot meet—multiple and abundant needs. If, as Tocqueville said, the art of association is the first law of democracy, then social justice is democracy's first virtue. And its tasks are never-ending. Families, schools, churches, and the media of communication need to instill this virtue incessantly; their own smooth running is this virtue's first fruit. Social justice is the one habit of the heart that unites humans in "little platoons" and "bands of brothers" for a variety of tasks and a rich budget of enjoyments.

How, then, is this virtue faring in America today?

THE "CIVIL SOCIETY" PROJECT

Some 30 years ago, fresh from melting-pot experiences in the U.S. armed forces in World War II (when it seemed that every platoon and squadron was made up of an O'Malley, Rodriguez, Holton, Kosloski, Regan, Jackson, and Rubenstein), the many peoples of the United States, the world's most planetary people deriving from every corner of the earth and constituting, in Ben J. Wattenberg's felicitous phrase, "the first universal nation,"[4] were engaged in one of history's great experiments in multiculturalism, setting the stage for the morally electrifying civil rights movement of the 1960s. In retrospect, to many of us, the ideal glimpsed in those days—the practice, we well remember, was far rougher and less just than the ideal—seems still to shimmer in our minds as a noble dream. We really could imagine then, with the Rev. Martin Luther King, Jr., a day when all our children would be judged, "not by the color of their skin, but by the content of their character." We imagined ourselves a "little League of Nations." There was conflict between neighborhoods and among peoples; there was hot passion and intemperate speech; there was prejudice and injustice, unfairness and bias. But we really did believe, every group among us, that "We shall overcome, some day."

Much as the Catholic Church had for centuries tried to unite the most diverse tribes, linguistic groups, nations, and races in one people of God, so in its way the United States, a nation of immigrants, imagined itself to be (and was taken to be) a model of pluralistic unity for a bitterly divided and often internally warring Europe—even a model for a future United States of Europe. America developed the sort of open, dynamic, and prosperous system in which the hostilities and hurts of the past could gradually be buried. Sometimes the route toward this union of many was portrayed as a melting pot, each child in native dress (as the grammar-school skit had it) filing behind a giant screen representing a huge black kettle to emerge on the other side in standard blue shorts or skirts, waving American flags—the meaning being to some *E pluribus unum* but to others "The only good American is an un-hyphenated American." More wisely (particularly in times of stress and crisis), the image was rather of a multiethnic stew (or even salad) in which each "ingredient" retained his or her historic group identity even while joining in collaborative efforts with others—all together as proud of the nation's diversity as of its unity.

The image of a symphony, however, seems more appropriate for embodied spirits such as human beings. In a symphony, each instrument and section retains its own character and plays its own distinctive melodic line, even while orchestrated into a more splendid whole than is attainable by any one instrumental section alone. But, of course, *no* metaphor is quite apt for all the virtualities of the human spirit, that most unique of God's creatures.

But the pursuit of social justice in matters of race and ethnicity in the United States somehow has gotten off track, and not all the huffings and puffings of today's multiculturalism will suffice to get it back on. Positively, one must applaud the shift represented by the usage "African–American" instead of "black American"— a shift from race to ethnicity; in effect, from genetic appearance to cultural difference. For this shift brings all human beings equally onto the same playing field of history and culture; it does not intransigently divide them by something over which no one has control: the accident of race. Negatively, multiculturalism is currently being used to single out certain cultures for special status, favors, discriminatory treatment, and—unintentionally—future disadvantage. When "multicultural" requirements have been established at universities, for example, they do not often make space for Slovak–Americans, Italian–Americans, Ukrainian–Americans, or Scots–Irish Americans (and certainly not WASPS of the George Bush variety, as described by Richard Brookhiser[5]) alongside various Third World cultures, gays, and feminists. The term, instead, has been given a decidedly anti-Euroethnic cast, as if distinctions within the "European" category have not been, and still are not, of significant cultural importance.

The truth is that those of us of Eastern and Southern European heritage, among others, seldom encounter in the standard curricula the images, history, ideas, or sensitivities of *our own* ancestral history. My children have learned (not entirely without profit), more of the history of British kings and queens than of the political history of our own ancestry. And was not the awful and tragic bargain at Yalta, so bitterly remembered in Central Europe today, due to the ignorance of American negotiators about precisely such matters?

Still, multiculturalism is a step beyond division merely by race. For the past 30 years, beginning perhaps with Mayor John Lindsay, the liberal Republican mayor of New York City in the 1960s, American urban politics was needlessly and tragically divided on racial lines. There was some justification for this, but it was most unwise. Its justification was the great sins of slavery and segregation in the American past, together with the terrifying emotions let loose (as Thomas Jefferson saw they would be) by the unjust master–slave relationship—terrifying both to the slaves and to the masters. A woman friend of mine who is white and has a black son from an early marriage has described to me in unforgettable words the "almost metaphysical" feelings that overwhelmed her talented son in his attempts to cope with the looks he met in the eyes of white society. The history of the inequality of the races in America does tempt the reformer, in the name of social justice, to select race as the rockbottom reality to be dealt with.

But it is not wise to do so. It is not wise, because that very choice secures the permanence of an unbridgeable split between the races. Our humanity is deeper than our racial differences. So is the capaciousness of our cultural ideals. In their light, the only wise and healing path of social justice is to stress those movements, reforms, associations, and actions that bring us together, and to avoid encasing in concrete those accidental differences, such as color, that divide us. To stress the factor of race is to relegate blacks, Indians, and others to permanent minority status and emotional isolation. Worse than that, the underlying justification for emphasizing race rather than culture is to address blacks of today as victims.

The chief reason why, many years ago, I had a special respect for Bobby Kennedy was his desire to speak to whites and blacks together. Consistently in the campaign of 1968, he won a majority of the votes both in urban black and urban white ethnic neighborhoods. He was one of the few politicians in that generation who put white and black together, spoke to them equally, and won the hearts of both. The more that white liberals tut-tutted about his alleged "ruthlessness," the more those who lived in these hard-pressed neighborhoods, white and black, turned to him for assistance.

Early in 1992, William Julius Wilson saw the same capacities (I do not know if he was right) in Governor Bill Clinton of Arkansas. Wilson wrote then of that presidential candidate:

> His message to the all-black audience could have been delivered to a solely white one. It included two important aspects: an explicit acknowledgement of the racial tension in America and the need for leadership to unite, not divide, the races; and a discussion of programs intended for all low- to moderate-income groups, not just minorities.
>
> Mr. Clinton has destroyed the myth that blacks will only respond if a candidate highlights race-specific issues and programs.
>
> But if the message emphasizes issues and programs that concern the families of all racial and ethnic groups, whites will see their mutual interests and join in a coalition with minorities to elect a progressive candidate.[6]

To define policies in terms of skin color is inherently divisive, for nothing can be done about skin color, while a great deal can be done (and has been done) about many other human characteristics. Since blacks make up just over 10 percent of the U.S. population, this rhetoric needlessly divides them 1-to-9 against nearly 90 percent of their fellow citizens. This rhetoric of race in the United States, particularly that of the state-dependent "civil rights" leadership, white and black alike, reinforces the paralysis of victimhood among blacks, and guilt among whites. It prolongs the mutually destructive master–slave syndrome. In self-parody, it has inspired legions of other would-be minorities (such as women, who are actually a majority) and would-be victims (Hispanics, Native Americans, gays, lesbians, the elderly, and children) to make a mockery of victimhood. This is not the rhetoric of a free people. It has written all over it: "No win."

Surely, children of one Creator are able to look at racial realities in another way—one that stresses economic opportunity, talent, and effort.

Consider first the record of black success on just these points. By contrast with the levels of education and skill brought to America by black immigrants today, the cultures of Africa from which in past centuries blacks were ripped by slave traders for sale in America were not cultures of literacy or high sophistication. Then the dreadful institution of slavery lasted just over 200 years—it was not ended in America until 1863 (about the same time as serfdom was brought to an end in Central and Eastern Europe). As recently as 1930, before the great northward migration, some 90 percent of all U.S. blacks lived in the mostly rural South. Most had been deliberately deprived of literacy, education, and instruction in those skills that might lead to independence and self-reliance.

Nonetheless, within the short 40 years between 1950 and 1990, more than two-thirds of this once desperately poor population had climbed above the poverty line (in 1990 about $13,400 for a family of four). At least one-half of all black married-couple families had an annual income over $33,000.[7] Some 1,268,000 black households had an income over $50,000.[8] The 29 million blacks of the United States had an aggregate income of $284 billion in 1991, higher than that of all but 10 nations on earth, and more than practically all of Black Africa combined.[9] In the spring of 1989, 1.94 million blacks held bachelor's degrees or higher.[10] By 1990, 32 percent of all blacks living in metropolitan areas lived in suburbs—including all or mostly black suburbs of considerable affluence, such as several in Prince Georges County, Maryland.[11]

This record of success amassed by American blacks since 1950 does not easily fit the conventional rhetoric of race. Instead, this remarkable success is usually dismissed—because it is in the interest of those whose aim is higher subsidies from the state to stress the negative and to ignore massive evidence of success (especially that achieved without dependency on government). But is that just or fair? Through this tactic African–Americans, alone of all ethnic groups, are denied public admiration for their collective achievements.

Nonetheless, highly visible and serious ills afflict those four million or so African–Americans (under 15 percent) crowded into America's hundred largest cities. During 20 years of "The War on Poverty," the federal government alone (not counting state and local agencies) expended many more billions of dollars per year than would have been required to raise every poor household above the poverty line with a direct grant (about $35 billion). Despite these sums, as we have seen, the morale of many—and the condition of their neighborhoods—is worse than it was in 1965. Hopelessness is often expressed by those who have worked for years to ameliorate this bleak picture.

Some statists say that all the poor need is more money. Fewer and fewer analysts find this claim convincing, since the poor neighborhoods of American cities now have more money flowing through them than ever before. Much of this money comes from welfare, a great deal from legitimately earned income, and unknown amounts from the drug trade and other illicit (and often violent) pursuits. Lack of money is by no means the central problem. For in many of those very same neighborhoods one sees many new nonwhite immigrants who have far less money than their American neighbors, but who avoid the welfare system like a plague, quickly gain a foothold on the way to prosperity. These immigrants may arrive poor in cash, but they do not think like poor people, they do not intend to remain poor, and they typically move out of poverty very soon. For them, the issue is not bread alone but those other things humans live by: spirit, ethos, family, a capacity for self-organization, initiative, hard work, and burning ambition. This constellation of attitudes and habits is called by social scientists "social capital." It is *the most important form* of capital.

This is the social capital that the "civil rights" leaders of the last 20-plus years have underpriced, whose development they have therefore neglected, and whose massive deterioration among young males in father-absent households bodes so pessimistically for such cities as Washington, DC, New York, Detroit, Los Angeles, Dallas, and a hundred others. Since it was the law that permitted slavery, and the law that imposed segregation, one can understand the civil rights establishment's preoccupation for several decades with law and government. And since the War on Poverty resulted in the hiring of scores of thousands of black professionals to run its agencies, one can also understand the pay-offs from such preoccupation.

Further, since government penalties attached at first to residual practices of segregation, and later even to numerical "under-representation" in government and private occupations, one can gauge the geometrically growing force of such preoccupation. Those whose power and money were dependent on the state became addicted to the state. This process strengthened leadership classes (although it kept them dependent), but it did little for those whose social capital—endowed in them by their Creator—remained undeveloped in home, neighborhood, and local institutions. A concentration on victimhood does nothing good for social capital; rather, by inducing passivity and bitterness, it *devalues* human capital.

Indeed, in the shocking riot in Los Angeles at the end of April 1992, which occurred just as I was writing these pages, the whole country came to see a major faultline in our national strategy since 1965. Following the "War on Poverty," declared at that time, highly race-conscious programs proliferated in the United States. "Don't blame the victim—send money and programs" was the dominant cry. And much good was done.

The justification for welfare reform, first announced in 1962 by President John F. Kennedy, was to defend and protect the strength of the American family.[12] Among the elderly, these reforms were a great success. In 1960, the single largest group among the poor was those over 65; by 1990, this was the *smallest* group among the poor. Enhanced social security benefits and Medicare coverage for health, along with great advances in medical technology, had given the American elderly a new lease on life. The number of those who passed the age of 85—now called the "elderly elderly"—surged dramatically. The vast majority over 65 finally felt secure enough to live alone, usually in homes that they owned. To repeat: Welfare programs for the elderly were a *great* success.

Among the young (particularly among young families), however, the picture was altogether different. The number of single heads of household, mostly female with children, grew rapidly until they constituted the largest and most rapidly growing portion of the poor. The deterioration of marriage and family under the unyielding assault of divorce, separation, and the very rapid growth in births out of wedlock (especially to the very young), resulted in poverty rates, for female-headed households with children, of above 30 percent.[13] The inherited sexual ethic had broken down. More and more of the young were having intercourse outside of marriage. The annual number of abortions rose rapidly after *Roe v. Wade* in 1973, until it reached about 1.6 million, disproportionately among blacks. Yet climbing with the number of abortions, the percentage of children born out of wedlock reached 70 percent or higher in urban poverty areas among blacks. (By 1985, more white women than black bore children out of wedlock—but statistically in lower proportion.)

Simultaneous, then, with the remarkable success of some two-thirds of the black population, the condition of the *urban black poor* deteriorated dramatically along such important indices as out-of-wedlock births (with associated medical and other ills); work force participation; unemployment (and, worse, unemployability); the completion of high school; involvement in criminal activities; homicides; and addiction to drugs and alcohol. Worse still, from the point of view of social psychology, the 1970s and 1980s were decades of high immigration—and most of those new immigrants, although nonwhite, were both seizing opportunity and succeeding quite well. Horatio Alger stories among them abounded. Asian students especially began appearing as high-school valedictorians, university prize-winners, and business entrepreneurs in almost unparalleled numbers. No longer could one argue that America is not an "opportunity society," since so many millions were seizing available opportunities. No longer could one argue, either, that America is in some simple sense a racist society, since so many from nonwhite races were succeeding brilliantly.

Although I was out of the country during most of the Los Angeles rioting, one fact about the events in Los Angeles from April 29–May 3, 1992, seemed to me (on reviewing the coverage later) dramatically underplayed, or even steadfastly ignored: The "racial" conflict involved was chiefly directed by black and other rioters against Asians. Surprisingly little of the coverage interviewed the Asian victims, despite the fact that "Eight out of ten Korean stores were burned or looted in the riots, 100 in Koreatown alone," and even in more peaceful times in South-Central Los Angeles, the riot zone, "Korean entrepreneurs . . . ran a 1 in 250 chance of being killed while pursuing their business there" each year. Stretched to a career of 30 years, "The chances go up to 1 in 16."[14] Arthur Hu, a columnist for *Asian Week*, continues this account thus:

> One-hundred-and-twelve-hour work weeks, plus un-paid family labor, is common among Koreans. Many have college degrees that won't get them decent jobs because of discrimination or language problems. Asian students who live in housing projects and go to inner-city schools rack up grades, test scores, and gradua-tion rates that are the envy of white suburban stu-dents. Koreans don't get special loans; they just work three jobs, save, sacrifice, and borrow from loan pools built by family and friends. It seems that Koreans are despised solely because they are the smallest local rep-resentative of the "capitalist system," or are of a dif-ferent race and culture.

Asians like Hu felt frustrated by the "double standard" employed by the American press. "Race" to too many meant only "black."

To repeat a theme raised earlier, this is one of the severe pen-alties levied against systems of political allocation based on race-conscious social strategies. This is bound to be especially divisive when implicitly those who do so only mean "black"; and when, even then, they do not count successful blacks, who are in the great majority, as "truly" black (using for them the contemptible racist slur "oreos," meaning that they are "white" on the inside—as if "black" *cannot* mean successful).

The preferred media word for the motives of the Los Angeles rioters was "rage," although some writers also saw the happy and massive looting of stores as an orgy of "greed," while only a few noted the rather more ominous and (some thought) preplanned raiding of gun stores in particular. But close observation of the exact and targeted deeds done—and many of the words publicly uttered—suggests that one especially neglected motivational word was "*envy*." Envy is, in fact, the *most* destructive social vice, more destructive even than hatred, since hatred is at least visible and widely recognized as evil. By contrast, envy never speaks its own name; rather, it hides behind such noble names as equality, fairness, and even (alas) social justice. And from that privileged vantage point it silently does its destructive work.

Galina Vishnevskaya tells a story of envy as it operates in Russia: An alien king condemns a Frenchman, an Englishman, and a Russian to death on the next Monday, but allows each of them to fulfill one wish over the weekend. The Frenchman wishes for a weekend in Paris with his mistress, no questions asked, no promises made. The Englishman wishes for a weekend walking the fields of Oxfordshire with his faithful setter, reciting Wordsworth and Shelley. The Russian wishes—that his neighbor's barn will burn down.

The young criminals who selectively burned down the successful shops in their own neighborhoods were not merely expressing blind rage, or whatever degree of greed, but also envy. And no other vice is more suited to destroying a free republic! It is like the story (again Eastern European) that describes God appearing to a Serbian peasant to allow him one wish for whatever he desires, on the condition that his neighbor will receive twice as much. The peasant immediately asks that one of his own eyes be plucked out. Now, to pluck out one's own eye in the hopes of wounding one's neighbor worse is envy of a very high order, indeed. One has to feel rather sorry for those afflicted with envy, because their spiritual state is far sadder than their physical condition.

Envy is *precisely* the spiritual condition that systems of political allocation cannot directly address—but civil society can. And must. Attention must be given to restoring *civil society* in poor neighborhoods; if not, all else will be in vain. *Government* can only circle in on this task from the outside (where it is destined to remain.) Since the 1960s the U.S. government has tried to manage the lives of the poor itself, in its efforts needlessly preempting many of the neighborhood, family, and ethnic associations that keep civil society healthy. It has unwittingly *replaced* civil society, instead of trying to support it from a discreet distance.

This may be a good place to summarize our findings so far. Let us start by saying that social justice is better served by focusing on the support and development of the social capital of the neediest than by emphasizing division by race and color. Indeed, during the 1970s and 1980s, the people of the United States received an object lesson in the superiority of this new vision of social justice. Almost as many legal immigrants came to the United States during those two decades as in our decades of highest immigration; and for the first time, most of these immigrants were nonwhite. Despite the conventional wisdom of the experts, such immigrants proved that America was *still* a land of opportunity for those willing to start wherever there was an opening—even at the bottom; that these openings were plentiful; and that menial jobs were not "dead-end" jobs but, rather, "jobs for starters." Arthur Hu puts this point dramatically:

> It is not as if Korean–Americans are far more economically powerful than black Americans. Even though household incomes were close to the national average, extended and intact families meant that Koreans in 1980 (the latest Census figures available) had a per capita income of only $5,544, which was closer to the $4,545 for blacks than the $7,808 for whites. The average small store brings in no more money than a good union manufacturing job. The difference is that Koreans have the highest number of self-employed of any ethnic group, and their willingness to work very hard for very little money gives them a competitive advantage in inner-city neighborhoods where supermarkets fear to tread. Blacks have also generally ceded the worst entry-level jobs such as janitors and maids to immigrants. Thus Latinos and Asians toil at subminimum wages, living in tiny cubicles and shacks in order to send money to their families in the old country, while many black teens turn their noses at jobs at McDonald's or Safeway at double the minimum wage.[15]

In addition, these immigrants knew how to work together as families, pooling earnings. They accomplished prodigies of savings and investment. They tried where they could to own a small business, however humble. Finally they understood the enormous advantages of disciplining their children so that they would perform at the upper limit of their abilities in school. A growing chorus of observers is being driven by experience to these old and hoary secrets. Their success has been proven worldwide.[16] The reappearance of these virtues among our new immigrants has restored the faith of many in their universal efficacy.

Thus, if social justice means an inner capacity to form associations for the sake of improving the community, it follows that by cooperating to improve the condition of their own families in the United States, immigrant workers are in fact practicing social justice. They follow others in learning to love the system through fulfilling its promise and vindicating its purpose.

A close observer will espy in such groups the vitality of several social principles—cohesion, mutual reinforcement, advice and counsel, credit arrangements (formal and informal), the building of networks to assist the perplexed in their many difficulties, and above all firm family discipline.[17] If the greatest social need of an immigrant group at one stage in its American story is to achieve economic survival, stability, and success, its members are by such joint activities exercising social justice first on their own behalf. (As the saying goes, "Charity begins at home.") The attainment of self-reliance by communities of immigrants helping each other is neither morally nor socially negligible. It is the first thrust of social justice. It deserves high and constant praise.

By contrast, to hold that social justice is a virtue only of those who act from *noblesse oblige*, such as those white liberals complacently referred to as "the justice community" (No Unjust Need Apply) is a horrible mistake. This was not the meaning of social justice lived by the workers who created this nation's industrial and craft unions. The full flowering of social justice means an opening of one's eyes, heart, and mind to the needs of others, as well as to the needs of one's society as a whole. But its first solid buds bloom at home.

The internal disorganization that undermines the four million members of the "underclass" who are concentrated in the high-density poverty tracts of American cities is not normal for black Americans. The "learned incapacity" involved in it, instilled by government programs, is something new. In today's urban public housing, residents have no power to manage their own buildings. Welfare clients are discouraged from ownership and prevented from saving. (In America, they alone are held captive by home-grown socialism.) It is not the values of the poor that are wrong; it is the system that they are obliged to accept. Government picks up the financial responsibility for those who bear children out of wedlock and, accordingly, an alienated and overburdened matriarchy is promoted. Up to 80 percent of all children born in urban poverty tracts are born out of wedlock, and reared without the presence of a father in the home. In such proportions, this never happened in America before. Worse, more than half of the nearly 1.6 million abortions performed annually in the United States are performed upon such mothers; and, in 1988, for example, 43 percent of the women aborting were repeaters.[18] The bleakness of such lives can hardly be overstated. One hears of babies reared by having bottles propped up for them as they lie for hours in front of blaring television sets. The apartment houses, belonging to nobody, are uncared for.

Worse still, young males in the "underclass" have few ways to learn the habits, expectations, and standards by which the larger society moves forward: Not learning to read at home; seldom seeing adults who work with regularity or at all; rarely having the advice or counsel of a father; never encouraged to read books; learning few skills with tools, or words, or ideas; abandoned for most hours of the night and day to their own devices and desires; seldom subjected to systematic correction of their speech, manners, dress, or behavior. Many such youngsters grow up physically strong and alert, but almost wholly unprepared for fatherhood, work, economic stability, social participation, and citizenship.

Among inner-city blacks, the socialization of young males seems virtually to have broken down, and traffic in drugs is cutting through their ranks like a scythe of death. In Washington, DC, at any given time 42 percent of black males are involved with the criminal justice system; over a lifetime 85 percent will be convicted of a crime.[19] The vast majority of these men grow up in a home with no father present to guide them through adolescence and young manhood. Constraints on their behavior and socializing influences are weaker than at any time in American black history, even under conditions of far more extreme poverty. Nor is this pattern unique to the United States. Rates of out-of-wedlock pregnancy in Sweden are even higher than in the U.S., and are growing rapidly in most welfare states.[20]

The devastation being wreaked on inner-city communities chiefly (but not solely) by fatherless young males threatens the whole of American society. In such areas, three or four random killings occur every night. Swagger and bullying, disregard for life, and lack of remorse are plainly visible. When the moral ethos dissolves, there are not enough policemen in the world to constrain behavior.

What does social justice require of the rest of us to reverse this breakdown of civilization, this shame of our cities? These problems are beyond the capacity of—indeed, they have unwittingly been *caused* by—the blunt-edged tool of government; they lie primarily in the realm of civil society. And to allow civil society to flourish again among the poor, the government must stop treating them as wards, dependents, mere numbers. It must alter its laws and procedures so as to encourage work, savings, investment, ownership, and personal accountability.

Then, too, leaders in every sphere of American life—not merely stepping back to "Let George do it"—need to bring to bear on these neediest of our citizens the respectful assistance of the larger community. Each of the major professions and occupational groups (doctors, lawyers, food distributors, realtors, bankers, clergy, carpenters, electricians, painters, and—perhaps above all—journalists) needs to be organized to concentrate healthy attention on the development of social capital in these neighborhoods.[21] This is a humanistic task; only human beings working one-on-one can do it. And this is precisely the point made by Pope John Paul II in *Centesimus Annus*:

> In fact, it would appear that needs are best understood
> and satisfied by people who are closest to them and
> who act as neighbors to those in need.[22]

As the Pope says, the welfare state erred "by intervening directly and depriving society of its responsibility." Civil society must be reawakened. The social isolation caused by skin color destroys confidence and trust. A personal offer of friendship across racial lines brings healing. Those who give their free hours to help the homeless, the pregnant, the unlettered, the ill, and the down-and-out in these most desolate communities practice social justice directly, not by proxy. They offer person-to-person counsel. They help to restore trust among the needy, through their own warm human engagement, not by hiring in their stead state bureaucrats.

We must not forget, meanwhile, that most American blacks have moved out of poverty, and work with remarkable amity among colleagues of other racial and ethnic backgrounds. So the social isolation of the few is not a preordained condition. It results, ironically, from misguided public policies and a wrongheaded way of discussing social reality. The self-censored words of the media, for example, reflecting the failed policies and attitudes of the recent past, are far out of touch with reality. Such policies (often launched in the name of social justice) have made matters far worse today than they need to be, given the good intentions and massive expenditures of social energy launched in the 1960s. Not everything called social justice by those who championed the social programs of the sixties worked as intended. The more-or-less single-minded turn to the state during that decade has not accomplished what it was supposed to accomplish. The mess that government has helped to make, it must begin to undo.

The first thing that government must do is halt the tidal wave of crime. Walking through a low-income, inner-city high-rise neighborhood is enough to scare the enamel off one's teeth; finding oneself alone there at night can be a terrifying experience.

Perhaps, too, there is some systematic, institutional way to bring educational help to the primary perpetrators of the crime that terrorizes these neighborhoods, young males between the ages of 14 and 26, to organize them in some way into neighborhood academies during after-school hours. What the military and high-school sports programs now do for some youths, the larger society must systematically provide to inner-city poverty areas. Perhaps the U.S. military could develop volunteer programs among demobilized soldiers willing to add a year or two of voluntary service to train youths in urban poverty areas. Here there could be special after-school academies: units would be formed, uniforms provided, instruction both in useful skills and in team morale instilled. Tests and graded performance levels would be established, with badges of accomplishment publicly bestowed. Inner-city parochial schools *already* do much of this, and other dedicated volunteers have started a variety of programs, from chess clubs to basketball leagues, that are designed to teach a lot more than chess or basketball. Every such effort helps, for civilization depends primarily on the civilizing of young males, and cannot long endure without it.[23] A liberal society that neglects this task is both naive and suicidal.

Halting crime by a positive program to civilize young males is the first thing (among many) that government must do—certainly not by itself but by providing leadership and openly encouraging voluntary efforts. The *best* thing government can do, in a positive way, is catalyze the efforts of civil society, so that the citizenry at large will bring its many diverse talents and resources to the assistance of the needy. Government does not itself have to do everything that a good society needs to have done. There is a great deal more that human beings can do for one another through the free associations of civil society than through government alone. But when government acts as a positive catalyst, more such activities can develop than through voluntarism alone. An activist government can be more imaginative than a merely passive one in inspiring, undergirding, and supporting the works of civil society. But to do so it must discipline itself to work indirectly, not directly, and to promote local responsibility, not passivity.

An activist government must design its laws, policies, and financial dealings in ways that encourage *citizens* to become activists on their own behalf. Government can also use, to inspiring effect, its unequaled capacity to direct the attention of the public to one necessary task after another in achieving the common good. For instance, more citizens belong to churches than to any other organization in civil society. Mayors can encourage church leaders and pastors to pair poor congregations with wealthier ones; but not only pastors—also the lawyers, doctors, and other professionals in each congregation.

Recall that the new definition of social justice given in Chapter 3 of this book aimed at highlighting the associative skills that an individual has to learn to practice social justice as a habit or steady disposition. Recall, too, that to regard social justice as a personal virtue is far different from regarding it as an abstract ideal. The latter gives rise to ideologies, models, and programs, whereas the fomer shapes a citizen's character and actions. As a virtue, social justice is the capacity to cooperate with others (social in the first sense) in achieving ends that benefit society either in part or as a whole. (In this way, it is social in a second sense, that of enhancing the good of society, as a work of justice.) For the more a society reflects the works of reason, cooperation, free initiative, and self-improvement, the more thoroughly that society favors the full development of the potential of its citizens.

The virtue of social justice aims at the improvement of the earthly city. A city so enlivened inspires its citizens to deepen and enrich the practice of that virtue, in a kind of beneficent circle. (In times of moral decline, the beneficent circle goes into reverse; the steady deterioration of society discourages even the virtuous from expending seemingly fruitless efforts—and moral decline thus accelerates.)

In matters of race and ethnicity, a wise focus for social justice is the development of human capital—especially social capital— among the most vulnerable. For the development of his or her own social capital is the chief ground on which an individual can build a sense of dignity, achievement, and pride. Moreover, the success of such efforts wins the admiration of others and underlines what the poor have in common with others.

Although this cannot be a book about concrete social programs (and although the public is rightly skeptical of the "ten-point programs" produced in such reckless abundance during the past generation), an American audience is trained to demand practical conclusions. Here are mine:

- Identify the core illness of the underclass as envy founded on a feeling of failure and incompetence in the arts of civil society.

- Stress in season and out the necessary role of parents (especially fathers) in teaching their children (especially their sons) these arts, since such responsibilities are now unfairly borne by females.

- Condition welfare supports for children on the work record and education record of *both* their mothers and their fathers.

- Give welfare benefits to young mothers of small children in *congregant* settings only (such as local churches or schools) in which they can be brought out of isolation and also learn how to care for children, how to study or work with others, and how to prepare themselves both for independent living and a potentially successful marriage.

- Shame the media (especially television) into recognizing their role as supports to conscientious parents. Entertainment is our society's most powerful and pervasive teacher, as Walt Disney understood. The makers of mass media entertainment bear an enormous moral responsibility for the deterioration of the human spirit during the present generation, especially among the most vulnerable, who lack other guidance. What do the omnipresent "boomboxes" ever at the ears of the underclass, and the undimmed television sets that are the only babysitters of thousands of the poor, now teach the young? Whose language, rhythms, and behaviors do the poor so obviously imitate?

■ Devise methods for helping the dependent poor become owners rather than renters or tenants. Stress capital ownership.

■ Give public-housing projects constitutions of self-government, with internal policing powers vested in duly appointed residents.

■ Turn every institution of civil society—businesses, schools, churches, professional associations, trade unions, and trade associations—to focus on the development of human capital in poor urban areas through the organization of academies, competitions, and skill-oriented and habit-developing training programs. Every young male in designated poverty areas should be given a chance to enter into such programs for some hours of every day. Among others, churches, religious lay groups, the U.S. military, auxiliary police forces, and sports associations—specialists in training young men— might run these programs. (Personally, I'd recommend the Marianist or Christian Brothers of old: tough disciplinarians, motivated by unsentimental love.)

■ Experiment with enterprise zones, with heavy emphasis on job training and apprenticeship programs within such enterprises.

■ Apprentice young blacks to local entrepreneurs to work the long hours and learn the skills it takes to build independent small businesses.

■ Demand courtesy, neatness, spic-and-span uniforms, promptness, and orderliness in schools, with long work–study programs for apprentices in the community after school.

- Demand ever more of the young. Give schools great leeway in methods of discipline.

But these are only suggestions meant to stimulate and to encourage the active and imaginative citizens already at work throughout our cities, and to give them a feeling of not being alone. Civil society *can* do what the state alone *cannot* do. What is asked of us in the current generation is the courage to be inventive, and the skills of social justice necessary to reach out to one another in free and generous cooperation. The state can't do it alone. It's up to us to do it. That is the meaning of social justice.

Yet the cultural institutions within which we live—families, churches, schools, associations, television networks, magazines, movies, and the like—make it either easier or harder for us to heed the call of moral imperatives that take priority over our own preferences, feelings, and interests. In 1776, Thomas Jefferson was supported by his culture when he wrote, "We hold these truths to be self-evident. . . ." Does the American culture of our time support Jefferson's conviction—or undermine it with relativism? That depends on which parts of American culture you turn to.

CHAPTER 8

AGAINST THE ADVERSARY CULTURE

Nowadays, there is a tendency to claim that
agnosticism and skeptical relativism are the philosophy
and basic attitude which correspond to democratic
forms of political life. Those who are convinced that
they know the truth and firmly adhere to it are
considered unreliable from a democratic point of view,
since they do not accept that truth is determined by
the majority, or that it is subject to variation
according to different political trends. It must be
observed in this regard that if there is no ultimate
truth to guide and direct political activity, then ideas
and convictions can easily be manipulated for reasons
of power. As history demonstrates, a democracy
without values easily turns into open or thinly
disguised totalitarianism.

Centesimus Annus, #46

AGAINST NIHILISM

THE MORAL–CULTURAL SYSTEM is crucial to the health of capitalist
democracies, and easily overlooked. By "system" I mean more
than the "ethos," the complex of social values that guides human
activities. I mean *institutions* and *habits*. I mean institutions such
as the churches, schools, families, universities, and media of com-

munication. These institutions tell citizens which of their behaviors will receive social approval or disapproval. These institutions help to form the inner life of individual citizens—their imaginations, aims, desires, and fears. These institutions inculcate habits, good and (sometimes, alas) bad. Such institutions are crucial because the primary form of capital is the human spirit, which is subject to decline as well as progress.

In any one generation, the moral life runs deeper than the busy mind easily discerns. Because the habits of the heart are learned in childhood, supplying reasons of which reason is not conscious, each generation lives off the spiritual capital of its inheritance, and may not even notice when it is squandering this treasure. By dint of habits of hard work and attentiveness parents sometimes grow successful, remain preoccupied, and leave their children barren of spiritual instruction. The moral and spiritual life of nations depends, therefore, on sequences of at least three generations. The habits inculcated by the first generation may be significantly abandoned by the second, and almost nonexistent in the third. Conversely, we do not always understand the treasures that, all unknowing, we have inherited from the hard experience of several faithful generations. In this ignorance lie the seeds of tragedy.

And such tragedy haunts the free society. A generation may not grasp until too late the full implications of altering the traditions of the past. Forgetting the principles on which their society has been constructed, any new generation may slide into behaviors and ways of thinking that set in motion its destruction. For example, the founders of the American experiment announced "We hold these truths to be self-evident," and took as a model Republican Rome, with its civic virtue. But a recent generation may brush aside this model, forget the truths once held to be self-evident, and abandon the daily disciplines that once kneaded such truths into civic virtues. A people that does let go like that of the intellectual and moral habits that hold its social system together is quite likely to fly apart. Is this not, indeed, the present greatest threat to the free societies of Western Europe and the United States?

The specific moral challenges to free societies today are perhaps too obvious to need elaboration. Precisely because such societies are affluent and free, they supply many allurements. Especially through the new technology of television, the solicitations of popular culture have come to occupy unprecedented space in the inner lives of the young—rock video, films of violence, sexual license, and the cultivation of passion and desire. Although counterbalanced by abiding moral seriousness on the part of many, there is, nonetheless, considerable evidence of mounting behavioral dysfunction among us: drugs, crime, births out of wedlock, children disoriented by divorce, teenage pregnancy, and a truly staggering number of abortions. Many of these behavioral dysfunctions result in various forms of social dependency. Thus a widespread loss of moral virtue creates larger and larger numbers of uncivic-minded hedonists on the one hand, and clients wanting to be supported by society on the other.

Indeed, although the phrase "liberal democracy" has a certain validity, there are now serious reasons for investigating whether there is a contradiction between "liberalism" (or at least a certain kind of liberalism) and democracy. In recent decades especially, at least in the United States, "liberal" has come to be associated both with a radical (and ultimately self-centered) individualism and with an insistence on doing not what one ought to do, but what one feels like doing. Radical individualism would be defective enough; it would destroy those bonds of sympathy, fellow-feeling, self-sacrifice, and sense of mutual obligation that nourish a lively community and civic responsibility. "Looking out for number one" would become a dagger in the heart of brotherhood, friendship, marriage, and family life. Worse, however, if the center of the self should slide away from its sense of duty, responsibility to others, and respect for the laws of nature and nature's God, and if it should come to pivot instead, on personal whim, feelings, or passions, the reflective self would no longer be the governor of its own behavior. When enough citizens can no longer govern their own passions and feelings, it is chimerical to imagine that they can maintain a self-governing republic.

Should this happen, a profound disorientation of intellectual habits would further undermine the truths a people once held to be self-evident, until such truths could no longer be intellectually defended. Thus Richard Rorty has propounded a "cheerful nihilism," in which any claim to "truth" independent of pragmatic social preference is to be joshingly brushed aside,[1] while Arthur M. Schlesinger, Jr., once argued—but has somewhat revised his view—that America was founded on "relativism."[2] Rorty would have us be kind and tolerant to one another, while happily refusing to offer an intellectual ("metaphysical") defense of our system.

Indeed, Rorty has become perhaps the best-known philosopher in America even while rejecting both "metaphysics" and the search for "foundations." His work, he thinks, constitutes a thorough-going rejection not only of Plato's ideal types (which Aristotle also rejected) but also a repudiation of any object "out there" which represents an "objective" (eternal, absolute) moral standard by which human deeds should be measured. Put another way, Rorty thinks it a waste of time (and an illusion) to search for an objective ground, standard, or mirror to which humans should look for nature's verdict on their beliefs or actions. There is no "mirror of nature."[3] All is flux; history, contingency, and random events go "all the way down." We have to accustom ourselves to this unanchored standpoint (or, rather, driftpoint). There are no foundations "out there" on which to base ourselves, no lighthouses by which to orient ourselves.

Some persons find this view liberating; it frees them from the preoccupations of the traditions they learned at home and at church. Others find it shocking, silly, or nihilistic.

To surprise the latter, Rorty denies that if there is no God, "everything is permitted." Those who hold to no objective stan-dard, and claim no foundation in universal reason or nature or God, he insists, nevertheless experience moral indignation about injustices that cause human beings to suffer. His nonbelieving "ironists" are quite capable of drawing lines to mark off what is morally unacceptable (to them), about which they can say with a certain kind of absoluteness: "Here I stand, I can do no other." He even notes that many people in the West have learned as much from Christ as from philosophy, including concern for the suf-fering of the vulnerable, a sort of kindness and gentleness, and a sense of solidarity with all humankind.[4]

These protestations, of course, don't satisfy those who find Rorty's rejection of objective standards, supplied by nature and nature's God, perilous and irresponsible.

In adjudicating this matter, I want to note that Rorty makes these points in response to Central Europeans such as Vaclav Havel and Jan Patočka, respectively the president (1990–1992) of Czech-oslovakia and Czechoslovakia's most important philosopher (1907–1977). Havel and Patočka maintained under persecution that a commitment to objective "truth" was essential in the struggle against the "lie" of totalitarian communism. Rorty argues that "we" Americans do not talk the language of "being" and "consciousness" that Havel, Patočka, and other Europeans have learned from Husserl, Heidegger, and ultimately Plato. "We" are not much troubled about rooting our actions in "foundations," "we" do not talk such "metaphysics," or try to figure out how to use "being" language. But this does not mean that "we" are indifferent to tyranny, regimes of the lie, or moral cowardice. On the contrary, even without metaphysics, simply with our humble pragmatism, "we" too know that there are some things we would not do, and some forms of politics we would resist.

Of course, it is easy for Rorty to boast about the heroic way in which he and others who hold his views would conduct themselves under totalitarian pressure; he has not been put to the test. Moreover, in his case, no matter of "truth" or "universal standard" or "nature" or "divine command" could be at stake. On his own intellectual premises, he could in Havel's place have found a pragmatic reason for treating totalitarian power with "irony," all the while conforming his behavior to its demands. He could have done so out of "temporary" necessity, absorbing one more contingency among the other absurd contingencies in life. No doubt, of course, Rorty would himself be willing to become a martyr; I do not doubt his own moral integrity. Yet even he must concede that not all those who hold his views would *in principle* feel obliged do so.

Some would surely find it possible to argue that their former liberal convictions were dependent on a quite different social context, which no longer exists, and that to adapt to another social system is no better and no worse, from a moral point of view, than to fail to adapt. After all, there is no "objective standard" compelling their consciences. They have nothing to lose, morally, in adjusting pragmatically to a new standard, even while maintaining a sense of irony and being as kind as possible to their loved ones. Social systems do differ, and one must survive as best one can. This vein of thought is especially compelling if, like Michel Foucault, one imagines that words are only a mask for power.

However such speculations may go, there are many of us in America who do not feel included under Rorty's "we." We *do* speak the language of moral foundations, being, and "laws of nature and nature's God." We do hold some truths to be foundational for a worthy social experiment ("testing whether this nation, or any nation so conceived and so dedicated, can long endure.") In distancing himself from such language, Rorty is not speaking for us. One may be quite sure that he does not speak for a majority of Americans. The moral views of the American public diverge significantly from those of humanists in our universities.

But is Rorty right? In a way, he can hardly be wrong, since he wants things both ways. He says there are no permanent, objective foundations "out there" in reality, independent of and authoritative for his consciousness. Nonetheless, he is conscious of holding certain moral standards that he will not violate. He is also confident that many others hold these standards now, and many will continue to do so. So it is false to hold that, in their case, "Without God, everything is permitted." He claims to have learned from Jerusalem as well as from Athens, from Christ as well as from Plato. Moreover, he speaks of such lessons from the past as though they constitute a more or less continuing tradition.

So what, really, does Rorty lack that would distinguish him from being a believer, say, in the Christian social gospel? Looking one way, he talks like a nihilist. Looking another, he acts more or less like the rest of us, except with a slight hint of moral superiority in his wan, ironic smile. If we pay attention to what he does, rather than to what he says, he behaves rather like a not very devout Christian, no better or worse than most others, and somewhat less dramatically than (say) Graham Greene, Albert Camus, or Gabriel Marcel. To take him seriously as a philosopher is not easy. Not even he acts as his theories would predict.

The same goes for Arthur Schlesinger, Jr. He sowed relativism, yet when the same relativism grew as high as his eye in the fields of academe under the guise of multiculturalism, and when young professors began to denigrate *his* values and loves, he tried desperately to uproot what he had sown.[5] Schlesinger cannot have it both ways. If "the truths we hold" are not "true" but merely "work well for us," they may be legitimately rejected by those who judge that they do not "work for them." (I much admire Schlesinger's elegant critique of recent racialist posturings and pretensions, and applaud his defense of our common culture. But I cannot share his insistence on cultural homogenization, on the one hand, as an answer to cultural relativism, on the other. Each of these two represents an extreme and dangerous position.) It is not so easy for Rorty and Schlesinger to get along without the word "true" as they think; they pay—and the country pays—a heavy price for their reliance on preference rather than truth.

The conception of "unalienable rights" on which the American experiment rests is intelligible only in terms of truth, nature, and nature's God. Against a background of "cheerful nihilism" this experiment makes no sense at all; it is only an assertion of arbitrary will. Cheerful nihilism would render the American experiment philosophically vulnerable to any adversarial will exercised with superior power and popular consent.

Quite unlike Rorty, others have argued that the philosophical background in which the American experiment was historically placed *is* congenial to the traditions of Christian philosophy and Christian belief. Among those who champion this view are John Courtney Murray, S.J., and Jacques Maritain.[6] Indeed, a large majority of American citizens shares the Christian intellectual tradition still today and understands the American experiment in its light. Rooted in a sense of transcendence, what Walter Lippmann has called "the public philosophy"[7] gives individual citizens an intellectual basis for resisting public expressions of arbitrary will and for vindicating their rights against aggression from any quarter. They believe these rights to be rooted not in human preference, will, or custom but in the intellect and will of God. This was the sort of belief from which the moral heroes in Eastern Europe— such as Orlov, Scharansky, Havel, Bratinka, and millions of their followers—drew the strength to overturn the most extreme totalitarian power in history.

Parallel to the task of renewing the moral foundation of free societies, therefore, is a further task of deepening their intellectual foundations. Certain classically inspired students of political philosophy, quite aware of the Enlightenment's deficiencies, have already engaged in a secular version of such a project; viz., such scholars as Leo Strauss, Allan Bloom, Francis Fukuyama, and, in his own fashion, Harry Jaffa.[8] It may even be the case that liberal institutions cannot be defended on the basis of the secular philosophies of the Enlightenment, but must be recast in more ancient terms, consistent with Jewish and Christian intellectual traditions.[9]

Furthermore, since democratic capitalist societies bring to the fore a new set of moral and intellectual virtues to complement the classical virtues, some new Aristotle should describe their actual practice today. Fresh thinking is needed on a whole range of traditional moral concepts, whose concrete embodiment is now quite different from that of the past. For example, such concepts as person, community, dignity, equality, rights, responsibilities, and common good are today enfleshed in new settings. Thus individuals today are citizens rather than subjects; they are expected to act for themselves, with initiative and enterprise, and not simply to wait for orders. In this respect, they require new virtues scarcely required of their ancestors in the classical period, such as civic responsibility, enterprise, free association, and (in the sense defined in Chapter 3) social justice. In the closing pages of this inquiry, we will return to the new virtues required of modern citizens.

Whether they always *act* as citizens, accepting their proper civic responsibility, is another matter. Americans being interviewed on television during presidential campaigns often speak as if they think of themselves primarily as workers and consumers, worried about "pocketbook issues." These considerations are not insignificant nor, given today's vast governmental intrusions into the economy, wholly irrelevant; but they are by no means the whole of citizenship. Of course, television journalists often act as if the chief responsibility for economic performance rests not with citizens acting in a free market as they will, but with the President and his economic policies. In public discourse, therefore, the language of citizenship has fallen into disuse—or, at least, more so than in the past.[10]

Reflection on other characteristics of moral life today suggests significant additions to our working concepts of community. Even with respect to purely economic activities, for example, large and broad markets work through voluntary choice, consent, and cooperation to achieve beneficial outcomes too complex for any one agency to direct, and such outcomes give rise to a new concept of common good quite unlike the simple common good defined by a tribal chief of yore.[11] Markets serve communities, even link and unify communities; to be excluded from them is more alienating than to be included within them.

Second, from infancy our young children—erroneously described as suffering from excessive individualism—are in fact immersed in social practices, group activities, cooperative projects, and group memberships of so many sorts that scarcely any human beings in history have been so thoroughly and complexly socialized.

Thus the work to be done in reform of our civilization's moral foundation—and even in our *ideas* about it—is quite immense.[12] For the main point of culture is to give character a shape.

CULTURE AND CHARACTER

We can imagine the white-haired Pope John Paul II, as he neared the end of *Centesimus Annus*, turning his attention from political and economic problems to matters closer to his own philosophical interests—those deeper (and more influential) questions of character, culture, and truth. "Of itself," he wrote, "an economic system does not possess criteria for correctly distinguishing new and higher forms of satisfying needs from artificial new needs that hinder the formation of a mature personality. *Thus a great deal of educational and cultural* work is urgently needed."[13]

Redoubtable social thinkers such as Joseph Schumpeter and Daniel Bell have also seen that the weakest link in the threefold system of the democratic republic and the capitalist economy is its moral and cultural system. Schumpeter in *Capitalism, Socialism and Democracy* and Bell in *The Cultural Contradictions of Capitalism* both argue that, in the long run, the American experiment is doomed,[14] and that this self-destruction will begin among the spiritual and intellectual elites. Both give long and vivid descriptions of the occupational vulnerabilities that promote this self-destruction. Both fear that this betrayal will spread outward rapidly, through the cinema and music, through magazines and newspapers, and through other fibers of the nation's spiritual nervous system.

What ultimately determine the character of a culture are its choices. As the Pope observed, "A given culture reveals its understanding of life through the choices it makes in production and consumption."[15] And again, "It is not wrong to want to live better; what is wrong is a style of life presumed to be better when directed towards 'having' rather than 'being.' "[16] Individuals, like cultures, reveal what they understand of life through their choices. A woman's inmost identity, like a man's, comes from the qualities of character revealed in her actions—from her very being, as she has shaped it by daily acts—and not from her possessions. "Even the decision to invest in one place rather than another, in one productive sector rather than another, is always a *moral and cultural choice*. The decision to invest, that is, to offer people an opportunity to make good use of their own labor, is also determined by an attitude of human sympathy and trust in Providence that reveals the human quality of the person making such decisions."[17]

"The first and most important cultural task is accomplished within man's heart. The way in which he builds his future depends on the understanding he has of himself and his destiny."[18]

The Pope's emphasis here on *being* (rather than having) represents another characteristic of the Catholic ethic. The dramatist and existentialist philosopher Gabriel Marcel dedicated a whole book to this topic,[19] and devoted considerable attention to it as well in many other books.[20] The insight into being, the fact of existence, is often held to be, in fact, a distinguishing trait of the perennial philosophy—that sharp sense of the difference between existing and not existing that one sometimes glimpses in those moments of exhilaration atop a mountain or in a boat on a still lake, when one is glad to be alive and poignantly aware of the swift slipping-away of life. To *ex-sist*, to stand out from nothingness if only for a moment, is not only to glimpse one's own fragility and dependency, and not only to give thanks for an unrequested and undeserved gift, but also to perceive a dimension of life that is often obscured in the rush and distraction of everyday pragmatism. It is to be overcome (momentarily) by wonder. The habit of making such moments more frequent during one's days is a habit important to Catholic life. It is reinforced by moments of frequent prayer and occasions of gratitude. (One meaning of "eucharist," indeed, is "gratitude").

The insight into being draws attention to what is truly central in life, uniquely and ultimately important, one's responsibility for saying "yes" to life, to the will of God Who created us to be where we are and to achieve all that we are capable of: Who gave us a vocation to wonder at His creation and to bring it to its latent perfection, so far as in us lies. From this attitude of wonder, reverence, and sense of vocation spring responsibilities for action and character development. The kind of person we become is far more important to God than the positions or possessions we may attain. This, in part, is "the truth about man."

The Pope praises democracy, the rule of law, and the separation of powers,[21] as well as the market economy and the virtues it nourishes. But always in his eyes is the pursuit of "the truth about man." Rejecting this search, socialism doomed itself to self-destruction. The same thing could happen to market democracies. Decadence, decline, and internal disintegration are latent possibilities. "From the open search for truth *the culture of a nation* derives its character," the Pope writes, adding: "when a culture becomes inward-looking, and tries to perpetuate obsolete ways of living by rejecting any exchange or debate with regard to the truth about man, then it becomes sterile and is heading for decadence."[22]

One can see why this Pope worries about the West, particularly America. We have already discussed what leading Americans today think of "truth." The nation's founding documents hold that the American experiment rests upon certain truths of nature and nature's God—that is, on a foundation beyond the power of any dictator to alter or to erase, a foundation worth giving one's life to uphold. Yet for many today "truth" is essentially a matter of taste and what "feels good for me." Others hold that *nothing* is either moral or immoral but personal opinion makes it so. Moral confusion is widespread (perhaps especially among the highly educated).

Those who welcome the Ten Commandments as a law beyond their power to wish away are sometimes ridiculed. Many who call themselves "liberal" cannot bear to call *anything* either "good" *or* "evil"; they seek every evasion possible. It has even become common to hear the essence of liberalism identified with relativism.[23] Thus an observer at a recent annual meeting of the American Academy of Religion in Kansas City had no difficulty citing many examples of the most rampant (and unchallenged) relativism.[24] Despite this *trahaison des clercs*, international survey data indicate that few peoples in the world are more religious than the people of the United States, both in belief and in activity.[25]

Nonetheless, the moral rot evident among Hollywood, television, and rock star elites, and the moral confusion evident in the professoriat seem steadily to be corroding the morals of ordinary people. It is not easy to explain away the extraordinarily high murder rates in U.S. cities; the prevalence of sex out of wedlock; the large proportion of female-headed households; and the moral equivalence asserted in public speech between homosexual acts and heterosexual married love. By traditional Jewish and Christian standards, certain features of current American culture bring to mind Sodom and Gomorrah, not "the city on a hill." Both on the intellectual and on the moral front, battle lines in a major cultural war are shaping up between those who cherish perennial truths and values and those who hold those truths and values in contempt.

In examining a nation's moral health, one must scrutinize especially the cultural elites who create the stories, images, and symbols of the nation's self-understanding and moral direction. The new frontier of the twenty-first century is likely to be contestation for the souls of both cultural and moral systems. Pope John Paul II calls for such criticism, both for its own sake and because U.S. culture, in particular, now exercises massive moral influence around the world.

AMERICAN FOUNDING PRINCIPLES, CURRENT PRACTICE

Like our own elites, most of the world still neglects the American Revolution. The failed French Revolution of 1789 is seized upon as the great symbolic center of the modern era of liberty. Even Cardinal Ratzinger ignored the American (and cited only the French) Revolution in his second "Instruction on Christian Freedom and Liberation."[26] "The sad truth of the matter," Hannah Arendt has written, "is that the French Revolution, which ended in disaster, has made world history, while the American Revolution, so triumphantly successful, has remained an event of little more than local importance."[27] How sad this really is becomes clear from Professor Arendt's earlier line: "The colonization of North America and the republican government of the United States constitute perhaps the greatest, certainly the boldest, enterprise of European mankind."

Intellectually isolated from Europe, and separated from it by hundreds of tacit understandings, customs, habits, laws, and institutions, the United States is still the world's most original and most profound counterculture. Its underlying presuppositions are unknown to, or left inarticulate by, even the larger part of its own intellectual elite—that "adversary culture" which Lionel Trilling was the first to analyze.[28] "It is odd indeed," Arendt writes, "to see that twentieth-century *American* even more than European learned opinion often inclined to interpret the American Revolution in the light of the French Revolution, or to criticize it because it so obviously did not conform to the lessons learned from the latter."[29]

The U.S. system was in its beginnings unlike the European, and the Framers were quite aware of their originality.[30] Do not deny to us, James Madison in effect wrote in *Federalist* 14, the originality of our *novus ordo seclorum*, through which the American people "accomplished a revolution which has no parallel in the annals of human society. They reared the fabrics of governments which have no model on the face of the globe."[31] One of the original features of the new system erected by the people of the United States was the primacy it afforded to the institutions of conscience, information, and ideas—precisely to its moral culture—over the realms of politics (limited government) and economics (the least statist in history).

Another (and at first more striking) novelty, Prof. Arendt writes, is that the American experiment drew Europe's long-slumbering attention to "the social question." "America," she wrote, "had become the symbol of a society without poverty. . . . And only after this had happened and had become known to European mankind could *the social question* and the rebellion of the poor come to play a truly revolutionary role."[32] The American example awakened the conscience of Europe. Poverty no longer being inevitable or irreparable, its continued existence became for the first time in history a problem for human conscience.

Indeed, long after one Frenchman, Crèvecoeur, had reported back to Europe the amazing prosperity of those Americans who had not long since departed from Europe bitterly poor,[33] and about the same time as another, Alexis de Tocqueville, was describing the systemic prosperity and ordered liberty that "the hand of Providence"[34] had launched in the world through the American experiment, Victor Hugo was still able to describe the dejection and virtual hopelessness of *Les Misérables* in the France of 1832. The poverty of the poor in France already had shocked Jefferson some 40 years earlier, and the French Revolution had done little to mitigate that poverty. Only gradually did the example of the United States, in moving so many millions of the poor out of poverty, awaken Europe to the social condition of its own poor.

In 1886 the Liberal party of France (the party of Tocqueville), seeking to awaken the world again to the difference that the United States had made to the history of liberty, commissioned and executed a magnificent gift to the United States: the Statue of Liberty. Imagine the work of its planning committee. "How shall we symbolize the specifically American idea of liberty?" they must have asked themselves. Being French, they decided the symbol would be in the shape of a woman, not a warrior. In this, they followed a tradition as old as the image of Lady Philosophy in Boethius's *The Consolation of Philosophy*: Woman as wisdom, bearing aloft in one hand the torch of understanding against the swirling mists of passion and the darkness of ignorance. In her other hand, they placed a book of the law, inscribed "1776" to signify the truths Americans hold dear. Her face would be resolute, serious, purposive. This Lady symbolized not the French *Liberté* (the prostitute on the altar of the Black Mass), but rather that "ordered liberty" to which Pope John Paul II was to call attention in Miami exactly 101 years later.[35] Thus the primacy of morals in the American idea was fully and rightly grasped by the Liberal party of France, heirs of Tocqueville.

Virtue is the pivotal and deepest American idea. Indeed, "Virtue" was the inscription (later supplanted by *Novus Ordo Seclorum*) at first inserted as the motto on the Great Seal of the United States. To imagine an experiment in republican government without virtue, Madison had told the Virginia Assembly, is "chimerical."[36] For how could a people, unable severally to govern their own passions, combine to govern their own body politic? Tied together in the then-novel conception of "political economy," neither a free polity nor a free economy can long survive an incapacity among the people for the virtues that make liberty possible.

According to the American idea (learned from Jerusalem, Athens, Rome, Paris, and London),[37] liberty springs from the human capacities for *reflection* and *choice*. These human capacities reflect the *Light* and *Love* that are the very names of God in Whose image humans are made, and by Whom they are endowed with "unalienable rights." Habits such as temperance, fortitude, justice, and prudence provide the calm that makes human acts of *reflection* and *choice* possible. The first paragraph of *The Federalist*[38] was addressed exactly to these capacities as the American people were making the precedent-shattering decision whether to constitute the new American republic or no.

The Framers appealed again and again to the primacy of morals, and indeed to God and to Providence (that is, the wise and knowing—"provident"—Creator) in whose image they believed the human capacities of reflection and choice were stamped. "The God who made us, made us free," Jefferson said. Hannah Arendt quotes John Adams (and could as well have quoted George Washington, Benjamin Franklin, James Madison, Alexis de Tocqueville, Abraham Lincoln, and others): "I always consider the settlement of America as the opening of a grand scheme and design in Providence for the illumination of the ignorant and the emancipation of the slavish part of mankind all over the earth."[39]

It is important to underline such a powerful stream of thought as this, and its embodiment in a thousand institutional and ritual ways, for it helps to understand how, to Americans, it is somehow fundamental to stand under the judgment of God. Like the ancient Israelites (to whom, John Adams said,[40] Americans owe more than to any other people), they know that no achievement of material prosperity or of military might would spare them a yet more demanding judgment. And this judgment would be rendered by a transcendent, almighty, and unswervingly *just* God, whose judgment was to be dreaded as "a terrible swift sword." The primacy of morals is written into America's very soul.

For this reason, Americans gave a privileged place to institutions of morals and culture: to churches preaching to the faithful, to universities (in whose support, more than any other people before or since, they have invested so many of their private and public energies), to learning, and to the press. Had he to choose between having a free government or a free press (and God forbid the choice, Jefferson said), he would prefer a free press.[41] If these moral and cultural institutions go sour, if that salt loses its savor, all the rest of ordered liberty is lost: The polity is doomed to division and self-destruction, the economy to hedonism and raw self-interest.

It is absolutely critical to the American experiment, therefore, that the institutions of conscience, information, culture, and moral reflection retain this primacy. Should there ever be a "treason of the clergy," all is lost.

We began with predictions of doom for American culture by Joseph Schumpeter and Daniel Bell. However accurate and penetrating their comments may be, their pessimism need not be paralyzing. For if the primary flaw in our political economy lies not so much in our political system (democracy being a flawed and poor type of governance, until compared to the alternatives), and not so much in our economic system (capitalism being a flawed and poor organization of economy, except compared to the alternatives), *but in our moral–cultural system*, then their prognosis may in the end be more hopeful than it first appears. For if the fatal flaw lies most of all in our ideas and morals, then its source lies not in our stars but in ourselves. And there, by the grace of God, we have a chance to mend our ways. Good ideas can (and often do) drive out bad ideas. If the flaw lies in ourselves—especially in our moral, intellectual, and cultural behavior—then we ourselves have a magnificent opportunity to do something about it. That is all that free women and men can ask. A chance. No guarantee, but a chance.

THE POPE'S CHALLENGE TO THE U.S.

If I am not mistaken, this is more or less the diagnosis that Joseph Cardinal Ratzinger and Pope John Paul II have for several years now been applying to the United States. They appeal to our elites, most of all, on the plane of ideas and on the terrain of morals and of faith. They call us to step back from ourselves and to look at ourselves as others abroad see us. They ask us to look at the moral decadence visible to outsiders in American films, videotapes, music, television shows, magazines, newspapers, novels, and books, all of which our culture sends as emissaries across the world. Are we not embarrassed by *Dallas*, spoof though it may be, a series (at last count) being shown in 77 different nations of the earth? Just recently a young Korean–American attorney in Washington, DC, wrote that the young people of his nation of origin, just two decades ago wildly pro-American, have come to hold our nation in contempt for its inconstancy and changeability, and for its public immorality. He begged the proper authorities to take American Armed Forces television off the airwaves, where it is shocking to South Koreans; but if we mean to keep it, at least to keep it on restricted cable lines which only Americans can watch, in quarantined self-corruption.[42]

In many ways, of course, U.S. culture is a much-admired model and pace-setter. Our films, our music, and even many of our books are both appreciated and imitated in every corner of the world. Nonetheless, it is also widely recognized that public exposure to various of the products of American pop culture do tend to generate a loosening of morals.

I do not think that our mass media are quite as decadent as some in our midst often say. Any well-told story requires the dramatization of the essential components of human moral action. Drama and narrative, even in the most attenuated forms, necessarily pay testimony to the basic capacities of the human soul for reflection and choice, and for the courage necessary to sustain both. Nonetheless, it can hardly be said that ours is an age of moral toughness, or that our public media of communication typically (or even often) present fully Christian or Jewish visions of the moral life. Such visions would have a great deal to say about our falls into temptation, about human sinfulness, and about the human weakness to which all of us are prey. It is not the portrayal of weakness and sinfulness that constitutes decadence; it is, rather, giving in to weakness and calling it virtue. It is not weakness that makes for decadence, but moral dishonesty. A fully Christian— or Jewish—vision cerainly would be much less likely than much of what we see today to call sin virtue, and virtue sin.

On a more profound level, the level of "serious" culture, Lionel Trilling—America's preeminent critic of culture—noted the detached (even hostile) point of view deeply embedded in today's cultural elites. It is not unusual for art to assume that at least some persons may "extricate themselves from the culture into which they were born." It is not odd in literature to take virtually for granted "the adversary intention, the actually subversive intention, that characterizes modern writing." There is not even anything surprising in its clear purpose of "detaching the reader from the habits of thought and feeling that the larger culture imposes, of giving him a ground and a vantage point from which to judge and condemn, and perhaps revise, the culture that produced him."[43]

This adversary intention in modern art is more than a century old, Trilling continues, but

> the circumstances in which it has its existence have changed materially . . . The difference can be expressed quite simply in numerical terms—there are a great many more people who adopt the adversary program than there formerly were. Between the end of the first quarter of the century into the present time there has grown up a populous group whose members take for granted the idea of the adversary culture. This group is to be described not only by its increasing size but by its increasing coherence. It is possible to think of it as a class. As such, it of course has its internal conflicts and contradictions but also its common interests and presuppositions and a considerable efficiency of organization, even of an institutional kind.[44]

Trilling notes that "Three or four decades ago, the university figured as the citadel of conservatism, even of reason." The phrase "ivory tower" suggested its safe removal from the acids of modernism. Taste, however, "has increasingly come under the control of criticism, which has made art out of what is not art and the other way around," and now this "making and unmaking of art is in the hands of university art departments and the agencies which derive from them, museums and professional publications."[45]

Trilling's is the classic text identifying a specific "adversary culture" within U.S. culture, a culture that now governs the mainstream in the universities, the magazines, movies, and television. Coincident with its rise is the gradual collapse of the prestige of scientific and technical elites, and even of the idea of progress. This adversary culture celebrates the antibourgeois virtues. By its own innermost intention, it defines itself *against* the common culture. It has increasingly lost its connection with ordinary people, whom it is inclined to scorn. *They* are religious, but the adversary culture is not. More than 100 million Americans attend church or synagogue every weekend, but the so-called popular culture of Hollywood and television is ignorant of this powerful vein of popular life.

The literature concerning the existence of this "new adversary class" is already vast.[46] Critics have long since linked Eastern European discussions of the new class in socialist societies, such as are found in the work of Milovan Djilas, with the adversary culture in Western societies.

Indeed, the hardest part of the moral task we now face is the immense power of that adversary culture. To oppose that power is to risk excommunication from the mainstream. Nonetheless, as Trilling (who loved modernist works) was compelled by intellectual honesty to state, the intention of the modernist project is to subvert the classic Jewish, Christian, and natural (as well as "bourgeois") virtues. It is to perform a massive transvaluation of values, to turn the moral world upside down. It is to insinuate that what Jews and Christians have for centuries called sin is actually a high form of liberation, and that what for centuries Jews and Christians have thought to be virtuous is actually vicious. It is to hate what Jews and Christians love, and to love what Jews and Christians hate.

Ironically, the very virtue of progressivism that is its most endearing quality—namely, its openmindedness—stands here defenseless. In trying to be broad-minded about the modernist subversion, even many Christians give it the best possible interpretation, and ascribe to the traditional Jewish and Christian agenda the most negative and hostile associations. Thus it happens that, in the name of launching a counterculture, some progressives baptize the worst features of the contemporary modernist project. In the name of openness, they try to shock the bourgeois middle class by collaborating in this deliberate transvaluation of values.

The truth is, there is all too little resistance to both the modernist project and the adversary culture. To oppose these would cause one to seem to be unsophisticated, backward, and unwashed. Thus does the treason of the intellectuals proceed as silently and effectively—and for the most part as undetectably—as a cloud of invisible but deadly gas.

To the extent that the Catholic Church is and must be countercultural, will it wish to link its criticism of U.S. culture with the criticism of that culture made by the new adversary class? This is certainly a temptation. It has tempted many socialists—particularly those in Latin cultures such as Southern Europe and Latin America who have become enamored of the project launched by the Italian communist Antonio Gramsci (1891–1937).[47] According to Gramsci, it is a mistake to understand socialism as an economoic doctrine, and thus to tie socialism to the outmoded economic theories of the Marxists of the nineteenth century. On the contrary, democratic and capitalist societies have proven that they can raise up the proletariat into the middle class rather quickly. Therefore, Gramsci argued, the true socialist project lies not in the realm of economics, but in the realm of culture. The true socialist is an adversary of Western culture, both in its Christian and in its bourgeois aspects. A "long march through the institutions" (to borrow a later phrase) must be undertaken to subvert Western culture and its fundamental values.

In reviewing Michael Barone's book *Our Country: The Shaping of America from Roosevelt to Reagan*,[48] James Q. Wilson asked: Why did the American elite, which seemed so confident of its own policies and of the basic goodness of our system of governance at the beginning of the 1960s, turn so violently against it in the years centering on 1967 and 1968? I know that *I* did, in "The Secular Saint" (1967) and *A Theology for Radical Politics* (1969),[49] too much moved by the war in Vietnam, the rise of "black power," the moral arrogance of liberal technocrats on the campuses, the assassinations of John F. Kennedy, Robert F. Kennedy, aned Martin Luther King, Jr. In any case, from pride in government service and optimism about "new frontiers," Jeff Bell points out, "Around 1967, the balance of powerful political and journalistic elites began to tip toward the views of society's harshest critics."[50]

Michael Barone, reviewing those events, writes: "The liberal elites, so smug and confident at the beginning of the decade, turned their face away from events that were in most cases the consequences of their own acts and found fault with the larger society instead."[51] Thus, the "adversary culture" of the 1950s became the "counterculture," a "movement" suddenly swollen by journalists, movie producers, TV stars, and radicalized professors whose favorite passion became rage—contempt for our own system.

As Jeff Bell shows, a great gap opened up between the elite and the people; a larger gap than ever. (This split is what worried me, and made me draw back, even in the last chapter of *A Theology for Radical Politics*.) It was particularly marked in the Democratic party, whose strength had theretofore come from close cooperation between the intellectual elites and the people of the neighborhoods, unions, and city "machines." The party split asunder, and the "Reagan Democrats" began to emerge. The key differences were moral. Moral relativism and equality of result held primacy in the counterculture; the great bulk of the population retained traditional values. This was the theme of *The Rise of the Unmeltable Ethnics*.

Is the adversary culture the counterculture that the Catholic Church ought to join? The Gramsci project is aimed specifically at intellectual elites not only in the universities but also in the organs of mass culture and in the governmental bureaucracies that have administrative powers over the works of culture, wherever radio, television, and the arts are supported by the state. In this respect, the term "intellectuals" is to be understood in a very broad sense; it signifies the whole range of intellectual workers in the realm of symbol-making and the propagation of values. Both politically and intellectually, therefore, the central debate of our time has switched increasingly from politics and economics to culture. Christian and Jewish intellectuals will need to be very careful in choosing where and how to direct their efforts in this more general debate. As the Church arrives on the field, the battles have already been joined. The question now appears to be: Having at last reached this crucial battleground, what should we do?

PROTECTING THE MORAL ECOLOGY

In the Jewish community, Irving Kristol has pointed out,[52] there has long been a division of labor. Receiving most notice down the ages have been the Jewish prophets of the Old Testament. But the prophets, Kristol notes, were relatively few in number and of considerably less than immediate relevance to the daily lives of most ordinary people. To meet these ordinary needs, the rabbinic tradition has nurtured the custom of practical commentary, carried through in the Talmud and in associated practical writings. The rabbis greatly outnumbered the prophets, not only in raw numbers but also in the magnitude of their daily influence.

In the Catholic tradition, by analogy, there have also been two major lines of development—one incarnational, the other eschatological. More than typical Protestant communities, the Catholic community has tried to emphasize the presence of Christ in daily physical life, the incarnation of Christ in culture. It has blessed harvests, tools, and objects of daily living. It has tried to awaken the baptized to the reality that the kingdom of God has already begun in them and among them. Catholic faith welcomes ordinary life, even blesses it; this is, so to speak, its priestly or rabbinic work.

On the other hand, not only through its tradition of celibacy and the "setting aside" of a special way of life for nuns, priests, and brothers, the Catholic tradition has also tried to maintain an eschatological witness, a sense of rupture with this world and its ordinary demands, an anticipation of the kingdom to come. This witness is akin to that of the prophets of old. It is not a gnostic witness. Consistently, the Catholic Church has set its face against the "spiritualizers" and the "enthusiasts"[53]—that is, against those who would interpret Christianity as a project for fleeing from the world, for rejecting the world, or for merely condemning the world. Since "God so loved the world that he gave his only Son" (John 3:16), it affirms the goodness of each being and every event within the providential order. In every aspect of being, it has seen mystery, fruitfulness, and the presence of God.

In one moment, then, the Catholic tendency is to affirm every culture in which it finds itself. In another moment, it has always called every culture beyond itself and toward the kingdom yet to come and, thus, has set itself up as a counterculture. For the

Catholic community to be truly Catholic, both moments are indispensable. Every Christian should represent in his or her own project in life both of these emphases. Each should be at home in the world, and work within it with affirmation and love; simultaneously, each should be in the world as a stranger.

But not so much as a stranger that one falls into uncritical lockstep with a treacherous ally. By now, the new adversary class has more than fulfilled its adversary intention. Hardly any aspect of the U.S. system—political, economic, and moral–cultural— escapes withering criticsm, often unfair and inaccurate criticism. Much of this criticism serves the self-interest of those who want to expand the powers and expenditures of the state. (There is profit in this prophet motive.) That such criticism is self-interested would matter little if it were accurate and fair. Most often, the appetite for prosecution outweighs the appetite for fair rebuttal. The sense of possessing a superior moral standing often overpowers a willingness to see the other side.

No democratic capitalist regime should pretend to be the kingdom of God. The U.S. regime, in particular, has been deliberately contrived to operate within a world of sin and fallibility, supplying to every ambition a counterambition. Such a political economy is self-consciously imperfect, flawed, and resolved to make the best out of the weak materials of human nature. "If men were angels, no government would be necessary," Madison wrote in *Federalist* 51. But men are not angels. Thus, criticism and prophecy do not of themselves injure a democratic capitalist regime. Even false prophecy and misplaced criticism may be put to creative use. Still, criticism and prophetic claims need to be assessed according to how accurately and creatively they are launched. Critics—and in particular the adversary culture—must in turn carry the burden of being *self*-critical. They must, if they are to be taken seriously, make sure that the interests they serve are truly just.

During the last 60 years or so, in interpreting the social doctrine of the Church, a great deal has been written about politics and (more recently) economics. No doubt this work has been necessary and valuable. It is surprising, however, to note the lack of sustained criticism regarding the culture of liberty. Neither a sound economy nor sound politics can be maintained for long in an atmosphere of decadence.

Pope John Paul II particularly has called upon U.S. Catholics to question our nation's widely diffused public morality as it is witnessed in the international media of communication that have so dramatic an effect upon the rest of the world. In raising this challenge, the Pope goes to the heart of our system's most glaring weakness (just when, ironically, many "progressive" Catholic theologians have been complaining that Rome does not understand U.S. culture). The Pope even raises the complementary question: Do American Catholic theologians *themselves* understand American culture? He has opened a debate about the true moral standing of U.S. culture: Is it really something that the rest of the world—including Rome—should emulate?

A distinction may be useful. There are certain virtues inherent in the successful practice of democratic polities and capitalist economies. These may be thought of as those parts of public morality that are embodied in *institutional* practices, and are accordingly thought of as the specifically "democratic" and "capitalist" virtues. But there are other virtues—equally necessary for the successful practice of democracy and capitalism—proper to the moral–cultural sphere itself.

When "progressive" Catholic theologians speak admiringly of the high moral standards of the U.S. experience, often they have in mind the panoply of virtues associated with democratic *institutions*: open inquiry, due process, judgment by a jury of one's peers, and the like. This, too, is a form of public morality. Both the political institutions and the economic institutions of the free society implicitly contain hidden references to the specific new virtues required to make these institutions function according to their own inner rules. Too seldom do we make these underlying virtues explicit in our thinking, despite the fact that they are quite different from the virtues of traditional societies. They include such modern virtues as the responsibilities of free, sovereign citizens, self-reliance, cooperativeness, openness, and personal economic enterprise. They are acquired during that long process of learning the habits of democratic living to which Tocqueville often refers. [54]

By comparison, the virtues proper to the moral–cultural system are distinct (but not separate) from the virtues proper to the political system. The founders of the U.S. order, such as Thomas Jefferson and James Madison, understood quite clearly the connection between the virtues of the moral order and those of the political order.

Thus, when Pope John Paul II suggests that the U.S. media

of communication may be undercutting the practice of the moral virtues, he is implying, as well, a threat to the survival of democratic institutions. If true, this is a devastating criticism. It suggests that the very qualities of U.S. institutions that the "progressive" Catholic theologians profess to admire are being undermined by the widely broadcast public morality of our country's major media of communication. This would represent a form of pollution in the moral order even more destructive than the pollution of the physical environment. There is, so to speak, an ecology in morals as well as in the biosphere.[55]

The analysis offered by the Pope seems to be well aimed. Many important moral virtues *are* required to make a free and democratic society function according to its own inner logic; there is a set of moral virtues without which democratic institutions *cannot* be made to work. The fundamental premise of republican life, as we saw in Chapter 4, is the concept of *ordered* liberty.[56]

The phrase "ordered liberty" follows the classical definition of practical wisdom, *recta ratio agendi* (the ordered reason in action). To hit the mark exactly, Aristotle observed, practical reason must be governed by (*recta*, corrected by) a good will. To do the truth, we must first love the truth—and love it well and accurately. In a similar way, to be truly free, our passions and appetites must be governed by a well-ordered love of the inner law of our humanity. In this sense, the exercise of freedom is a form of obedience to the truth—the truth about our own human nature.[57] For Christians, this truth is revealed only in Christ, the Logos "in whom, by whom, and with whom" were made all the things that were made. For those who are not Christian believers, the outlines of an analogous truth are also revealed in "the things that were made"—the habitual weakness of humans, combined with possibilities of love and renewal.[58]

THE INSTITUTIONAL TASK

All around the world people who have suffered under socialist and traditionalist institutions are longing for a freer life. They dream of living under institutions that would liberate their human capacities for reflection and for choice. There is a longing in the human heart to live under a system of natural liberty—that is, under those sorts of institutions that allow the human soul to express itself naturally in all three major fields of life: political, economic, and moral–cultural. The vast majority of peoples on this planet, in the past and still today, have not lived under such institutions. But the broad outlines of these institutions are now fairly well known to most of the peoples of the world. They have glimpsed these outlines through their own harsh experiences under meaner alternatives.

Thus, with Pope John Paul II, most people seem to understand today that their best protection from torture, tyranny, and other forms of political oppression derives from living under institutions that are (a) subject to the consent of the governed, (b) protective of minority rights, and (c) designed around internal sets of checks and balances. We have in fact been hearing a great deal more about "democracy," even in cultures in which the very word has long been spoken of (as in "bourgeois democracy") with much disdain.

Similarly, since neither communist nor traditionalist societies seem to be capable of producing the goods which the poor of the world need and desire, the reputation of the hitherto much-scorned system, capitalism, is growing. In an ever-increasing number of countries one hears the demand for freer markets, for private property, and for incentives that reward greater labor and superior skills. Human beings can scarcely help desiring to express in their institutions and daily practices their God-given capacities for personal economic intitiative and creativity.

Finally, in such places as the former Soviet Union and the Peoples Republic of China, in South Africa and throughout Black Africa, in Latin America and elsewhere, the cry of most people is for "openness"—for institutions that permit the free exercise of liberty of conscience, inquiry, and expression.

In sum, most citizens of the world seek the three basic institutional liberations of human life: a free polity, a free economy, and a free moral–cultural system. This is seldom today a matter of ideology; it has arisen from harsh lessons of trial and error. One cannot speak of these three liberations without also speaking of *institutions*. And one can hardly speak of institutions without speaking of the *moral virtues* that sustain them.

For human rights are not protected by words on parchment. They are protected by habits, free associations, and independent judicial institutions. Moreover, the institutions that protect human rights do not *coerce* conscience, or *force* citizens to develop their individual moral and spiritual capacities. Those institutions create space for those achievements—but do not automatically produce them. Thus, the mere achievement of the basic institutions of political and economic liberty will not itself fulfill human moral and spiritual longing. Politics and economics are not enough. That is why the next frontier for those who think counterculturally concerns the moral and spiritual dimension of culture.

We come around then to the theme that Pope John Paul II set forth in the beginning as the *leitmotif* of his pontificate: the primacy of morals. Here is where the next and most important battles lie.

> Solving serious national and international problems is not just a matter of economic production or of juridical or social organization, but calls for ethical and religious values. There is hope that the many people who profess no religion will also contribute to providing the necessary ethical foundation. But the Christian churches and the world religions will have a preeminent role in . . . building a society worthy of man.[59]

Building up civilizations that respect the true and nature-fulfilling "moral ecology" in which the virtues of ordered liberty flourish is a demanding task which will occupy the human race throughout the coming ages.

In this task, the institutions of the mass media—the much-vaunted "entertainment industry"—incur very high responsibilities, which they have barely begun to face. They, too, must be held to account. Because their influence upon the moral air we breathe and on the moral ecology we inhabit is vast, the prospects of the free society, and the virtues proper to ordered liberty, depend on their performance. The moral nobility of their task is far greater than they seem yet to recognize.

EPILOGUE
The Creative Person

SEVEN MORAL THEMES

In the tradition of papal social thought from 1891 to 1991, seven moral themes particularly stand out, although a whole family of special words surrounds them. These seven, in particular, may be thought to add something to the Protestant ethic, as Max Weber defined it. They represent a distinctive Catholic contribution to the universal effort to develop a social ethic appropriate to our time. We have so far dealt with all seven:

- Recognition of the social nature of the human person, exercised in the family, in friendship, in civil society, and in universal solidarity

- The principle of subsidiarity, put in practice by the virtue of social justice

- The liberty and responsibility (hence the dignity) of persons

- The virtues necessary for exercising personal responsibility

- Creative subjectivity

- Unity amid diversity

- Emphasis on being rather than having; on character; and on grace

These seven terms recur, to be sure, in the context of other special terms characteristic of Catholic social ethics, such as justice and charity, *Imago Dei*, the preferential option for the poor, the social dimensions of the sacraments, the role of prayer, and the role of Jesus Christ as the Logos through Whom all humans (and all things) were made and as the measure of humans. In a well-considered network of terms, every term bears on every other. (Catholic theology is nothing if not highly specialized and well-considered, every term thoroughly meditated on worldwide for its ramifying meanings.)

In this book I have not developed the specifically Christological themes of Catholic social thought, since this volume is intended mostly for non-Catholics. For those who are chiefly interested in the bearing of this social theory on their own understanding of society, rather than in an exposition of the depths of Catholic faith (which they do not share), these seven themes point to an ethic accessible to all. For those who would like to explore further the role of Christ in giving final shape and measure to Catholic life, I recommend the writings of Hans Urs von Balthasar, and especially his *Theo-Drama*.[1] This highly original Swiss theologian and literary critic uses the categories of theater more than those of logic as the backbone of his exposition of theology.

It is not just to Catholics that modern encyclicals ("letters to the whole circle of nations") have been addressed. Encyclicals do not demand that Jews, Muslims, Hindus, Buddhists, ethical humanists, or atheists think as Catholics in order to understand them. They try to reach common universal ground. In this spirit, then, let us review and extend the argument.

THE RIGHT STUFF

If Pope John Paul II in *Centesimus Annus* did not give two cheers for democracy and capitalism, he did give at least one cheer. From a church that has passed through many bad systems in history, and whose main business is eternal life, one cheer for *any* worldly system is quite a lot. For in Christian eyes, no worldly system deserves three cheers. All are flawed.

Consider democracy. Democracy, Reinhold Niebuhr once said (even before Winston Churchill did) is a poor form of government—but other forms are worse. Under democracy, the tyranny of a majority is as much a danger to minorities and individuals as is a single tyrant. Unbridled democracy, unchecked by protections for individual rights, unbalanced, irresponsibly exercised, is a misfortune.

Religious power has also often been abused, especially when intermixed with the power of the state. The medieval dream of close union between church and state, however understandable in its naiveté, compromised both religion *and* society.

It should not surprise us, therefore, that "unbridled capitalism" and even the "unbridled pursuit of wealth creation"—indeed, an unbridled *anything*—arouses fears in ordinary people. This is true even of unbridled liberty of thought and expression, although philosophers might offer better reasons for laissez-faire in this sphere than in any other.[2]

Thus, free societies in the West have in practice approached the institutionalization of liberty cautiously, by balancing one liberty against another. Under such practical arrangements, no liberty runs entirely unchecked. Every power is assigned its counterpower, every office its countervailing force.

The reason behind these checks and balances is a classical Christian and Jewish observation: *Every human sometimes sins.* From this fact is drawn a political principle: *Trust no one with excessive power.* Trust no institution, either.

In most free societies, therefore, the three great systems of human life are placed in balance against one another, like the three points of a triangle: the political system, the economic system, and the moral–cultural system. No person can easily master all three of these forms of power, and each of them in any case has internal interests contrary to the other two. In the struggle for equilibrium among all three systems, the hope is that none of the three will gain excessive power.

In our day, for example, the media of communication are central to the exercise of most forms of power; through them the intellectuals, artists, journalists, experts, and clergy exert considerable control over public perception. But they do not control everything.

In counterpoise queens, prime ministers, party leaders, parliamentarians, judges, and political activists exercise considerable social power through the levers of the state, which today in some ways exceeds the power of all previous states. But they do not control everything—not the opinions of the idea class, perhaps not the compliance of their own bureaucracies, and certainly not economic realities (which may undo them).

Finally, leaders of commerce and industry, bankers, brokers, advertisers, labor union leaders, consumers, and many other economic agents exercise considerable social power. But their power, too, is severely limited. For one thing, they rank low in the esteem of clergymen, intellectuals, artists, and journalists, and their failures and achievements are seldom treated without remarkable antipathy. For another, government can do more to them than they can do to government; through regulations, laws, rulings, and taxes, government coerces them into compliance. Conflict between the two systems is inherently tilted toward the power of government.

The system as a whole is meant to be this way, so that its three major systems are internally divided against one another. That tripartite counterpoise is called by several names: the mixed economy, capitalist democracy, democratic capitalism. In some places, "social democracy" might be a more acceptable term, as in the historical context of 1945–48 the Germans chose the term "social market economy." By this term they meant to emphasize an analogous set of checks and balances—the market *and also* the constraints imposed upon it by society from several different directions. My aim is not to argue about nomenclature. The important thing (set forth in *Centesimus Annus*, #42) is the tripartite structure of checks and balances.

The question Pope John Paul II asks is: What is the main *religious* justification for a capitalist system so understood—balanced by a constitutional democracy protecting individual rights, on the one side, and by moral–cultural institutions such as those of Jewish, Christian, and humanist traditions, on the other?

For many persons, the primary moral justification for capitalism is a combination of the free space it creates in society, the independence of property owners, the freedom of economic choices, and ample civic liberties. For others, the primary moral justification is the widespread social prosperity that capitalism brings, ending famine and destitution while steadily bringing about improvements in the living standards of the poor. It is not difficult to accept these moral claims as valid, at least when the only contemporary alternatives are "real existing socialism" and Third World mercantilism. Nonetheless, the Pope's primary moral claim for capitalism calls attention to a different moral strength. Its processes embody signficant moral values and virtues.[3]

Two of my closest intellectual colleagues in the discussion of capitalism, Peter Berger and Paul Johnson, prefer to describe capitalism as a set of purely technical and instrumental arrangements, attributing to the surrounding cultural ethos any discernible moral qualities.[4] They would explain the cultural differences between Japanese and American capitalism, for example, by differences in culture, as if to say that the institutions and practices of capitalism are relatively invariant even while being flexibly adaptable to diverse cultures. Moreover, Berger attributes to modernity many of the characteristics that are sometimes attributed solely to capitalism, such as pragmatism, instrumentalism, and impersonality. Such characteristics are just as discernible in socialist as in capitalist nations, Berger observes.

My reasons for diverging from my colleagues on this point are several. First, the shift from precapitalist to capitalist cultures did, in fact, entail significant changes in the moral assessment of passions and interests, the national purpose, the possibility of overcoming age-old poverty, and the classic tables of natural virtues. Second, when a country moves from being a traditionalist society to becoming a market society, the moral habits of its people generally show improvement—at least in certain specific ways. Traditionalist societies have usually been heavily state-controlled and riddled by corruption and dishonest practices. Capitalism requires a significantly higher level of honesty, rule-abidingness, and self-reliance. As the formerly socialist nations of Eastern Europe move from socialism to capitalism, for example, one notes in them a quickening of certain crucial moral virtues, including a sense of personal and civic responsibility, habits of initiative and enterprise, friendliness, openness, a regard for truth-telling, and a decisive rejection of the spirit of envy. I do not mean to suggest that in the moral order everything in such transitions is gain. History doesn't work that way. Normally, from one form of society to another there are some *gains* and some *losses*. But the historical evidence now seems clear that the move from traditional (and socialist) societies to capitalist societies is a move to *higher* moral standards, particularly with respect to improvement in the condition of the poor and the development of "middle-class" virtues such as initiative and social responsibility, institutions of human rights, and civic respect for liberty under law.

Third, the rise of capitalism brought with it a marked rise in social compassion among the bourgeoisie, beginning with the conviction that the grinding poverty of the poor (merely taken for granted in earlier history) could and should be alleviated, and moving onward to the need to overcome illiteracy, disease, and other physical infirmities. It is more plausible to hold that many, if not most, of these changes in modern attitudes arose from the habits and assumptions of capitalist practice, reinforced by the historical success of those habits, than that they inhered in precapitalist cultures. Otherwise, why did they not emerge before capitalism?

Fourth, Berger and Johnson are left, it seems to me, with an inadequate description of an obvious reality of our time, which is that millions of persons in noncapitalist lands migrate at great cost to themselves toward capitalist lands, and with great idealism and hope. To say that these immigrants seek mere technical efficiency and material increase seems to me not quite exact. In addition to material improvement, capitalist institutions convey dignity and opportunity to individuals, along with a sense of open horizons and personal responsibility. Indeed, it is the high morale of such immigrants that is their most compelling characteristic.

In short, capitalist institutions present themselves to millions of outsiders as more attractive morally, psychologically, and spiritually than the existing alternatives. Moreover, capitalism as experienced by immigrants endows them with a new sense of self-worth, responsibility, and challenge. They enjoy the free air, and they even walk the walk of the free. Most assuredly, for them capitalism is seen to be far more than just a set of technical arrangements.

Finally, considerable moral gain arises from conceptualizing capitalism as having an inbuilt ethos, partial but real. This ethos sets a standard to which cultures must measure up. Certain kinds of moral ethos are incompatible with capitalist practice; other kinds favor it. Several different types of cultures favor capitalist success: Protestant, Confucian, Jewish, Northern European Catholic. All of these have in common a certain rigor and austerity, an almost Stoic sense of sobriety and responsibility, and a certain disdain for corruption. In such cultures capitalism grows speedily. By contrast, cultures in which the state controls everything seem to breed habits of bribery, favoritism, nepotism, and rule by personal favor rather than rule by law. In many Third World cultures people may be very loving within their families, but hardened against outsiders; or soft and gentle in personal relations, but indifferent to general laws; faithful to those they love, but not so reliable (perhaps as a survival mechanism) in the world outside. In cultures of this second type, the moral demands inherent in capitalist practices and necessary for their successful implantation, can scarcely take root. Where there is systematic dishonesty, the free cooperation required by capitalist institutions finds no firm ground on which to rest its foundations.

These are among the reasons why I do not conceptualize capitalism as a merely technical institution with an *anima technica vacua*, "an empty technical soul." Its institutions, rather, make sufficient demands on citizens who would live under them to be thought of as a "way of life" (but only in a secondary sense; the phrase "way of life" has two different meanings).[5] Such institutions encourage citizens to be law-abiding, cooperative, and courteous even to strangers (such as customers), but without predetermining the actual beliefs and spirit with which individuals infuse these behaviors. The *inner* qualities of capitalist societies are much more deeply shaped by the *particular* culture that infuses individual action—by Christianity and Judaism in the United States, by Confucianism and Shinto in Japan, and so on. Capitalism itself is not even close to being the kingdom of God; indeed, it is not a religion—or even a philosophy. Its construction is not designed to fill the soul, or to teach a philosophy, or to give instruction in how to live. Compared to socialist and traditional cultures, however, its institutions do set a higher moral standard, and do insist on certain basic moral habits. Up to some low threshold, then, it *is* a way of life, and not merely a neutral technique. Beyond that threshold, it is open to a great many quite diverse cultural specifications. It *is* pluralistic—but it is *not* consistent with any and every cultural form.

The presuppositions, ethos, moral habits, and way of life required for the smooth functioning of democratic and capitalist institutions are not a full expression of Christian or Jewish faith, and are indeed partially in conflict with the full transcendent demands of Christian and Jewish faith. Nonetheless, they by no means *exclude* the exercise of full Christian or Jewish faith. One may be both a Catholic saint *and* a patriotic, law-abiding American; a devout Jew *and* a democratic capitalist. There is no radical contradiction between the two; nor a perfect identity, either. Historically speaking, modern democracy, capitalism, and pluralism emerged in the West both deeply affected by and in large part inspired by Christian and Jewish beliefs and practices. Even today, the shortest route to defending the truths we hold is to ground them in the Jewish and Christian doctrine of Creation, as the Framers often did.

Moreover, once the threefold division of systems appears in history—dividing the political, economic, and moral–cultural systems into the custody of mutually independent elites—it is entirely open to Christians and Jews to supply for these institutions a thoroughly Christian or Jewish rationale, and to encourage one another to live out their vocations in the fullness of God's presence, and to reach for the highest forms of sanctity. There is no "internal logic" in democracy, capitalism, or pluralism requiring that anyone live as an atheist, agnostic, secularist, or practical materialist, or in any state less profound than that of a holy life. A saint committed to ordinary life in the world might well be expected to be a good democrat, a creator and distributor of wealth, and a pluralistic respecter of the dignity and faith of others, all three in one.

In brief, a democratic capitalist society is merely a thisworldly form, perhaps the most responsive to the social implications of the gospels yet developed by the human race—but, nonetheless, quite imperfect. Such a regime is designed for sinners (the only moral majority there is), and burdened by "structures of sin," as is the fate of all human societies. It must not be confused with the kingdom of God on earth. Nonetheless, it did not develop in history merely formless. Its inner form, although thisworldly, springs from inspirations derived in good measure from Jewish and Christian sources. And this historical form is subject to *further* specification by a more perfect practice of Christian and Jewish life.

In other words, the more closely attuned to Christian and Jewish faith that its citizens become, the better democracy, capitalism and pluralism should function. As Tocqueville acutely noted, religion is the single most important political agency in democratic regimes. One reason why religions are critical to the life of democracy is that they stand over against it in transcendent judgment upon the merely worldly. They open citizens to the perspective of transcendent life *outside* the state, to the judgment of the Almighty, to an *immortal* destiny. To think of religion in this way is not to think of religion as an instrument of the state, or even as a pillar of the state. It is to value religion as an end in itself and *because it is* an end in itself. Citizens of free societies sorely need such spiritual independence of the state.

To complement Max Weber's thesis about the new sense of order needed to transform a traditional society into a capitalist society, and the role of certain Calvinist traditions in supplying that sense, I have followed Pope John Paul II in stressing the Catholic (and catholic) ethic of the human person as an active and creative person, in realizing her or his vocation to create, to show initiative, and to accept responsibility. A complementarity between the Catholic (and catholic) ethic and the free society is implied by this argument.

Following World War II, as we have seen, German liberals and reformers faced the daunting problem of reconstructing a social order on three fronts at once. They needed to reconstruct democracy, to replace Nazi morals with the Christian and humanistic morals that had been the glory of German thought, and to put in place an economy safe against the monopolies and cartels that Hitler had so easily taken over after his election in 1934. For this daunting task, they needed a new theory of order. A group of thinkers gathered around Walter Eucken and the journal *Ordo* had been working on the foundations of such a theory during the war years. They called this inquiry *Ordotheorie*, and they later called the concrete social order they intended to put in place "the social market economy."[6] They did not have the luxury of relying, as English liberals had, on a continuous tradition of parliamentary democracy and sound common-sense morals, and so their philosophical inquiries were correspondingly broader and deeper. Their conception of *Ordo* is helpful in trying to understand Max Weber.

This is because, as David Little has shown,[7] the key to Weber's theory about the Protestant ethic lies in his keen awareness that the new order introduced by what he called capitalism was different from the economies of the traditional order, even though it had in common with them a reliance on market exchange, private ownership, and the legitimacy of private profit. This order was different because it was not patrimonial; that is, it was ordered neither to political nor to moral authorities (kings, nobles, prelates). It represented instead a new conception of order, less concerned with enhancing political or religious power but rather more autonomous, open to all, and governed by meritocratic procedural rules.[8] Weber named the two different types of economy, based on two different conceptions of order, "patrimonial capitalism" (serving the rulers) and "rational capitalism" (serving fair and open procedures). It is true, as Trevor–Roper and Samuelson have pointed out, that there *were* good entrepreneurs and industrialists in the patrimonial era, prior to the era of rational capitalism.[9] But the early existence of such great capitalist families as the Colberts and the Fuggers does not contradict Weber's thesis, as these writers alleged; it in fact confirms it. The wealth of such families served the Crown, and thus the Crown protected their privileges. The patrimonial capitalist system remained centrally organized, elitist, and subordinate to the old order.

One sees in this paradigm, as Weber recognized, a key difference between the patrimonial capitalism of Latin America, with its allegiance to the old order, and the gathering strength in North America of a new order grounded in a more open, law-like, and fair "rational capitalism." And Weber saw, or claimed to see, the inner source of this new order in the new conception of order (moral, political, and economic) carried forward by specific forms of Calvinism which, as it happened, were both especially vigorous in numbers and favored by circumstance in North America (which had no preexisting class structure, for example).

LATIN AMERICA

In recent years, this Weberian thesis has been applied to the case of new forms of rational capitalism breaking through the old order of patrimonial capitalism in Latin America, especially (but not solely) associated with the newly burgeoning ranks of evangelical Protestants there. David Martin's full development of this thesis in *Tongues of Fire*[10] is one of those works for which the word "brilliant" is justly employed. He points out how the impact of the moral/religious conversion that marks the "acceptance of Jesus as personal Savior" transforms those who experience it by replacing in their consciousness the static old order, in which they had earlier felt mired, by a new sense of self, hope, possibility, and the moral legitimacy of self-initiated action. The newly converted feel that they no longer have to wait for someone else's approval. They break with the past order by feeling empowered to begin a new one, at least in their own lives and in the new circles of association into which they are drawn, whose burgeoning ranks they expand. They feel within themselves a new capacity to become "acting persons," determining for themselves their own moral, political, and economic behavior, under a scheme of legitimacy that is quite different from that of the old order to which they had been accustomed.

Of course, as Martin points out,[11] some of their newly self-appropriated Christian identity is accessible, as well, to evangelical and charismatic Catholics, who also experience a highly personal conversion to Christ and a fresh sense of community. But the Protestants experience, in addition, both an advantage and a disadvantage. Their advantage is that Protestantism affords a clearer break from the old order, which had an established Catholic foundation in the classical patrimonial order of the Holy Roman Empire. The Protestant disadvantage, and Catholic advantage, is that the Catholic body carries within it the philosophical and theological resources for a wide-ranging conception of the entire social order (political, economic, and moral), whereas the evangelical Protestant language, while very rich for private life, is far less adequate for the articulation of a full public morality.

Martin's work shows how the old order of patrimonial capitalism in Latin America is today being slowly subverted by all these new energies, both Catholic and Protestant (but especially Protestant), at the bottom of society. He does not stress, although it is also true, that several liberal macroeconomic experiments have also been undertaken, more or less successfully, within entire nations (such as Chile, Mexico, and Argentina), and that these also have been moving the economic debate in Latin America away from the old order. In any case, the discrediting of the socialist idea in Eastern Europe and Cuba has had a great impact on ideas of order and legitimacy in Latin America.

The weakest part of Weber's thesis, we have seen, lay in its theological analysis.[12] For it may well be true that the effects of the Protestant ethic, whether in the countries singled out by Weber or in Latin America today, lie far less than Weber thought in strict ideas of predestination and calling, and rather more in the delegitimizing of the old order effected by a new nonestablished religion, whose converts feel free at last to be acting persons in their own right. Thus Jews, Catholics, and indeed other men and women who have rejected the old order in the name of initiative and creativity have done as well as the Calvinists Weber singled out.

In any case, Pope John Paul II has supplied just such a new rationale for the building of a new order, through his own concepts of the acting person; the unalienable right to personal economic initiative; the virtues associated with the act of enterprise; and human creativity grounded in the *Imago Dei* endowed in every woman and man by the Creator Himself.

Often, in Latin America, I am met with the following objection: "If Max Weber is right, then we in Latin America, Catholic countries, don't have a chance." Well, it is quite true that without a stronger work ethic than now prevails in Latin America, and without a change in the anticommercial climate of Latin American governments, aristocracies, and churchmen, the future *does* look bleak. But one key point of this inquiry has been to show that the Catholic tradition also carries within it a powerful ethic of capitalism—indeed, a fuller and deeper ethic than was available to the first Puritans. This ethic goes beyond the need for hard work and doing one's duty; it appeals to one's capacities for creativity and community. It is blended together with a strong affirmation of the natural, created order. It is open to grace, while certainly being aware as well of the sinfulness and fallibility of human beings. It is, on the whole, a marvelously inspiring, positive, and creative force. And it makes possible social justice, the virtue by which free persons freely organize themselves to improve the life of the community.

THE NEW VIRTUES REQUIRED

Moreover, the new virtues that modern experience has taught the Catholic Church to add to the ancient and medieval lists of the virtues also play a role in building a new Christian humanism. Some persons have the capacity to act with enterprise and imagination without waiting for instructions from others; they do this often, regularly—they have the "habit" of so doing.

Among these virtues, at least a few may be singled out:

1. *Initiative.* If citizens are sovereign, they must be the first to discern coming dangers and opportunities, and to be the originating sources of social actions designed to meet them squarely.

2. *Enterprise.* Particularly (but not only) in the economic sphere, citizens dare not sit back and wait for "others" (or the state) to supply the goods and services necessary for the improvement of daily life, but must exercise the insight and the organizing skills to accomplish these tasks themselves. The human person is not merely an individual, in the way that every cat or every tree is an individual—that is, merely different from every other. More than that, the human person is an originating source of insight and action. Made in the image of God, each person is intended by God to be a creator and called to show imagination, creativity, and a capacity for achieving self-directed purposes. Enterprise is the name for the habit of doing this. Like other habits, it is acquired by practice, by trial and error, and by perseverance.

3. *Social cooperation.* We have seen that Tocqueville regarded the art of association as the first law of democratic living. What "subjects" historically waited for the aristocracy or for the state to do, "citizens" must associate together to do for themselves. It was a Communist lie that the only way to overcome excessive individualism was to wait for the Party or the state to give social directives. Free citizens are entirely capable of mobilizing their own imaginations and social skills, under their own initiative and guidance, to accomplish great social tasks for themselves.

As we have seen, it is the capacity of free citizens to form free associations among themselves of their own initiative that gives the adjective "social" its force in the modern term social justice, a term developed precisely for the era of free societies. When grievances arise, as they always must, citizens have both the right and the duty to form associations to seek redress, even against the state. When new needs arise, free citizens again form associations to meet them. It is a primitive error to think of social justice as an activity of the state or a synonym for statist justice. Social justice is, properly, a form of free association. Only as a last resort, and after taking due precautions against the excessive bureaucratic power of the modern state, do free citizens sometimes assign some of the power that belongs to themselves to a state agency in order to achieve their purposes through certain limited activities.

4. *Public spiritedness and civic responsibility.* When citizens are no longer subjects, they inherit grave responsibilities not solely

for their own personal and familial purposes but also for the whole range of the common or public good. They are the stewards of their own well-being. They must see to the beautification of their cities, the vitality of the arts and sciences, the provision of public monuments, and all the daily public necessities such as power and water, roads and bridges, the economic vitality of their communities, and the protection of the environment. They will be wise not to entrust all these responsibilities purely and simply (without checks and balances) to the state. The more they can secure ways to provide for these goods privately, rather than through the state, the more vital, various, and free their society is likely to remain. Naturally, they will carefully designate certain responsibilities to mixed public/private agencies, and to other proven mechanisms of carefully monitored responsibility. The fact remains that the greater the sense of civic responsibility and public-spiritedness exercised by the citizens themselves, the freer—and more splendidly various—their society will be.

Other virtues essential to the maintenance of a free society might be mentioned:

5. *The habit of acting as a "loyal opposition"* —which is to say of registering dissent without obstructionism.

6. *The art of compromise on practicalities,* even with those with whom one in principle disagrees, so that the perfect will not become the enemy of the good.

7. *The habit of showing respect to persons,* even when disagreeing with their *opinions.*

8. *The art of speaking kindly,* even of those one opposes, in order to protect possibilities of future practical cooperation.

As these last three habits suggest, democratic living demands a very high degree of *civility* in argument and action, even under conditions of intense opposition. It should not be objected that, since civility requires a kindly bearing even toward those whose views one loathes, civility entails a certain "hypocrisy." For the procedures of democracy are in a way like those of a formal dance, and the common good requires a certain check on primitive feelings. It is necessary and right to obey the formal rules, even when one does not "feel" like it—and in this way to tutor one's feelings to the amity and equanimity proper to a civilized people.

Although a few theorists of capitalism concentrate tightly on the economic system alone, nearly all would freely recognize that capitalism depends upon the evolution of law, tacit customs, responsible ethical practices, and limited government. Friedrich Hayek was tone-deaf to religious language for most of his life, as he freely admitted toward the end, but in establishing the possibility of the free economy he emphatically affirmed the roles of culture, virtue, and limited government.[13] Others among us are willing to go further than Hayek in recognizing the role of certain interventions by government, particularly on behalf of the poor and the vulnerable. But even he saw the need for government to establish the basic rules of the game that are necessary to the workings of liberty. Like him, and like Tocqueville in his fear of a new "soft depotism," we keep our eye on how much damage the "tutelary force" of government may do to the individual's capacity for initiative and enterprise.

Democratic capitalism sets in motion a tripartite system. That system is designed to serve individuals, not for individuals to serve it.

THE HEART OF THE MATTER: CREATIVITY

By way of summary: The deepest moral justification for a capitalist system is not solely that—poor system that it is—it serves liberty better than any other known system; nor even that it raises up the living standards of the poor higher than any other system; nor that it improves the state of human health and maintains the balance between humans and the environment better than either socialist or traditional Third World societies. All these things, however difficult for some to admit, may be empirically verified. In fact, the true moral strength of capitalism lies in its promotion of human creativity.[14]

Here let me again dampen enthusiasm. Like democracy and like organized religion, capitalism has many faults, liabilities, and worrisome tendencies. These are daily chronicled in our newspapers, television, and cinema. Nonetheless, no other known system better cherishes, nourishes, supports, and strengthens human creativity than the tripartite free society. Since its establishment in law barely two centuries ago in a handful of nations, the tripartite free society (free in its polity, economy, and culture) has, in the words of Marx, "transformed the productive capacity of the earth."

Yet there is still vast hunger and destitution in large parts of the world, and there is still shocking poverty within advanced countries. Not so long ago in human history, universal poverty was no moral scandal. It was simply a fact of life. But so transformed have been the conditions of life—transformed by human creativity, seeking out the secrets of the earth hidden in reserve by a loving Providence—that no national leader today can plausibly say, "My people are poor, and we intend to keep them poor." Today poverty *anywhere* on earth is displayed on TV and movie screens as a moral affront. So much has the human capacity for economic creativity transformed the moral calculus of humankind that grinding poverty *anywhere* on earth is seen to be morally repugnant. And it is because of this economic creativity that we can foresee the day when every man and woman upon this earth will be liberated from poverty's prison.

This is the dynamic intention of the tripartite free society as it is practiced in societies of Jewish, Christian, and humanistic culture; it is the inner dynamic of the system itself. For, based upon the capacity of humans to create, and (further) upon a panoply of institutions designed to support the full exercise of that capacity, such a system cannot rest until every single able person is *exercising* that capacity. We mean by this, as Pope John Paul II writes, "a society of free work, of enterprise, and of participation." And he also writes (and here I quote him so as to end where we began):

> Indeed, besides the earth, man's principal resource is man himself. His intelligence enables him to discover the earth's productive potential and the many different ways in which human needs can be satisfied. It is his disciplined work in close collaboration with others that makes possible the creation of ever more extensive working communities which can be relied upon to transform man's natural and human environments. Important virtues are involved in this process such as diligence, industriousness, prudence in undertaking reasonable risks, reliability and fidelity in interpersonal relationships as well as courage in carrying out decisions which are difficult and painful, but necessary both for the overall working of a business and in meeting possible setbacks.[15]

One important point remains to be made. To establish the moral, philosophical, and religious case for wealth creation is one thing; to find the practical institutions that reach all of the destitute, poor, and vulnerable on this planet and include them in the creative economy is yet another.

Yet is that search for sound institutions not itself a task for creativity? For enterprise? For invention? In any case, that practical task appears now to be the primary vocation of all those of genuinely good will in our generation—as hopefully it will also be in the next. We need to think hard and with practicality about how to include the poor of Ghana, Bolivia, and many other Third World nations within systems that concentrate on developing their innate human capital. We need to put in place institutions that liberate and empower that creativity: private property, access to markets, ease and rapidity of incorporation, access to credit, practical tutorials in the elements of creative economic practices, and a legal system structured to spread opportunity to the poor rather than (as at present) to protect the advantages of the rich.

The Third World, as John Paul II suggests, needs a thoroughgoing, lawful and peaceful revolution. Such a revolution will be constituted by many institutional changes designed to remove the weighty restrictions that today repress the economic creativity of millions of persons on this planet. This practical task is immense. Unfortunately, it is obvious that neither our university nor our business elites have yet begun to imagine its full practical dimensions.

If we lose our own souls in the process, it will not profit us to save the poor of the entire world. But insofar as the moral test we face is "the option for the poor," it is not those who cry "The poor! The poor!" who will pass that test, but those who actually put in place the practical institutions that help the poor to throw off their poverty. My own hope is that the poor of Eastern Europe and Latin America (for whom this book is chiefly written) will soon join other formerly poor peoples—from South Korea, Taiwan, Singapore, Hong Kong, and so on—who have demonstrated that poverty is *not* an immutable condition.

New wealth can be created. Human beings themselves are the primary cause of the wealth of nations. Human creativity is nature's primary resource. Removing the institutional repression that now stifles that creativity is the immense task to which the Catholic (and catholic) ethic calls us.

NOTES

INTRODUCTION

1. On Weber's family see Arthur Mitzman, *The Iron Cage: An Historical Interpretation of Max Weber* (New York: Knopf, 1970), 15–38.

2. According to Viner:

> Weber, like his followers, generalizes freely about the actual economic behavior of Calvinists or "Puritans" in the seventeenth century; but he seems to rely on common knowledge and gives no detailed historical evidence. . . .
> His final opinion on the subject . . . amounted to a positive rejection of the possibility of a reversal of his thesis; it was not conceivable, in his view, that the bare existence of capitalism could suffice to generate a unified ethic, let alone a communal religious ethic (Jacob Viner, *Religious Thought and Economic Society: Four Chapters of an Unfinished Work*, ed. Jacques Melitz and Donald Winch [Durham, NC: Duke University Press, 1978], 156, 159).

3. See *The Culture of Entrepreneurship*, ed. Brigitte Berger (San Francisco: ICS Press, 1991).

4. Max Weber, *The Protestant Ethic and the Spirit of Capitalism*,

trans. Talcott Parsons (New York: Charles Scribner's Sons, 1958), 176–77, emphasis added.

5. Ibid., 51, emphasis added.

6. Ibid., 53–54, emphasis added.

7. Viner, 151–89.

8. Ibid., 152.

9. Ibid., 174–75.

10. Ibid., 172.

11. Hugh Trevor–Roper, "Religion, the Reformation and Social Change," in *The European Witch-Craze of the Sixteenth and Seventeenth Centuries and Other Essays* (New York: Harper & Row, 1969), 1–45.

12. It is true, however, that some of these families depended largely on governmental arrangements, a fact that made their version of capitalism, in Weber's view, less than full-blown. Thus, David Little offers a rejoinder to Trevor–Roper: Weber did not mean by "capitalism" any large-scale industry or any practice of enterprise at all, but only those undertaken independent of princes and rulers, on the one hand, and only those undertaken in a certain spirit. But this is to make the task too easy and virtually circular—as if Weber had limited "the capitalist spirit" to "the Protestant capitalist spirit." As perhaps he did. See David Little, *Religion, Order, and Law: A Study in Pre-Revolutionary England* (Chicago and London: University of Chicago Press, 1969), 226–27.

13. See Weber, 17, 60, 20; see also Little, 12.

14. Little, 6–32.

15. Aristotle, *Nicomachean Ethics* 4. 1–3. 1119^{b}21–1125^{a}35.

16. Part of this agony, as Perry Miller explains it, is the fate of being wrong even when you're right; the wealth that industrious habits tend to produce is simultaneously a sign of moral success and of unchristian worldliness. See Little, 233–34.

17. Kirzner's is the most brilliant exposition of this insight, developed by him from the work of Hayek and Schumpeter. See his *Discovery and the Capitalist Process* (Chicago and London: University of Chicago Press, 1985).

18. Berger summarizes his findings in a hypothesis:

These reflections all tend toward a simple but far-reaching hypothesis: *Capitalism is a necessary but not sufficient condition of democracy.* As pointed out before, the proposition refers to modern conditions only. It goes without saying that a theory of democracy (as distinct from a theory of capitalism) will have to be vitally concerned with those *other* conditions that may be deemed to be sufficient for the democratic phenomenon; indeed, most recent theorists of democracy have dealt with precisely this issue. As to falsifi-

cation of the above hypothesis, the most convincing one
would be the emergence, in empirical reality rather than in
the realm of ideas, of even one clear case of democratic socialism. That such a society will emerge in the future is, of
course, the fondest wish of democratic socialists. The future
is always open, and social science is not capable of making
definitive statements about it. It is clear, though, that the
above hypothesis implies that the future emergence of a
democratic socialism is very improbable (Peter L. Berger,
*The Capitalist Revolution: Fifty Propositions about Prosper-
ity, Equality, and Liberty* [New York: Basic, 1986], 81).

19. For an historical chart of "Liberal Democracies Worldwide" see
Francis Fukuyama, *The End of History and the Last Man* (New York:
Free Press, 1992), 49–50.

20. *Capitalism and Freedom* (Chicago and London: University of
Chicago Press, 1962).

21. In addition to Meir Tamari, *"With All Your Possessions": Jewish
Ethics and Economic Life* (New York: Free Press, 1987), see also the
essays by Milton Friedman, Aaron Levine, and S. Herbert Frankel in
Walter Block, Geoffrey Brennan, and Kenneth Elzinga, eds., *Morality
of the Market: Religious and Economic Perspectives* (Vancouver, British
Columbia, Canada: Fraser Institute, 1985), 401–59.

22. For example Alan Macfarlane, *The Culture of Capitalism* (Oxford:
Basil Blackwell, 1987). See also Jean Baechler, John A. Hall, and Michael
Mann, eds., *Europe and the Rise of Capitalism* (Oxford: Basil Blackwell,
1987); and Roy Porter and Mikulas Teich, eds., *Revolution in History*
(Cambridge: Cambridge University Press, 1986). Most recently, see
Louis Baeck, "The Economic Impact of the Cistercian Order," *Notes
et documents* 32 (September–December 1991): 42–56.

23. After a condemnation of socialism even more severe than Leo
XIII's, Pius XI made this asymmetry explicit in #101 of *Quadragesimo
Anno* (1931):

It is clear then that the [liberal] system as such is not to be
condemned. Surely it is not vicious of its very nature; but it
violates right order whenever capital so employs the working or wage-earning classes as to divert business and economic activity entirely to its own arbitrary will and
advantage without any regard to the human dignity of the
workers, the social character of economic life, social justice
and the common good.

24. David Martin, *Tongues of Fire: The Explosion of Protestantism in Latin America* (Oxford: Basil Blackwell, 1990).
25. Ibid., 288–93.
26. See George Weigel, *The Final Revolution* (New York: Oxford University Press, 1992).

1. CATHOLICS AGAINST CAPITALISM

1. Amintore Fanfani, *Catholicism, Protestantism and Capitalism* (Notre Dame, IN: University of Notre Dame Press, 1984), 28–29.
2. Ibid., 39.
3. Elisa Carillo, *Alcide de Gasperi: The Long Apprenticeship* (Notre Dame, IN: University of Notre Dame Press, 1965); Mario Einaudi, *Christian Democracy in Italy and France* (Notre Dame, IN: University of Notre Dame Press, 1952); and Terence Prittie, Horst Osterheld, and François Seydoux, *Konrad Adenauer* (Bonn: Aktuell, 1983).
4. Thomas T. McAvoy, *The Great Crisis in American Catholic History* (Chicago: Regnery, 1957).
5. Michael Novak, *The Spirit of Democratic Capitalism*, 2d ed. (Lanham, MD: Madison Books, 1991).
6. Michael Novak, "On the Governability of Democracies: The Economic System: The Evangelical Basis of a Social Market Economy," in Luigi Lombardi Vallauri and Gerhard Dilcher, eds., *Cristianesimo secolarizzazione e diritto moderno 11/12* (Milan: Giuffre Editore; Baden–Baden: Nomos Verlags-gesellschaft, 1981), 497–525; reprinted as "The Economic System: The Evangelical Basis of a Social Market Economy," *Review of Politics* 43 (July 1981): 355–80.
7. Tocqueville, as if in response to such criticisms, wrote that "Americans, on the contrary, are fond of explaining almost all the actions of their lives by the principle of interest rightly understood; they show with complacency how an enlightened regard for themselves constantly prompts them to assist each other, and inclines them willingly to sacrifice a portion of their time and property to the welfare of the State." Moreover, "The inhabitants of the United States almost always manage to combine their own advantage with that of their fellow-citizens." Alexis de Tocqueville, *Democracy in America*, trans. Harry Reeve, 2 vols. (New York: Schocken Books, 1961), 2: 146–47.
8. Nicholas Phillipson, "Adam Smith as Civic Moralist," in Istvan Hont and Michael Ignatieff, eds., *Wealth and Virtue: The Shaping of Political Economy in the Scottish Enlightenment* (Cambridge: Cambridge University Press, 1983), 179–202.

9. But Douglas Rasmussen and Douglas Den Uyl, in *Liberty and Nature* (LaSalle, IL: Open Court, 1991) try to draw both from the Thomistic–Aristotelian tradition and from Ayn Rand.

10. See for example Lincoln's Annual Address Before the Wisconsin State Agricultural Society, Milwaukee, WI, September 30, 1859, in Abraham Lincoln, *Speeches and Writings 1859–1865: Speeches, Letters, and Miscellaneous Writings, Presidential Messages and Proclamations*, ed. Don E. Fehrenbacher (New York: Library of America, 1989), 90–101. For a discussion of Lincoln's thesis see Terry Hall, "Abraham Lincoln on the Priority of Labor," *Catholicism in Crisis* 2 (July 1983): 8–9.

11. Nathan Rosenberg and L. E. Birdzell, Jr., *How the West Grew Rich* (New York: Basic, 1986). "Growth is a form of change. Change implies innovation; and the Western system of innovation had depended upon wide diffusion of the power to undertake and use innovations, coupled with ample rewards for success and penalties for failure" (266). "The origins and forms of industrial research in the United States *were* diverse. What seems to have been most significant in the American experience was precisely the institutional flexibility that ensued" (261). "[Between 1880 and 1914] The United States, which experimented most, also made the greatest economic gains" (238).

12. "I doubt whether men were more virtuous in aristocratic ages than in others; but they were incessantly talking of the beauties of virtue, and its utility was studied only in secret. . . . In the United States hardly anybody talks of the beauty of virtue; but they maintain that virtue is useful, and prove it every day." Tocqueville, *Democracy in America*, 2: 145–46.

13. Handlin writes of William H. Harriman, a nineteenth-century businessman–dreamer, that he "wanted to build a transportation system that would circle the globe. He wanted to be able to get on a railroad in New York and go all the way around the world, through China, Russia, and Western Europe, crossing the water by steamship, and return to New York all on the same line. This idea made neither economic nor political sense, but Harriman spent years of his life and millions of dollars trying to realize it." Oscar Handlin, "The Taxonomy of the Corporation," in Michael Novak and John W. Cooper, eds., *The Corporation: A Theological Inquiry* (Washington, DC: American Enterprise Institute, 1981), 24.

14. See Paul Johnson, "Is There a Moral Basis for Capitalism?" in Michael Novak, ed., *Democracy and Mediating Structures: A Theological Inquiry* (Washington, DC: American Enterprise Institute, 1980), 54.

15. Jacques Maritain, *Creative Intuition in Art and Poetry*, Bollingen Series (New York: Pantheon Books, 1953); and *The Person and the Common Good*, trans. John J. Fitzgerald (New York: Charles Scribner's Sons, 1947).

16. Tönnies described one such application of the typology:

"In the history of the great systems of culture," he wrote, "a period of Gesellschaft follows a period of Gemeinschaft." The latter period begins with social relations based on family life and on domestic economy; later, with the development of agriculture and rural village life, there is a shift to cooperative patterns based on locality. Then follows the growth of town life and the mental community of religious faith and artistry. The Gesellschaft period of history opens with the growth of city life based on trade and contractual relationships. Industrialization and the rational manipulation of capital and labor are accompanied by the growth of the state and of national life. Cosmopolitian life, toward which Tönnies thought society was moving, would be based on the ultimate expressions of rational will-science, informed public opinion, and control by "the republic of scholars" (*International Encyclopedia of the Social Sciences*, ed. David L. Sills, 17 vols. [New York: Macmillan & Free Press, 1968], s.v. "community–society continua").

The reference to Tönnies is to Ferdinand Tönnies, *Gemeinschaft und Gesellschaft*, trans. and ed. Charles P. Loomis (East Lansing: Michigan State University Press), 231.

17. One of the best efforts to understand the new liberal ideal of community is Peter L. Berger and Richard John Neuhaus, *To Empower People: The Role of Mediating Structures in Public Policy* (Washington, DC: American Enterprise Institute, 1977). For an original thesis on the role that ideals of community have played in American politics see William A. Schambra, "The Quest for Community and the New Public Philosophy," *Catholicism in Crisis* (April 1984): 16–21; (May 1984): 7–12.

18. Little, 71 n., 161, 257–58.

19. Fanfani, 24.

20. Cf. *Populorum Progressio*, ##76–77; "Reflections by Cardinal Maurice Roy on the Occasion of the Tenth Anniversary of the Encyclical 'Pacem in Terris' of Pope John XXIII," #143; and *Centesimus Annus*, #52.

21. Fanfani, 24 (emphasis added).

22. For an excellent explanation of Smith's ideal see Gertrude Himmelfarb, "Adam Smith: Political Economy as Moral Philosophy," in *The Idea of Poverty: England in the Early Industrial Age* (New York: Alfred A. Knopf, 1984), 42–63.

> The argument of [Adam Smith's *Theory of*] *Moral Senti-
> ments* is subtle, complicated, and not without difficulties,
> but even the barest statement of it is enough to demonstrate
> that Smith was hardly the ruthless individualist or amoralist
> he is sometimes made out to be. Whatever difficulties there
> may be in the reconciliation of *Moral Sentiments* with the
> *Wealth of Nations*, it is clear enough that Smith intended
> both as parts of his grand 'design'—that he had the *Wealth
> of Nations* in mind even before he wrote *Moral Sentiments*,
> reissuing and revising it long after the *Wealth of Nations*
> was published.
>   A close reading of the *Wealth of Nations* itself suggests
> that political economy as Smith understood it was part of a
> larger moral philosophy, a new kind of moral economy.
> Schumpeter complained that Smith was so steeped in the
> tradition of moral philosophy derived from scholasticism
> and natural law that he could not conceive of economics
> per se, an economics divorced from ethics and politics (48).

For a discussion of the hidden similarities between the Catholic tradition
and the liberal tradition, especially their shared sense of realism, see
Michael Novak, *Catholic Social Thought and Liberal Institutions: Freedom with Justice*, 2d ed. (New Brunswick: Transaction, 1989), 16–38.
    23. "Unlimited greed for gain is not in the least identical with capi-
talism, and is still less its spirit. Capitalism *may* even be identical with
the restraint, or at least a rational tempering, of this irrational impulse."
Weber, 17.
    24. Fanfani, 137–38.
    25. Ibid.
    26. Maritain says he encountered in the United States the "industrial
civilization which I had learned to know in Europe . . . [as] everywhere
in the world, inhuman and materialist." By contrast, he also recognized
a people who were "freedom-loving and mankind-loving . . . clinging
to the importance of ethical standards, anxious to save the world, the
most humane and the least materialist among modern peoples which had
reached the industrial stage." How would this tension work itself out?
Maritain says, ". . . the more I lived in this country, the more I realized
that . . . the vital, pragmatic, completely unsystematic pressure exercised by the American people and the American soul on the structures
of our modern industrial civilization is transforming from within the
inner dynamism and historical trends of the industrial regime. . . . The
people have thus vanquished the inner logic of the industrial regime
considered in its first historical phase, and have, almost without knowing
it, inaugurated a really new phase in modern civilization." Jacques Mar-

itain, *Reflections on America* (New York: Charles Scribner's Sons, 1958), 21–23.

27. James Madison stated this principle in *Federalist* 10: "The regulation of these various and interfering interests forms the principal task of modern legislation." Alexander Hamilton, James Madison, and John Jay, *The Federalist*, ed. Clinton Rossiter (New York: The New American Library, 1961), 79.

28. See F. A. Hayek, ed., *Capitalism and the Historians* (Chicago: University of Chicago Press, 1954).

29. Peter Berger, "Capitalism and the Disorders of Modernity," *First Things* (January 1991): 19.

2. SOCIALISM, NO! CAPITALISM? MAYBE (LEO XIII)

1. Such a letter, called an encyclical, has a well-defined role in papal ministry. See *The Church Speaks to the Modern World: The Social Teachings of Leo XIII*, ed. Etienne Gilson (Garden City, NY: Image Books, 1954), 3–4:

> What is an encyclical letter, or, as it is more simply called, an encyclical? It is a pastoral letter similar to those which bishops frequently address to the Catholics of their dioceses, but of greater scope. Since the Pope is Bishop of Rome and the successor of St. Peter, he can address some of his pastoral letters to all the Christians now living in all the countries of the earth. As often as not, the Pope will address all men without any distinction of race, of language, or even of religion.

2. Brochure for "A Conference to Mark the Centenary of Pope Leo XIII's Social Encyclical *Rerum Novarum*," Von Hügel Institute, St. Edmund's College, Cambridge, England, 1991.

3. Robert Heilbroner, "Was the Right Right All Along?" *Harper's* 282 (January 1991): 18–22. Reprinted from "The World After Communism," *Dissent* (Fall 1990).

4. Hannah Arendt, *On Revolution* (New York: Viking, 1963), 63.

5. See Joseph Schumpeter, *History of Economic Analysis* (New York: Oxford University Press, 1954), 765–66; and *Capitalism, Socialism, and Democracy* (New York: Harper & Row, 1975), 344–45.

6. In his first use of the term, the Pope says, "Socialists, exciting the envy of the poor toward the rich, contend that it is necessary to do away with private possession of goods and in its place to make the goods of individuals common to all, and that the men who preside over a mu-

nicipality or who direct the entire State should act as administrators of
these goods. They hold that, by such transfer of private goods from
private individuals to the community, they can cure the present evil
through dividing wealth and benefits equally among the citizens." *Rerum Novarum*, #7.

7. Leo XIII, *Rerum Novarum*, #10.

8. Ibid., #23.

9. Ibid., #36. "The fact that God gave the whole human race the
earth to use and enjoy cannot indeed in any manner serve as an objection
against private possessions. For God is said to have given the earth to
mankind in common, not because He intended indiscriminate ownership
of it by all, but because he assigned no part to anyone in ownership,
leaving the limits of private possessions to be fixed by the industry of
men and the institutions of peoples." *Rerum Novarum*, #14.

10. Ibid., #9.

11. Ibid., #16.

12. Ibid., #22.

13. Ibid., #26.

14. Ibid., #55.

15. Kevin Acker, " 'Poisoning of the Soul': New Leaders of Russia
and Central Europe Talk About the Evil Empire," *Policy Review* (Winter
1991): 60–65. Quotations nn. 16–20 are drawn from this article.

16. Tzvetan Todorov, Bulgarian author, *The New Republic* (June 25,
1990).

17. Tatyana Zaslavskaya, Soviet sociologist, in *Voices of Glasnost*.

18. Gavrii Popov, Mayor of Moscow, Cato Institute/Soviet Academy
of Sciences, September 10, 1990. "How can you say you have a moth-
erland when you don't own a single square meter of land which you can
leave to your grandchildren?" (Suyatoslav Fyodorov, Soviet laser scientist, *New York Times* [March 11, 1990].) "We are consciously limiting
the role of the state in the economy. It is no longer the supermanager
of a superfactory, the main boss and the main controller, the main
storekeeper and the main distributor of goods and services. Several dozen
years of costly experience have shown that the state cannot do this well,
and, in partiuclar, cannot inspire energy in people so that they may work
productively, efficiently, and economically." (Tadeusz Mazowiecki,
Prime Minister of Poland, before the *Sejm* [Polish Parliament], January
18,1990.) "When people are compelled to look only one way, when they
are deprived of information and the possibility to compare things, they
stop thinking. Well-informed people, ones who have access to versatile
information, inevitably begin to think. The very system invites lies."
(Oleg Kalugin, former KGB Major-General and USSR People's Deputy,
Moscow News [July 1, 1990].) "In a totalitarian situation people conform

outwardly to the prevailing morals and isolate themselves in microso-
cieties where they live, work, and die. People act according to moral
double standards, an unwritten social contract that everyone knows.
Workers are allowed to idle and steal, as long as they come to party
meetings and applaud. Only a small mafia of party bosses and enterprise
bosses took it seriously; the rest of the people cut themselves off." (Valtr
Komarek, Deputy Prime Minister of Czechoslovakia, *NRC Handelsblad*
[Rotterdam], February 6, 1990.)

19. Timisoara Declaration, Romania, March 11, 1990.

20. Vaclav Havel, President of Czechoslovakia, *Izvestia* (February
23, 1990).

21. *Rerum Novarum*, ##4–5.

22. Ibid., ##11–12.

23. Mises argues as follows:

> Under Socialism . . . the economic administration may in-
> deed know exactly what commodities are needed most ur-
> gently. But this is only half the problem. The other half,
> the valuation of the means of production, it cannot
> solve. . . .
> The problem of economic calculation is the fundamental
> problem of Socialism. . . .
> To prove that economic calculation would be impossible
> in the socialist community is to prove also that Socialism is
> impracticable (Ludwig von Mises, *Socialism*, trans. J. Ka-
> hane from 2d ed. of 1932 [Indianapolis: Liberty Classics,
> 1981], 103–104, 116–17).

24. According to Heilbroner:

> The Soviet system has long been dogged by a method of
> pricing that produced grotesque misallocations of effort.
> The difficulties were not so visible in the early days of So-
> viet industrialization or in the post–Second World War re-
> construction period. . . . Inefficiency set in when projects
> had to be joined into a complex hole—a process that re-
> quired knowing how much things should cost. Then, as
> Mises foresaw, setting prices became a hopeless problem
> because the economy never stood still long enough for any-
> one to decide anything correctly (Robert Heilbroner,
> "After Communism," *The New Yorker* [September 10,
> 1990]: 92).

25. Hayek contrasts two norms of rationality:

> The main point of my argument is . . . that the con-
> flict . . . is due to a factual error. . . . As a question of fact,
> this conflict must be settled by scientific study. Such study
> shows that, by following the spontaneously generated
> moral traditions underlying the competitive market order
> (traditions which do not satisfy the canons or norms of ra-
> tionality embraced by most socialists), we generate and gar-
> ner greater knowledge and wealth than could ever be
> obtained or utilized in a centrally-directed economy whose
> adherents claim to proceed strictly in accordance with "rea-
> son." Thus, socialist aims and programs are factually im-
> possible to achieve or execute; and they also happen into
> the bargain as it were, to be logically impossible (F. A.
> Hayek, *The Fatal Conceit* [Chicago: University of Chicago
> Press, 1988], 7).

26. From Zamyatin's novel *We*: "The state poet wrote a poem,

> Eternally enamored two times two
> Eternally united in the passionate four,
> Most ardent lovers in the world—
> Inseparable two times two . . .

The state newspapers stated: You are perfect. You are machinelike. The road to one hundred percent happiness is free. . . ." Quoted by Mihajlo Mihajlov, "Life = Freedom: The Symbolism of $2 \times 2 = 4$ in Dostoevsky, Zamyatin and Orwell," *Catholicism in Crisis* 3 (October 1985): 20–24.

27. According to the historical account given by A. M. C. Waterman, between 1798 and 1832 the new science of political economy was fully integrated into contemporary Christian social theory and the ethical implications of a market economy had been rigorously analyzed from the standpoint of trinitarian orthodoxy. "Christian political economy" became the inheritance of English-speaking culture from then on. By contrast, the Church of Rome knew no such debate, its chief intellectual institutions having been destroyed after 1789. As a result, when Leo XIII turned belatedly to economic matters in 1891 he issued an anti-socialist tract that steered well clear of any recognition of market forces in the social order. Waterman's article discusses the "three most important elements of the explanation: a misunderstanding of classical political economy, a misperception of the European economy in the nineteenth century, and philosophical commitment to a purely Scholastic understanding of liberty." A. M. C. Waterman, "The Intellectual Con-

text of *Rerum Novarum,*" *Review of Social Economy* 49 (Winter 1991): 465–82.

28. Vaclav Klaus, Finance Minister of Czechoslovakia, in Acker, 63–64. Original citation from *Reason* (June 1990). Klaus goes on to say, "The market is indivisible; it cannot be an instrument in the hands of central planning."

29. Anatoly Sobchak, Mayor of Leningrad, in Acker. Original citation from Cato Institute/Soviet Academy of Sciences (September 11, 1990).

30. Yuri Afanasyev, USSR People's Deputy and Rector of the Moscow Historical Archival Institute, in Acker. Original citation from *Dagens Nyheter* (Stockholm), (January 3, 1990).

31. See, e.g., the opinions of St. Ambrose:

> Ambrose apparently believes that almost all methods of acquiring wealth are unjust. That is certainly true of trade, which he regards with the abhorrence of a Roman aristocrat brought up in traditional values. Trade is based on lying and cunning, for the seller tries to make the merchandise appear more valuable than it is, and the buyer does the exact opposite. He goes so far as to declare that to use the sea for commerce is to twist its purpose, for the sea was given in order to produce fish and not in order to be sailed. . . . For Ambrose, travel to distant lands to procure what is not available locally is one more consequence of greed, of not being content with what is readily at hand (Justo L. Gonzalez, *Faith and Wealth: A History of Early Christian Ideas on the Origin, Significance, and Use of Money* [New York: Harper & Row, 1990], 189. Gonzalez cites St. Ambrose, *De Officiis* 3. 37, 57, 65–66, 71–72).

32. *Rerum Novarum*, #6.
33. See, e.g., ibid., ##8–9:

> It is fully in accordance with nature to own property privately. The truth is that it is only when men cultivate it skillfully that the earth provides in plenty all that men need for the preservation of life and still more for its higher development. Thus, when a man expends the activity of his mind and the strength of his body in procuring the goods of nature he makes his own that part of nature's resources which he brings to completion, leaving on it, as it were, in some form, the imprint of himself. This being so, it cannot but be right for him to possess that part as his very own, nor can it be lawful for anyone to violate that right in any way.

It is amazing that some people dissent from arguments
as powerful as these and seek to resurrect bad opinions long
since outworn. Enjoyment only of the different products of
the soil is all they are willing to concede to a private person. They flatly deny the existence of any right of freehold
possession, whether of the land on which a man has built
or of a farm which he has cultivated. They do not see that
in making these denials they defraud a man of part of the
produce of his labor. For the soil which is cultivated with
toil and skill is greatly changed in condition: the wilderness
is made productive, the infertile fruitful. That which has
improved the soil becomes so completely mingled with it as
to inhere in it and become to a large extent utterly inseparable from it. Does justice allow any man to seize and enjoy
something which another man has stained with his sweat?
As effects follow their cause, so is it right for the fruit of
labor to belong to those who have given their labor. It is
with good reason, then, that the common opinion of mankind has found no merit in the dissenting opinions of a
few. Making a close study of nature, men have found in nature's law the basis for a distribution of goods and for private ownership and have been fully convinced that these are
in the highest degree in conformity with the nature of man
and with peace and tranquility.

Cf. also #36:

A characteristic of a well constituted state is an abundance
of material goods, 'the use of which is necessary to virtuous
action' [Thomas Aquinas, *De Regimine Principum*, 1. 15].
Such goods cannot be provided without the highly productive, skilled and painstaking labor of the unpropertied
workers who are employed in farms and factories. So great
is their vigor and efficiency in this regard that it may truly
be said that it is only by the labor of working-men that
states grow rich.

34. Ernest L. Fortin, " 'Sacred and Inviolable': *Rerum Novarum* and
Natural Rights," *Theological Studies* 53 (June 1992): 203–33.

35. *Rerum Novarum*, #46.

36. "When the 'sacredness of property' is talked of, it should always
be remembered, that any such sacredness does not belong in the same
degree to landed property. No man made the land. It is the original
inheritance of the whole species. Its appropriation is wholly a question

of general expedience." John Stuart Mill, *Principles of Political Economy: With Some of Their Applications to Social Philosophy*, ed. William Ashley [1909] (Fairfield: Augustus M. Kelley, 1976), 233.

37. *Summa Theologica*, II–II, q. 66, art. 1–2.

38. "Reflection on the Scholastic procedure for distributive justice helps clarify the conception of exploitation implicit in the Pope's condemnation of the evils of capitalism." In Scholastic theory, distributive justice depends on a sense of community based on the "*ontological* kind of reason mankind needs in order to perceive the good and the beautiful." Only by this kind of reason can we recognize persons as ends, not mere means. By demoting this kind of reason to a status below that of *instrumental* reason, capitalism may undercut the ontological dignity of human beings, using them merely as means. This is "exploitation derived from the demotion of reason, whereby a community is deprived of the vision required to perceive and appreciate instantiations of the good and the beautiful." Stephen T. Worland, "Exploitative Capitalism: The Natural-Law Perspective," *Social Research* 48 (Summer 1981): 294–95, 299, 304–5.

39. *Rerum Novarum*, #15.

40. See Madison's remarks in *Federalist* 51:

> Ambition must be made to counteract ambition. The interest of the man must be connected with the constitutional rights of the place. It may be a reflection on human nature that such devices should be necessary to control the abuses of government. But what is government itself but the greatest of all reflections on human nature? If men were angels, no government would be necessary. If angels were to govern men, neither external nor internal controls on government would be necessary. In framing a government which is to be administered by men over men, the great difficulty lies in this: you must first enable the government to control the governed; and in the next place oblige it to control itself. A dependence on the people is, no doubt, the primary control on the government; but experience has taught mankind the necessity of auxiliary precautions.
>
> This policy of supplying, by opposite and rival interests, the defect of better motives, might be traced through the whole system of human affairs, private as well as public. We see it particularly displayed in all the subordinate distributions of power, where the constant aim is to divide and arrange the several offices in such a manner as that each may be a check on the other—that the private interest of every individual may be a sentinel over the public rights.

These inventions of prudence cannot be less requisite in the distribution of the supreme powers of the States.

41. Heilbroner, "Was the Right Right All Along?" 20. Cf. Vaclav Klaus, Finance Minister of Czechoslovakia: "We wanted to create a new man, with only unselfish thoughts. I am afraid it is not possible." Acker, 62.

42. Such "private life," of course, can be socially organized and publicly active; some forms of it (unions, associations, nonprofit organization) may be legally incorporated and thus, in a sense, "public." We should not confine the word "public" only to the action of the state.

43. Long before Marx was on the scene, Madison stated the problem in *Federalist* 10:

> The most common and durable source of factions has been the various and unequal distribution of property. Those who hold and those who are without property have ever formed distinct interests in society. Those who are creditors, and those who are debtors, fall under a like discrimination. A landed interest, a manufacturing interest, a mercantile interest, a moneyed interest, with many lesser interests, grow up on necessity in civilized nations, and divide them into different classes, actuated by different sentiments and views. The regulation of those various and interfering interests forms the principal task of modern legislation, and involves the spirit of party and faction in the necessary operations of the government. . . . The apportionment of taxes on the various descriptions of property is an act which seems to require the most exact impartiality; yet there is, perhaps, no legislative act in which greater opportunity and temptation are given to a predominant party to trample on the rules of justice. Every shilling with which they overburden the inferior number, is a shilling saved to their own pockets.
>
> It is vain to say that enlightened statesmen will be able to adjust these clashing interests, and render them all subservient to the public good. Enlightened statesmen will not always be at the helm.

Madison suggests the solution in No. 51: "It is of great importance in a republic not only to guard the society against the oppression of its rulers, but to guard one part of the society against the injustice of the other part. Different interests necessarily exist in different classes of citizens. If a majority be united by a common interest, the rights of the minority will be insecure." The method of providing "against this evil . . . will be exemplified in the federal republic of the United States. Whilst all authority in it will be derived from and dependent on society, the society itself will be broken into so many parts, interests and classes of citizens, that the rights of individuals, or of the minority, will be in little danger from interested combinations of the majority."

44. John Locke, *Two Treatises of Government*, Second Treatise, #41.

45. Roy Porter, "The Heart of the Country," *The New Republic* (May 4, 1992): 37. Speaking of the book by E. P. Thompson that he is reviewing, Porter says: "He seems reluctant to concede the possibility that the true historical strength of capitalism may lie in the extensive and essentially voluntary uptake of market opportunities by great, middling, and small folks alike." These issues go to the heart of Thompson's prejudices, Porter adds, and illustrate what is wrong with English Marxist historiography. Marxists are characteristically nostalgic about an "older, rural England"; their Marxism has a "highly patrician timbre" and may assume a paternalistic mission to rescue the wretched. They experience great "difficulties in coming to terms with the bourgeoisie—a repugnance that has all too commonly been the telltale trademark of elite, ex–public school English Marxist intellectuals." The latter disdain to consider all the small advances in activity (shops, newspapers, factory-made goods) and "domestic plenty" that made "the bourgeois world of family life" a signal improvement over rural poverty.

46. Robert Rector, "How 'Poor' Are America's Poor?" *Heritage Foundation Backgrounder*, No. 791 (September 21, 1990); "How the Poor Really Live: Lessons for Welfare Reform," *Heritage Foundation Backgrounder*, No. 875 (January 31, 1992).

47. Boris Yeltsin, speech at Columbia University, 1990, cited in Acker, 64.

48. "The fundamental impulse that sets and keeps the capitalist engine in motion comes from new consumers' goods, the new methods of production or transportation, the new markets, the new forms of industrial organization that capitalist enterprise creates. . . . This process of Creative Destruction is the essential fact about capitalism," Schumpeter, *Capitalism, Socialism and Democracy*, 83.

49. See Friedrich A. Hayek, "The Use of Knowledge in Society," in *Individualism and the Economic Order* (Chicago: Gateway, 1972), 77–91.

50. Kirzner sees "market capitalism not simply as a set of institutions governing exchanges . . . but as an ongoing process of creative discovery. What one witnesses in a market economy, at any point in time, are nothing but attempts by market participants to take advantage of newly discovered or created possibilities. . . . The process of creative discovery is never completed, nor is it ever arrested." Kirzner, ix–x.

51. For example, *The American Heritage Dictionary* (1976) defines capitalism as "An economic system characterized by freedom of the market with increasing concentration of private and corporate ownership of production and distribution means, proportionate to increasing accumulation and reinvestment of profits." For others see Novak, *Spirit*, 430 (new Afterword).

52. George Gilder quoting Mikhail Gorbachev, "Freedom and the High Tech Revolution," *Imprimis*, Vol. 19, No. 111 (November 1990): 1.

3. SOCIAL JUSTICE REDEFINED (PIUS XI)

1. *Quadragesimo Anno*, ##105–108.
2. Alan Peacock and Hans Willgerodt, eds., *Germany's Social Market Economy: Origins and Evolution* (New York: St. Martin's Press, 1989).
3. In the words of Nell-Breuning himself:

> It is clear to me today that the insertion of Pius XI's comments on fascism bears the chief blame for the total misunderstanding of the picture of order, or rather outline of a social order, developed in *Quadragesimo Anno* which in the German translation is called by the unhappy word "occupational" and in the French by "corporatism." This is no excuse for the inadequate delineation, that was my responsibility exclusively. On the contrary, I blame myself. I became confident because the Pope did not complain in any way about my exposition; and I blame myself far more because I approved the supplement to it written by him. I lulled myself into a false sense of security and undertook no further reflections (Oswald von Nell-Breuning, S.J., "*Quadragesimo Anno*," *Stimmen der Zeit*, no. 187 [1971]: 294).

4. Nell-Breuning, *Reorganization of Social Economy* (New York: Bruce Publishing, 1939), 5.
5. See for instance the three-volume *Law, Legislation and Liberty* (Chicago: University of Chicago Press, 1976–77); *The Constitution of Liberty* (Chicago: University of Chicago Press, 1960); and *The Road to Serfdom* (Chicago: University of Chicago Press, 1944).
6. Friedrich Hayek, "Opening Address to a Conference at Mont Pelerin," in *Studies in Philosophy, Politics and Economics* (London: Routledge & Kegan Paul, 1967), 155.

7. Hayek, *The Mirage of Social Justice*, 62–100. For a discussion of these four points see John Gray, "Social Injustice: What Hayek Taught Communists, He Can Now Teach Us," *Crisis* 8 (September 1990): 30–32. As Gray describes them, the four objections are as follows:

> 1.   Market distributions of income and capital are to a considerable extent a matter of chance and are therefore unpredictable, and so uncontrollable, by government.
>
> 2.   Typical criteria of conventional conceptions of social justice are that resources be allocated according to need or merit. Hayek's insight is, first, that we have among us no consensus as to what constitutes need or merit. More exactly, we lack sufficient consensus on relative degrees of merit and need for communally acceptable judgments to be made.
>
> 3.   The pursuit of social justice will . . . harm the efficiency of the market system since it will alter the signals which tell persons where the most profitable opportunities lie. . . . The pursuit of social justice involves accepting a lower level of production than might otherwise be achieved.
>
> 4.   In the absence of clearly applicable and conflict-free criteria, the idea of social justice will be deployed by established interest groups to promote their entrenched interests. Social justice becomes, in effect, the slogan of those who wish to resist the negative feedback that is inseparable from market processes.

8. But cf. Aquinas's account, in which the virtue of justice is different from the other cardinal virtues precisely because of its ordination to a state of affairs external to the agent:

> Accordingly, that which is right in the works of the other virtues, and to which the intention of the virtue tends as to its proper object, depends on its relation to the agent only, whereas the right in a work of justice, besides its relation to the agent, is set up by its relation to others. . . . And so a thing is said to be just, as having the rectitude of justice, when it is the term of an act of justice, without taking into account the way in which it is done by the agent; whereas in the other virtues nothing is declared to be right unless it is done in a certain way by the agent (II–II, q. 57, a. 1).

Hence, justice is more oriented to outcomes or to what Hayek calls "states of affairs."

On this account, some say, Hayek may have imposed a false dichotomy between the personal and the social. But Hayek's real point is
not that dichotomy but, rather, the difference between matters affected
by human volition and matters settled independent thereof, by processes
that are systemic and, on other grounds, better for human societies than
any known alternative. His point is *epistemic*: We cannot know enough
to produce the outcomes we desire by forethought and deliberation
without doing more harm than good.

9. Hayek, *Mirage*, 63–64. See also "The Atavism of Social Justice,"
67–68 in F. A. Hayek, *New Studies in Philosophy, Politics, Economics
and the History of Ideas* (Chicago: University of Chicago Press, 1978).

10. Writing in 1976, Hayek says: "The use of the term 'social justice'
in this sense is of comparatively recent date, apparently not much older
than a hundred years" (*Mirage*: 63). While explaining that the term was
used many years before, Nell-Breuning says: "The Encyclical *Quadragesimo Anno* has finally and definitely established, theologically
canonized, so to speak, social justice" (*Reorganization of Social Economy*: 5).

11. See Michael Novak, *This Hemisphere of Liberty* (Washington,
DC: The AEI Press, 1990), 3:

> In some sense, the Catholic Whigs resemble progressives.
> They believe in the dignity of the human person, in human
> liberty, in institutional reform, in gradual progress. But
> they also have a deep respect for language, law, liturgy,
> custom, habit, and tradition that marks them, simultane-
> ously, as conservatives. With the conservatives, the Catho-
> lic Whigs have an awareness of the force of cultural habit
> and the role of passion and sin in human affairs. With the
> liberals, they give central importance to human liberty, es-
> pecially the slow building of institutions of liberty.
>
> The Catholic Whigs see liberty as *ordered* liberty—not
> the liberty to do what one wishes, but the liberty to do
> what one ought—much as Thomas Aquinas saw practical
> wisdom as ordered reason, *recta ratio*. Often embattled by
> the Church's traditionalists and fundamentalists, the Catho-
> lic Whigs have championed the value of progress in history,
> progress above all along the axis of liberty; but their pro-
> gressive instincts are tempered by an acute sense of irony,
> tragedy, and contingency. They prefer to stress steady insti-
> tutional progress, achieved gradually and solidly, and well
> rooted in cultural habit. They distrust merely abstract prin-
> ciples and spasms of revolutionary fervor.

See also especially Chapter 1, and the Appendix: "Thomas Aquinas, The First Whig": 107–123.

12. Nell-Breuning, *Reorganization of Social Economy*, 251.

13. Hayek, *Mirage*, 65. He continues: "People may dispute whether or not the particular measure is required by 'social justice.' But that this is the standard which ought to guide political action, and that the expression has a definite meaning, is hardly ever questioned. In consequence, there are today probably no political movements or politicians who do not readily appeal to 'social justice' in support of the particular measures which they advocate."

14. Karl Rahner et al., eds., *Sacramentum Mundi: an Encyclopedia of Theology*, 6 vols. (New York: Herder and Herder, 1968–70).

15. Johannes Messner, *Social Ethics: Natural Law in the Western World*, rev. ed. (St. Louis: B. Herder Book Co., 1965). The discussion of the idea of social justice takes up about one page (320–21), out of the more than 1,000 pages in the book. Messner says:

> In origin, the expression "social justice" refers especially to the economic and social welfare of "society," in the sense of the economically cooperating community of the state. . . . Social justice . . . imposes obligations on employer and on employee in the course of negotiations of collective labor agreements. It not only demands a just distribution of the social product, but also binds the groups cooperating in society to make the efforts in rendering their services, necessary for the firm estabishment and development of the common good in all spheres and for economic and social progress.

16. Ernest Fortin, "Natural Law and Social Justice," *American Journal of Jurisprudence* 30 (1985): 1–20.

17. Jean-Yves Calvez, S.J. and Jacques Perrin, S.J., *The Church and Social Justice: Social Teaching of the Popes from Leo XIII to Pius XII*, trans. J. R. Kirwan (London: Burns and Oates, 1961), esp. 145–53.

18. William J. Ferree, S.M., *Introduction to Social Justice* (Dayton, OH: Marianist Publications, 1948), 12. Ferree says that two levels of justice are distinguished in *Quadragesimo Anno*:

> On the one level of commutative or individual justice the employer is *helpless*, and note that this happens "all too frequently." Now evidently, if he is really helpless to do full

justice, he does not sin when out of sheer necessity he falls short of justice. In individual justice the case is closed, for the employer can do nothing about it; and the injustice must be allowed to continue out of sheer inability to stop it.

Above this field of individual justice, however, there is the whole field of Social Justice, and in this higher field the case is *never* closed. The "helplessness" of individuals comes from the fact that the *whole industry* is badly organized ("socially unjust"). Social Justice demands that it be *organized rightly* for the common good of all who depend upon it for their welfare and perfection. Therefore, employers have the duty—the rigid duty of Social Justice which they cannot disregard without sin—to work *together* (socially) to reorganize their industry. Once this reorganization (act of Social Justice) has been accomplished by group (social) action, then the employers will no longer be helpless in the field of individual justice, and will be under obligation to meet their strict duties in this field.

19. Ernest Fortin, "Natural Law and Social Justice," 14–15.
20. Ibid., 15–16.
21. Aristotle, *Nicomachean Ethics*, 5.1.1129^{a}1–1129^{b}24. Note esp. 1129^{b}15–20: "Now all the various pronouncements of the law aim either at the common interest of all, or at the interest of a ruling class determined either by excellence or in some other similar way; so that in one of its senses the term 'just' is applied to anything that produces and preserves the happiness, or the component parts of the happiness, of the political community."
22. Aquinas, *Summa Theologica*, IIa–IIae, q. 58, art. 5–6. For a fuller discussion see Calvez and Perrin, 139–45.
23. According to Nell-Breuning, Pesch called social justice "the spiritual foundation and supporting pillar of Christian solidarity" (*Reorganization of Social Economy*, 5).
24. Pius XI identifies social justice with the requirements of the common good:

Free competition, and especially economic domination,
must be kept within definite and proper bounds, and must
be brought under effective control of the public authority,
in matters pertaining to the latter's competence. The public
institutions of the nations should be such as to make all
human society conform to the requirements of the common
good, that is, the norm of *social justice*. If this is done, that
very important part of social life, the economic system, will

of necessity be restored to sanity and right order (*Quadragesimo Anno*, #110).

25. Cited in Ferree, 7.

26. *Quadragesimo Anno*, ##57, 58, 71, 88, 101, 110, and 126. Social justice is referred to, but not named, at #74 and #88. At least two central themes emerge from these ten usages. First, social justice is a prescriptive canon by which current social conditions are measured; second, social justice is the end of a society and polity that pursues the common good.

An example of the former is #71, where Pius XI says: "Every effort must therefore be made that fathers of families receive a sufficient wage adequate to meet ordinary domestic needs. If in the present state of society this is not always feasible, social justice demands that reforms be introduced without delay which will guarantee every adult working man just such a wage."

The second usage is found (among other places) at #101: "It is clear . . . that the system as such is not to be condemned. Surely it is not vicious of its very nature; but it violates right order whenever capital so employs the working or wage-earning classes as to divert business and economic activity entirely to its own arbitrary will and advantage without any regard to the human dignity of the workers, the social character of economic life, social justice and the common good."

27. Nell-Breuning, *Reorganization of Social Economy*, 250, emphasis added.

28. Ibid., 250–51.

29. See Nell-Breuning, "*Quadragesimo Anno*," *Stimmen der Zeit* 187 (1971): 293–94: "already in my Commentary of 1932 and later, I continually interpreted these statements of Pius XI as diplomatic irony and I could refer to Mussolini for the correctness of this interpretation."

30. Ibid. Mussolini "understood the encyclical as such an unfavorable criticism of him that he unleashed his anger over it against the Italian Catholic youth organizations. The Pope complained that Mussolini reacted so spitefully to the 'benevolent nod' that he had given him."

31. *Quadragesimo Anno*, #120. "Christian socialism," said the Pope, implies "a contradiction in terms. No one can be at the same time a sincere Catholic and a true socialist." Socialism is "founded upon a doctrine of human society peculiarly its own, which is opposed to Christianity."

32. Nell-Breuning, *Reorganization of Social Economy*, 250.

33. Ibid., 247–48. Nell-Breuning refers to #88 of *Quadragesimo Anno*, where the Pope says: "Free competition . . . though within certain limits just and productive of good results, cannot be the ruling principle of the economic world; this has been abundantly proved by the consequences that have followed from the free rein given to these

dangerous and individualistic ideals. It is therefore very necessary that economic affairs be once more subjected to and governed by a true and effective guiding principle." The market cannot "be curbed and governed by itself. More lofty and noble principles must therefore be sought in order to control this supremacy sternly and uncompromisingly; to wit, social justice and social charity."

34. Ibid., 248–49.
35. See *Quadragesimo Anno*, #25.
36. A concise contemporary definition of subsidiarity:

> Derived from Roman Catholic teaching, this concept holds that any social task should be performed in the smallest of available units: in the family before the neighborhood; or in local governments, before the central state. As Bildt (Prime Minister of Sweden) explains: "The subsidiarity principle means that society is built from the bottom up, with a departure point from the individual's and the family's need, instead of from the top down, with the departure point in an abstract political doctrine" (Allan Carlson, "Forward to the Past: Rebuilding Family Life in Post-Socialist Sweden," *The Family in America* 6 [July 1992]: 4).

Nell-Breuning points out that:

> Long before the encyclical *Quadragesimo Anno* (1931) proclaimed the principle of subsidiarity as "*in philosophia sociali gravissimum illud principium*," Abraham Lincoln had formulated it thus for practical use: "The legitimate object of government is to do for a community of people whatever they need to have done but cannot do at all, or cannot so well do for themselves in their separate and individual capacities. In all that people can individually do as well for themselves, governments ought not to interfere" (Nell-Breuning, "Social Movements: Subsidiarity," *Sacramentum Mundi*, 6 vols., ed. Karl Rahner [New York: Herder & Herder, 1968–70], 6: 115).

37. Nell-Breuning, *Reorganization of Social Economy*, 251.
38. Alexis de Tocqueville, *The Old Regime and the French Revolution*, trans. Stuart Gilbert (Garden City: Doubleday, 1955), 206.
39. Michael Novak, *Will It Liberate? Questions About Liberation Theology*, rev. ed. (Lanham, MD: Madison Books, 1991).
40. See Friedrich A. Hayek's objections in *Law, Legislation, and Lib-*

erty, Vol. 2: *The Mirage of Social Justice* (Chicago: University of Chicago Press, 1976), Chapter 9, "Social or Distributive Justice," 62–100.

41. In *The Mirage of Social Justice*, Hayek characterizes the "Great Society" as a society in which the range of production and service is so extended that, unlike a traditional society, chief among its beneficiaries are strangers and foreigners. This extended chain of production is brought about because transactions are regulated by rules of just conduct that are the same for all participants. These rules, moreover, make possible both social peace and "individual liberty and all its values." This transformation changes the small society into the Great Society. Thus Hayek writes that "The Great Society arose through the discovery that men can live together in peace" and mutually benefit each other "without agreeing on the particular aims which they severally pursue." The discovery of the substitution of "abstract rules of conduct for obligatory concrete ends made it possible to extend the order of peace" beyond small groups pursuing the same ends, "because it enabled each individual to gain from the skill and knowledge of others whom he need not know and whose aims could be wholly different from his own." (109)

42. Nell-Breuning writes in *Reorganization of Social Economy*, 53:

> *Organized self-help* alone can be really successful. For this
> reason Leo XIII recommended the organization of societies.
> Pius XI rightly observes that this recommendation found
> the people well prepared and consequently resulted in an
> unprecedented movement of founding societies. At the start
> considerable obstacles had to be overcome. It is to Leo
> XIII's greatest praise that he contributed decisively to the
> conquest of these obstacles; he is the great champion of
> *freedom of association.*

43. For a fuller discussion of the concept of civil society, see Adam Seligman, *The Idea of Civil Society* (New York: Free Press, 1992).

44. For a discussion of the concept of catallaxy, see Friedrich A. Hayek, *The Mirage of Social Justice*, 107–109:

> The term "catallactics" was derived from the Greek term
> *katallattein* . . . which meant, significantly, not only "to
> exchange" but also "to admit into the community" and "to
> change from enemy into friend." . . . From this we can
> form an English term *catallaxy* which we shall use to de-
> scribe the order brought about by the mutual adjustment of
> many individual economies in a market. A catallaxy is thus
> the special kind of spontaneous order produced by the market

through people acting within the rule of the law of property, tort and contract.

45. Calvez and Perrin, *The Church and Social Justice*, 151–52.

46. Michael Novak, *Free Persons and the Common Good* (Lanham,
MD: Madison Books, 1989).

47. Ibid., 138: "Taken as a benchmark . . . the concept of the common good obliges the citizens of any particular society to lift up their
eyes in order to see how well they are doing, by some standard that
transcends present achievement."

48. See the Afterword to the second edition of my *The Spirit of Democratic Capitalism* (Lanham, MD: Madison Books, 1990), 432: "The
decisive move that distinguishes capitalism from all preceding systems,
as well as from socialism, is its social organization around the principle
that the primary cause of wealth is *caput* (mind)."

49. "[The] right of economic initiative," explains the Pope, "is a right
which is important not only for the individual but also for the common
good. Experience shows us that the denial of this right, or its limitation
in the name of an alleged 'equality' of everyone in society, diminishes,
or in practice absolutely destroys the spirit of initiative, that is to say,
the creative subjectivity of the citizen. As a consequence, there arises,
not so much a true equality as a 'leveling down'." *Sollicitudo Rei Socialis*,
#15.

50. As I have written elsewhere:

> Religious thinkers, in the main, have not assessed economic
> history. In few seminaries are courses in economics manda-
> tory, although courses in politics, sociology, and psychol-
> ogy increasingly are. Theologians, therefore, face two
> challenges simultaneously. First, they need to acquire some
> of the basic concepts and methods of economic analysis.
> Second, they must master factual materials concerning do-
> mestic and international economic activities, about which
> they are concerned to render judgment.
>
> To meet this need, I hope that a significant number of
> economists will turn their attention to the economic ques-
> tions being raised by official and unofficial church bodies.
> As religious leaders make more and more pronouncements
> about economic matters, they must receive prompt and ef-
> fective feedback. Otherwise, unchallenged assertions will
> begin to acquire the weight of conventional wisdom and of-
> ficial tradition. If mistakes are being made, they need to be
> corrected before they solidify. For the churches represent
> not only a legitimate but also a significant institutional force

within democratic capitalist societies. The elites of economics and of religion have weighty responsibilities each toward
the other (Michael Novak, *Catholic Social Thought and
Liberal Institutions* [New Brunswick, NJ: Transaction
Books, 1989], 15).

51. Amartya Sen, "Some Contemporary Economic and Social Issues,"
Social and Ethical Aspects of Economics. A Colloquium in the Vatican,
1992.
52. See George Weigel, *Liberty and Its Discontents: Catholicism Con-
fronts Modernity* (Washington, DC: Ethics and Public Policy Center,
1991).

4. THE SECOND LIBERTY

1. James M. Buchanan, "Economics in the Post-Socialist Century,"
Economic Journal 101 (January 1991): 15–21.
2. *Social and Ethical Aspects of Economics.* A Colloquium in the
Vatican, 1992.
3. David Martin, *Tongues of Fire: The Explosion of Protestantism in
Latin America* (Oxford: Basil Blackwell, 1990), 9–14.
4. Lord John Emerich Edward Dalberg-Acton, *Selected Writings of
Lord Acton*, 3 vols., ed. J. Rufus Fears (Indianapolis: LibertyClassics,
1988), 3: 491.
5. Ibid., 3: 29.
6. Ibid., 3: 491.
7. Ibid., 3: 489.
8. Ibid., 2: 99.
9. Ibid., 3: 491.
10. Ibid., 3: 490–91.
11. Michael Ignatieff, "Suburbia's Revenge," *The New Republic* (May
4, 1992): 11.
12. Buchanan, 15.
13. In *Centesimus Annus*, #42, Pope John Paul II asks:

Can it perhaps be said that, after the failure of communism,
capitalism is the victorious social system, and that capitalism should be the goal of the countries now making efforts
to rebuild their economy and society? Is this the model
which ought to be proposed to the countries of the Third
World which are searching for the path to true economic
and civil progress?
If by "capitalism" is meant an economic system which

recognizes the fundamental and positive role of business,
the market, private property and the resulting responsibility
for the means of production, as well as free human creativity in the economic sector, then the answer is certainly in
the affirmative, even though it would perhaps be more appropriate to speak of a "business economy," "market economy," or simply "free economy."

14. Quoted in Andrea Rutherford, "Soviets Pin Hopes on Mom 'n'
Pop Stores," *Wall Street Journal* (April 23, 1991): A19.

15. Tzvetan Todorov, *New Republic* (June 25, 1990), cited in Kevin
Acker, "Poisoning the Soul: New Leaders of Russia and Central Europe
Talk About the Evil Empire," *Policy Review*, No. 55 (Winter 1991): 62.

16. See p. 47 above.

17. Buchanan, 17–18.

18. For an account of the hostility of preachers and theologians to
commerce and industry, see Bernard Groethuysen, *The Bourgeois: Catholicism vs. Capitalism in Eighteenth-Century France*, trans. Mary Il-
ford (New York: Holt, Reinhart & Winston, 1968), 184–225.

19. Pope John Paul II says:

[*Rerum Novarum*] and the related social teaching of the
Church had far-reaching influence in the years bridging the
nineteenth and twentieth centuries. This influence is evident
in the numerous reforms which were introduced in the
areas of social security, pensions, health insurance and com-
pensation in the case of accidents, within the framework of
greater respect for the rights of workers. . . .

Thus, as we look at the past, there is good reason to
thank God that the great encyclical was not without an
echo in human hearts and indeed led to a generous response
on the practical level. Still, we must acknowledge that its
prophetic message was not fully accepted by people at the
time. Precisely for this reason there ensued some very serious tragedies. . . .

Following the destruction caused by the [Second World]
War, we see in some countries and under certain aspects a
positive effort to rebuild a democratic society inspired by
social justice, so as to deprive Communism of the revolutionary potential represented by masses of people subjected
to exploitation and oppression. In general, such attempts
endeavor to preserve free market mechanisms, ensuring by
means of a stable currency and the harmony of social relations, the conditions for steady and healthy economic

growth in which people through their own work can build
a better future for themselves and their families. At the
same time, these attempts try to avoid making market
mechanisms the only point of reference for social life, and
they tend to subject them to public control which upholds
the principle of the common destination of material goods.
In this context, an abundance of work opportunities, a
solid system of social security and professional training, the
freedom to join trade unions and the effective action of
unions, the assistance provided in cases of unemployment,
the opportunities for democratic participation in the life of
society—all these are meant to deliver work from the mere
condition of "commodity," and to guarantee its dignity
(*Centesimus Annus, #*19).

20. Jacob Viner, "Early Attitudes towards Trade and the Mer-
chant," in *Essays on the Intellectual History of Economics*, ed. Douglas
A. Irwin (Princeton University Press, 1991), 39–40.

21. Alexis de Tocqueville explains: "When the world was under the
control of a few rich and powerful men, they liked to entertain a sublime
conception of the duties of man. It gratified them to make out that it is
a glorious thing to forget oneself and that one should do good without
self-interest, as God himself does. That was the official doctrine of morality at that time." Alexis de Tocqueville, *Democracy in America*, ed.
J.P. Mayer (Garden City: Anchor Books, 1969), 525.

See also Michael Novak, *This Hemisphere of Liberty* (Washington,
DC: AEI Press, 1990), 13–14: "The distinctive originality of the modern Whigs lay in discerning clearly the liberating role of the humble
sphere of commerce—so much disdained by earlier philosophers—
and not only the nobler spheres of politics, civic life, and desires of
the human spirit. Classical writers, they believed, had turned too early
to these nobler spheres and too much neglected such lowly matters as
the 'merely useful.' Upon the stone that earlier builders had rejected
they built."

22. He discussed reforms in the following spheres:

Of itself, an economic system does not possess criteria for
correctly distinguishing new and higher forms of satisfying
human needs from artificial new needs which hinder the
formation of a mature personality. *Thus a great deal of educational and cultural work* is urgently needed, including
the education of consumers in the responsible use of their
power of choice, the formation of a strong sense of responsibility among producers and among people in the mass

media in particular, as well as the necessary intervention by
public authorities. . . .

Authentic democracy is possible only in a State ruled
by law, and on the basis of a correct conception of the
human person. It requires that necessary conditions be
present for the advancement both of the individual through
education and formation in true ideals, and of the "subjectivity" of society through the creation of structures of participation and shared responsibility (*Centesimus Annus*,
##36, 46).

23. See n. 49, chap. 3 above.
24. For a fuller discussion see Novak, *This Hemisphere of Liberty*,
63–88. Also in Peter L. Berger, ed., *The Capitalist Spirit: Toward a
Religious Ethic of Wealth Creation* (San Francisco: ICS Press, 1991), 51–
80.
25. Buchanan, 15.
26. Among the texts of Aquinas on the *imago Dei*:

While in all creatures there is some kind of likeness to God,
in the rational creature alone we find a likeness of
image . . . ; whereas in other creatures we find a likeness
by way of a *trace*. Now the intellect or mind is that
whereby the rational creature excels other creatures; where-
fore this image of God is not found even in the rational
creature except in the mind; while in the other parts, which
the rational creature may happen to possess, we find the likeness of a *trace*, as in other creatures to which, in reference to such parts, the rational creature can be likened. We
may easily understand the reason of this if we consider the
way in which a *trace*, and the way in which an *image*, represents anything. An *image* represents something by likeness in species, as we have said; while a *trace* represents
something by way of an effect, which represents the cause
in such a way as not to attain to the likeness of species. For
imprints which are left by the movements of animals are
called *traces*: so also ashes are a trace of fire, and desolation
of the land a trace of a hostile army (St. Thomas Aquinas,
Summa Theologiae, I, q. 93, art. 6).

Reason in man is rather like God in the world (St. Thomas
Aquinas, Opusc. XI, I *de Regno*, 12).

In intellectual natures, where forms are received without
matter, the full play of freedom is ensured and with it the

ability to will. To material things, then, natural appetite is attributed; to animals a sensitive appetite; to intellectual substances a rational appetite or will, and the more spiritual they are the greater the power of will. Since God is at the summit of spirituality, he possesses supremely and most properly the character of will (St Thomas Aquinas, Disputations, XXIII *de Veritate*, I).

27. Letter to UN Secretary General Waldheim, December 2, 1978. Cited in George Weigel, "Religious Freedom: The First Human Right," *This World* 21 (Spring 1988): 41.

28. *Sollicitudo Rei Socialis*, #33.

29. Ibid., #15. (Italics in text)

30. *Laborem Exercens*, #25.

31. *Sollicitudo Rei Socialis*, #15.

32. Cf. Francis Fukuyama, *The End of History and the Last Man* (New York: Free Press, 1992).

33. For a splendid argument on this point see Peter Berger's "Capitalism and Cultural Disorders of Modernity," *First Things*, no. 9 (January 1991): 14–19. "The market allows latitude for every sort of belief or way of life because . . . money knows neither color nor creed: Your sauerkrautist dollar is as good as my Presbyterian one, and if you can find a market niche for your particular form of *mishugas*, who am I to deny it to you?" (p. 19).

34. Sen, 105–106.

5. CAPITALISM RIGHTLY UNDERSTOOD

1. *Centesimus Annus* commemorates the hundredth anniversary of Pope Leo XIII's 1891 encyclical *Rerum Novarum*, considered the beginning of modern Catholic social teaching. Since then, the essential documents have been: Pius XI's *Quadragesimo Anno* (1931); John XXIII's *Mater et Magistra* (1961) and *Pacem in Terris* (1963); Paul VI's *Octogesima Adveniens* (1971); and John Paul II's *Laborem Exercens* (1981) and *Sollicitudo Rei Socialis* (1987).

2. Karol Wojtyla, *The Acting Person*, trans. Andrzej Potocki (Boston: D. Reidel, 1979). Originally published as *Osoba i Czyn* (Cracow: Polskie Towarzystwo Teologiczne, 1969).

3. According to this report:

When all the speechmaking is done and the writings published, it is quite possible that the most prominent advocacy of socialist democratic values in Europe this year will not

come from the likes of Willy Brandt, Felipe Gonzales or
even Neil Kinnock, but from Karol Wojtyla, the Polish
Pontiff whose frequently controversial views suggest a quiet
loathing for aspects of liberal capitalism. . . .

The Vatican is nervous about acquiring political labels,
but John Paul II has long been one of Europe's leading socialists. . . .

The impression the Pope gives is that he can find little
more to praise in liberal capitalism than in marxist communism (John Wyles, "Vatican Prepares Attack on Sins of
Capitalism," *Financial Times*, March 9–10, 1991, Sect. 2,
1).

4. A French journal has reported that the draft of *Centesimus
Annus* prepared by the Institute of Justice and Peace was unsatis-
factory to Pope John Paul II, who had a new draft prepared more
in harmony with American ideas of markets and enterprise. See Gi-
ancarlo Zizola, "Les revirements d'une encyclique," *L'Actualité religieuse dans le monde*, #90 (June 1991): 10–11. Other sources offer
support for this view. Moreover, Zizola reports that the chief author of
the final version was the highly esteemed Italian philosopher Rocco
Buttiglione.

In fact, Buttiglione visited the United States two months before the
encyclical was published, and said on that occasion (he lectured at Catholic University in Washington, DC) that the Holy Father was very
interested in being clearly understood in America. Several sources, including Zizola, offer as a reason for this papal interest a desire to balance
the public criticism voiced by the Holy Father against the UN war to
drive Iraq out of Kuwait, led by the United States.

But this deduction is not credible. The Pope's criticism aroused
little comment in America, and to the extent that it did, most observers thought it helpful for the Christian Pope to make clear that
the action could not be interpreted as in any sense a religious war.
Others found it entirely proper for a religious leader to speak for
peace and against war. Many, indeed, hoped until the very end that
war would not be necessary. The Pope lost no popularity whatever, and
certainly no moral standing, for his principled activities regarding the
Gulf War.

5. *Centesimus Annus*, #42.

6. "The expression 'subdue the earth' has an immense range. It
means all the resources that the earth (and indirectly the visible world)
contains and which, through the conscious activity of man, can be discovered and used for his ends." *Laborem Exercens*, #4.

7. "Very seldom has the role of entrepreneurship as the creative

side of human work been so clearly seen and so highly evaluated as in this encyclical [*Centesimus Annus*]." Ibid., 2.

8. See n. 19 in this chapter for the reference in *Sollicitudo Rei Socialis* to the right of economic initiative.

9. "By intervening directly and depriving society of its responsibility, the Social Assistance State leads to a loss of human energies and an inordinate increase of public agencies, which are dominated more by bureaucratic ways of thinking than by concern for serving their clients, and which are accompanied by an enormous increase in spending." *Centesimus Annus*, #48.

10. Ibid., #32.

11. Ibid.

12. The Pope describes the reform program:

> *Rerum Novarum* and the related social teaching of the church had far-reaching influence in the years bridging the nineteenth and twentieth centuries. This influence is evident in the numerous reforms which were introduced in the areas of social security, pensions, health insurance and compensation in the case of accidents within the framework of greater respect for the rights of workers.
>
> *Rerum Novarum* points the way to just reforms which can restore dignity to work as the free activity of man. These reforms imply that society and the state will both assume responsibility, especially for protecting the worker from the nightmare of unemployment. Historically, this has happened in two converging ways: either through economic policies aimed at ensuring balanced growth and full employment or through unemployment insurance and retraining programs capable of ensuring a smooth transfer of workers from crisis sectors to those in expansion (*Centesimus Annus*, #15).

13. David Little interprets Locke in this way:

> "God . . . hath given the world . . . to Mankind in common," Locke writes, and therefore all human beings share exactly the same common rights in using the earth to preserve life. Each individual is entitled to use what is needful so long as everyone's equal need is respected: "The same Law of Nature, that does . . . give us Property, does also *bound* that *property* too." Individuals must always observe the equal rights of others, they may not cause waste by taking more than they need, and they must leave "enough

and as good . . . in common for others" [emphasis in original].

The idea here is that because property originally belongs to all in common, all individuals by birthright possess certain prior "inclusive rights" to it. In other words, everyone possesses an enforceable title, or what might be called a fair survival share, not to be excluded from access to the means of preservation and sustenance. Accordingly, all human beings have an inclusive natural right to use property for the sake of survival (David Little, "A Christian Perspective on Human Rights," in Abdullahi Ahmed An-Na'im and Francis M. Deng, eds., *Human Rights in Africa: Cross-Cultural Perspectives* [Washington, DC: Brookings Institution, 1991], 74).

14. Russell Hittinger, "The Problem of the State in *Centesimus Annus*," *Fordham International Law Journal* 15 (1992): 952–96.
15. *Centesimus Annus*, #49.
16. Ibid., #60.
17. Ibid., #33.
18. Ibid., #53.
19. *Sollicitudo Rei Socialis*, #15.
20. *Centesimus Annus*, #13.
21. Ibid., #54.
22. Ibid., #25.
23. Ibid.
24. Ibid.
25. Hamilton asks rhetorically:

Have we not already seen enough of the fallacy and extravagance of those idle theories which have amused us with promises of an exemption from the imperfection, the weaknesses, and the evils incident to society in every shape? Is it not time to awake from the deceitful dream of a golden age and to adopt as a practical maxim for the direction of our political conduct that we, as well as the other inhabitants of the globe, are yet remote from the happy empire of perfect wisdom and perfect virtue? (*The Federalist Papers*, No. 6).

26. *Centesimus Annus*, #25.
27. On this coincidence of self-interest and public interest, see the "accord" reached by Jacques Maritain, Yves R. Simon, and Charles de Konnick as reported by Michael Novak, "When Personal and Communal

Good Are One," in *Free Persons and the Common Good* (Lanham, MD: Madison Books, 1989), 30–35.

28. The Pope roots the ecological question in anthropology:

> Equally worrying is the ecological question which accompanies the problem of consumerism and which is closely connected to it. In his desire to have and to enjoy rather than to be and to grow, man consumes the resources of the earth and his own life in an excessive and disordered way. At the root of the senseless destruction of the natural environment lies an anthropological error, which unfortunately is widespread in our day. Man, who discovers his capacity to transform and in a certain sense create the world through his own work, forgets that this is always based on God's prior and original gift of the things that are. Man thinks that he can make arbitrary use of the earth, subjecting it without restraint to his will as though it did not have its own requisites and a prior-God-given purpose, which man can indeed develop but must not betray. Instead of carrying out his role as a cooperator with God in the work of creation, man sets himself up in place of God and thus ends up provoking a rebellion on the part of nature, which is more tyrannized than governed by him (*Centesimus Annus, #37*).

29. Here are some relevant passages:

> The Church found herself facing a historical process which had already been taking place for some time but which was by then reaching a critical point. The determining factor in this process was a combination of radical changes which had taken place in the political, economic and social fields, and in the areas of science and technology, to say nothing of the wide influence of the prevailing ideologies.
>
> In the sphere of economics, in which scientific discoveries and their practical application come together, new structures for the production of consumer goods had progressively taken shape. A new form of property had appeared—capital; and a new form of labor—labor for wages, characterized by high rates of production which lacked due regard for sex, age or family situation and were determined solely by efficiency, with a view to increasing profits (*Centesimus Annus, #4*).

The Pope and the Church with him were confronted, as
was the civil community, by a society which was torn by a
conflict all the more harsh and inhumane because it knew
no rule or regulation. It was *the conflict between capital
and labor* or—as the encyclical puts it—the worker question (*Centesimus Annus, #5*).

30. See n. 19 above.
31. The pope writes about:

the tragic series of wars which ravaged Europe and the
world between 1914 and 1945. Some of these resulted from
militarism and exaggerated nationalism, and from related
forms of totalitarianism; some derived from the class struggle; still others were civil wars of an ideological nature.
Without the terrible burden of hatred and resentment which
had built up as a result of so many injustices both on the
international level and within individual states, such cruel
wars would not have been possible in which great nations
had invested their energies and in which there was not hesitation to violate the most sacred human rights, with the ex-
termination of entire peoples and social groups being
planned and carried out. Here we recall the Jewish people
in particular, whose terrible fate has become a symbol of
the aberration of which man is capable when he turns
against God (*Centesimus Annus, #17*).

The pope later refers to the Cold War:

Extremist groups . . . found ready political and military
support and were equipped and trained for war. . . . In addition, the precariousness of the peace which followed
World War II was one of the principal causes of the mili-
tarization of many Third World countries and the fratricidal
conflicts which afflicted them as well as of the spread of
terrorism and of increasingly barbaric means of political and
military conflict (*Centesimus Annus, #17*).

32. Pope John Paul II explains that Leo XIII anticipated "real existing socialism" in *Rerum Novarum*:

It may seem surprising that "socialism" appeared at the beginning of the Pope's critique of solutions to the "question
of the working class" at a time when "socialism" was not

yet in the form of a strong and powerful State, with all the
resources which that implies, which was later to happen.
However, he correctly judged the danger posed to the
masses by the attractive presentation of this simple and radical solution to the "question of the working class" of the
time—all the more so when one considers the terrible situation of injustice in which the working classes of the recently industrialized nations found themselves (*Centesimus
Annus*, #12).

In describing today's world, the Pope takes many pains to distinguish
concrete differences among systems in different parts of the world. On
Latin America, e.g., see #20; on Asia, #22; on the advanced democratic
and capitalist countries, #19.

33. Pope John Paul II cites Leo XIII's teaching that it is a:

"natural human right" to form private associations. This
means above all the right to establish professional associations of employers and workers or of workers alone. Here
we find the reason for the Church's defense and approval of
the establishment of what are commonly called trade
unions: certainly not because of ideological prejudices or in
order to surrender to a class mentality, but because the
right of association is a natural right of the human being,
which therefore precedes his or her incorporation into political society (*Centesimus Annus*, #7).

Apart from the family, other intermediate communities exercise primary functions and give life to specific networks
of solidarity. These develop as real communities of persons
and strengthen the social fabric, preventing society from becoming an anonymous and impersonal mass, as unfortunately often happens today. It is in interrelationships on
many levels that a person lives, and that society becomes
more "personalized" (*Centesimus Annus*, #49).

See also #13:

The social nature of man is not completely fulfilled in the
state, but is realized in various intermediary groups, beginning with the family and including economic, social, political and cultural groups which stem from human nature

itself and have their own autonomy, always with a view to
the common good. That is what I have called the "subjectivity" of society which, together with the subjectivity of
the individual, was canceled out by "real socialism."

34. *Centesimus Annus*, #48.
35. Some considerations on these limits follow:

[One] task of the State is that of overseeing and directing
the exercise of human rights in the economic sector. However, primary responsibility in this area belongs not to the
State, but to individuals and to the various groups and associations which make up society. The State could not directly ensure the right to work for all its citizens unless it
controlled every aspect of economic life and restricted the
free initiative of individuals (*Centesimus Annus*, #48).

36. Ibid., #42.
37. The encyclical links economic health to moral principles:

In general, such attempts endeavor to preserve free-market
mechanisms, ensuring by means of a stable currency and
the harmony of social relations the conditions for steady
and healthy economic growth in which people through
their own work can build a better future for themselves and
their families. At the same time, these attempts try to avoid
making market mechanisms the only point of reference for
social life, and they tend to subject them to public control,
which upholds the principle of the common destination for
material goods (ibid., #19).

Germany, after World War II, had to restructure its political, economic,
and moral systems simultaneously. To emphasize both "markets" and
political–moral constraints upon them, they called their new system the
"social market economy." For a report on its successes and failures, see
Alan Peacock and Hans Willgerodt, *Germany's Social Market Economy:
Origins and Evolution* (New York: St. Martin's Press, 1989).
38. Among other texts of Hayek, see:

There probably never has existed a genuine belief in freedom, and there has certainly been no successful attempt to
operate a free society, without a genuine reverence for

grown institutions, for customs and habits and "all those
securities of liberty which arise from regulation of long pre-
scription and ancient ways." Paradoxical as it may appear,
it is probably true that a successful free society will always
in large measure be a tradition-bound one (Friedrich A.
Hayek, *The Constitution of Liberty* [Chicago: University of
Chicago Press, 1978], 66).

Bruno Leoni was a great champion of custom, common sense, and trial-
and-error, rather than of reformist legislation. He wrote, e.g.:

Legislation appears today to be a quick, rational, and far-
reaching remedy against every kind of evil or inconveni-
ence, as compared with, say, judicial decisions, the settlement of disputes by private arbiters, conventions, customs,
and similar kinds of spontaneous adjustments on the part of
individuals. . . .
    Both Roman and English history teach us . . . a com-
pletely different lesson from that of the advocates of in-
flated legislation in the present age. . . . Both the Romans
and the English shared the idea that the law is something to
be *discovered* more than to be *enacted* and that nobody is
so powerful in his society as to be in a position to identify
his own will with the law of the land. The task of "discovering" the law was entrusted in their countries to the juris-
consults and to the judges, respectively (Bruno Leoni,
Freedom and the Law [Los Angeles: Nash Publishing,
1961], 5, 10).

39. Michael Novak, *The Spirit of Democratic Capitalism*, 2d ed.
(Lanham, Md.: Madison Books, 1991), 56–57.
40. This tripartite division is foreshadowed in the three chapters into
which the Constitution on the Church in the Modern World, *Gaudium
et Spes*, is divided.
41. *Centesimus Annus*, #32.
42. Ibid., #37.
43. Ibid., #43.
44. Ibid.
45. Some texts from *Sollicitudo*:

Peoples or nations too have a right to their own full development, which while including . . . the economic and social

aspects, should also include individual cultural identity and openness to the transcendent. Not even the need for development can be used as an excuse for imposing on others one's own way of life or own religious belief (*Sollicitudo Rei Socialis*, #32; italics in original).

When individuals and communities do not see a rigorous respect for the moral, cultural and spiritual requirements, based on the dignity of the person and on the proper identity of each community, beginning with the family and religious societies, then all the rest—availability of goods, abundance of technical resources applied to daily life, a certain level of material well-being—will prove unsatisfying and in the end contemptible. The Lord clearly says this in the Gospel, when he calls the attention of all to the true hierarchy of values: "For what will it profit a man, if he gains the whole world and forfeits his life?"

On the internal level of every nation, respect for all rights takes on great importance, especially: the rights to life at every stage of its existence; the rights of the family, as the basic social community, or "cell of society"; justice in employment relationships; the rights inherent in the life of the political community as such; the rights based on the *transcendent vocation* of the human being, beginning with the right of freedom to profess and practice one's own religious belief (*Sollicitudo Rei Socialis*, #33).

46. The pope links initiative and creative subjectivity in *Sollicitudo Rei Socialis*, #15, where he says that political structures must not diminish or destroy "the spirit of initiative, that is to say, the creative subjectivity of the citizen."

47. Kirzner describes his work as an "attempt to understand the systematic character of the capitalist process in terms of entrepreneurial discovery." He says:

To understand the systematic forces at work in markets, we must introduce into our analysis the element of undeliberate but motivated *discovery*. . . .

A misallocation of resources occurs because, so far, market participants have not noticed the price discrepancy involved. This price discrepancy presents itself as an opportunity to be exploited by its discoverer. *The most impressive aspect of the market system is the tendency for such opportunities to be discovered* (Israel Kirzner, *Discovery and the Market Process* [Chicago: University of Chicago Press, 1985], 14, 30; emphasis in original).

48. "This principle directly concerns the process of production: In this process labor is always a primary efficient cause, while capital, the whole collection of means of production, remains a mere instrument or instrumental cause." *Laborem Exercens*, #12.

49. Abraham Lincoln, *Annual Message to Congress*, December 3, 1861 in *Lincoln: Speeches and Writings, 1859–1865*, ed. Don E. Fehrenbacher (New York: Library of America, 1989), 296.

50. On invention and discovery Lincoln says:

> I know of nothing so pleasant to the mind, as the discovery of anything which is at once *new* and *valuable*—nothing which so lightens and sweetens toil, as the hopeful pursuit of such discovery. And how vast, and how varied a field is agriculture for discovery. The mind, already trained to thought, in the country school, or higher school, cannot fail to find there an exhaustless source of profitable enjoyment. Every blade of grass is a study; and to produce two, where there was but one, is both a profit and a pleasure (Abraham Lincoln, "Address to the Wisconsin State Agricultural Society, Milwaukee, Wisconsin," September 30, 1859, in *Abraham Lincoln: Speeches and Writings, 1859–1865* [New York: Library of America, 1989], 99).

51. On the patent laws, Lincoln says:

> These began in England in 1624; and, in this country, with the adoption of our constitution. Before then, any man might instantly use what another had invented; so that the inventor had no special advantage from his own invention. The patent system changed this; secured the inventor, for a limited time, the exclusive use of his invention; and thereby added the fuel of *interest* to the *fire* of genius, in the discovery and production of new and useful things (ibid., 10–11).

52. *Centesimus Annus*, #31.
53. Under the heading of "Great Society," Mises says:

> Society is joint action and cooperation in which each participant sees the other partner's success as a means for the attainment of his own.

The ascendancy of the idea that even in war not every
act is to be considered permissible, that there are legitimate
and illicit acts of warfare, that there are laws, i.e., societal
relationships which are above all nations, even above those
momentarily fighting one another, has finally established a
Great Society embracing all men and all nations. The various regional societies were merged into one ecumenical society.

Society . . . always involves men acting in cooperation
with other men in order to let all participants attain their
own ends (Ludwig von Mises, *Human Action* [New Haven:
Yale University Press, 1949], 168–69).

See also n. 41, chap. 3 above.

Among contemporary economists, not many besides Hayek and
Mises have had the philosophical drive to imagine themselves following
in the footsteps of Aristotle and offering large-scale theories of action,
society, law, and liberty; and not many have had the perspicuity to
discern in enterprise the dynamic element in capitalism. Though both
write as atheists, and develop an anthropology in certain key ways opposed to Christian values, nonetheless the full sweep of their theories
and their commitments to reason and freedom make them stimulating
interlocutors—at least for those trained in the Aristotelian and Thomist
passion for systematic reasoning. In their philosophical interests, moreover, Hayek and Mises are so much deeper than the mainstream economists who rely on utilitarian categories. Of these, the *reductio ad
absurdum* is Richard Posner's utilitarian discussions of sex in *Sex and
Reason* (Cambridge, MA: Harvard University Press, 1992).

54. *Centesimus Annus*, #31.

55. See Michael Novak, *This Hemisphere of Liberty* (Washington,
DC: The AEI Press, 1990), 51: "Those who wish to liberate human
beings from poverty within their nation should look to its primary resource, the minds and spirits of the citizens *at the bottom* of society.
The cause of the wealth of nations is the empowerment of such persons.
To empower people is the indispensable first step toward rapid economic
development."

I expand this point elsewhere:

The heart of the capitalist idea is to begin *at the bottom*, by
releasing the economic creativity of the poor. Several nations of the East Asian rim—Hong Kong, Singapore, Taiwan, and South Korea—observed the lessons to be learned
from the Fabian socialism of India and from Communist
socialism in China and North Korea. They also observed

Japan. Like Japan, they had suffered in the war. They had extremely low standards of living. They had virtually no natural resources. Their populations, already large, were growing rapidly. Per capita income in Taiwan in 1945 was an incredibly low $70. By 1980, it has reached $2,280. The real GNP of Taiwan doubled every seven years—in 1980 it was *eleven* times greater than in 1952. Destitution is gone, and Taiwan's income distribution is among the most equal in the world. The case is similar in South Korea, racked not only by severe Japanese repression during World War II but suffering horribly during the long Korean war of 1949–1953. In 1962, per capita income was $87. Twenty years later, it was $1,600. The average increase in real wages exceeded seven percent per year during the same twenty years (Michael Novak, *Will It Liberate? Questions about Liberation Theology* [Mahwah, NJ: Paulist Press, 1986], 90).

The Pope makes a similar point about unleashing the creative potential of the poor: "This is the culture which is hoped for: one which fosters trust in the human potential of the poor and consequently in their ability to improve their condition through work or to make a positive contribution to economic prosperity. But to accomplish this, the poor—be they individuals or nations—need to be provided with realistic opportunities." *Centesimus Annus*, #52.

56. Ibid., #32.
57. Ibid.
58. Ibid.
59. Ibid.
60. Ibid.
61. Ibid.
62. Ibid., #35.
63. Ibid.
64. See *Wall Street Journal*, February 11, 1992, "There's More Than One Kind of Team," A16.
65. *Centesimus Annus*, #35.
66. Joseph Schumpeter, *Capitalism, Socialism and Democracy* (New York: Harper & Row, 1950), 83.
67. *Centesimus Annus*, #33.
68. Ibid., #34.
69. Ibid., #33.
70. Ibid.
71. Ibid., #35.
72. Ibid., #34.
73. Ibid., #35.

74. Ibid.

75. Ibid., #42.

76. Gary M. Walton, ed., *The National Economic Policies of Chile* (Greenwich, Conn.: Jai Press, 1985).

77. Writing from Italy, for instance, Rocco Buttiglione explains that whereas in the United States "Capitalism is a thoroughly positive and respectable word," in Europe "As a rule, we have a different perception of the same word. Here capitalism implies rather the exploitation of large masses through an elite of tycoons who dispose of natural and historical resources of the land and expropriate and reduce to poverty large masses of peasants and artisans." Rocco Buttiglione, "Behind *Centesimus Annus*," *Crisis* 9 (July–August 1991): 8. See also Rocco Buttiglione, "Christian Economics 101," *Crisis* 10 (July–August 1992): 32–36.

78. In addition, "democratic capitalism" has three other advantages. In the political order, it stresses the democratic ideal. It underlines the role of *caput* or "human capital" in the modern economic order. And it parallels closely the classic phrase "political economy." (That phrase does *not* mean that the economy is political, and its parallel does not mean that capitalism is internally democratic.)

79. See n. 28 above.

80. "Certain objectives stated by *Rerum Novarum* remain valid, and, in some cases, still constitute a goal yet to be reached, if man's work and his very being are not to be reduced to the level of a mere commodity. These objectives include a sufficient wage for the support of the family, social insurance for old age and unemployment, and adequate protection for the conditions of employment." Ibid., #34.

81. "Even prior to the logic of a fair exchange of goods and the forms of justice appropriate to it, there exists *something which is due to man because he is man*, by reason of his lofty dignity. Inseparable from that required 'something' is the possibility to survive and, at the same time, to make an active contribution to the common good of humanity." Ibid. (Emphasis in original.)

82. "It would appear that, on the level of individual nations and of international relations, *the free market* is the most efficient instrument for utilizing resources and effectively responding to needs." Ibid.

83. See n. 19 above.

84. See Thomas S. Johnson, "Capitalism after Communism: Now Comes the Hard Part," in John A. Coleman, S.J., ed., *One Hundred Years of Catholic Social Thought: Celebration and Challenge* (Maryknoll, NY: Orbis, 1991), 247.

85. Julian L. Simon, *The Ultimate Resource* (Princeton: Princeton University Press, 1981).

86. *The Progress*, June 30, 1991.

87. "After Communism," *Commonweal*, 118 (June 1, 1991): 355.

88. Jim Hug, "*Centesimus Annus*: Rescuing the Challenge, Probing the Vision," *Center Focus*, No. 102 (August 1991): 1 ff.

89. "A decent provision for the poor is the true test of civilization. . . . The condition of the lower orders, the poor especially, was the true mark of national discrimination." Samuel Johnson quoted in James Boswell, *The Life of Samuel Johnson*, LL.D., Great Books of the Western World (Chicago: Encyclopaedia Britannica, 1952 [1st ed., 1791]), 182.

90. Hug, 3.

91. *Centesimus Annus*, #33.

92. David Hollenbach writes:

> In February 1990 (thus more than a year before *Centesimus Annus* was issued), Brazilian theologian Leonardo Boff attended a series of meetings in what was then East Germany to discuss the significance of the events of 1989 for the future of liberation theology. In his reflections on these discussions, he maintains that what failed in Eastern Europe was "command socialism," "patriarchal socialism," or "authoritarian socialism." Following the dictatorial model developed by Lenin, after the Second World War so-called scientific socialism was imposed on Eastern Europe from "outside" and "above" by Soviet troops. The breakdown of this kind of socialism is beneficial for everyone. But this does not mean the end of all socialist models (David Hollenbach, S.J., "Christian Social Ethics after the Cold War," *Theological Studies* 53, no. 1 [March 1992]: 77).

93. Hollenbach, 95.

94. Mead's studies of the effect of work in reducing poverty would be especially useful in the perspective of Pope John Paul II's emphasis on human work. See Lawrence M. Mead, *The Politics of Poverty* (New York: Basic Books, 1992).

95. U.S. Bureau of the Census, Current Population Reports, Series P-60, No. 166, *Money Income and Poverty Status in the United States: 1988 (Advance Data from the March 1989 Current Population Survey)* (Washington, DC: U.S. Government Printing Office, 1989), 9.

96. Hollenbach, 83.

97. *Centesimus Annus*, #33.

98. See Hernando De Soto, *The Other Path: The Invisible Revolution in the Third World* (New York: Harper & Row, 1989).

99. U.S. Bishops' Pastoral Letter, *Economic Justice for All: Catholic Social Teaching and the U.S. Economy* (November 13, 1986), #77.

100. *Centesimus Annus*, #33. Emphasis added.

101. In *This Hemisphere of Liberty*, I offered ten practical proposals, a political platform for the party of liberty:

- To recognize in law the inalienable right of personal economic initiative

- To allow the multitudes who labor in the informal or illegal sector swift, easy, and inexpensive access to legal incorporation (ideally by mail, within 14 days, for a modest registration fee of about U.S. $30)

- To empower all citizens now in the informal sector with all relevant legal and social supports for their economic activities and to build institutions designed to instruct them in how to make use of them

- To establish institutions of credit accessible to the poor, which also give professional advice on how to make their enterprises successful

- To favor by law and tax incentives virtually universal home ownership, land ownership, or both with full rights of ownership in perpetuity (including rights to buy or sell)

- To grant workers in state industries, utilities, and the like stock ownership in these enterprises, through employee stock ownership plans

- To sell off most state enterprises to the public, that is, to "privatize" them, through as wide a system of public ownership as possible, approximating universal participation in ownership

- To give primacy among social welfare expenditures to building systems of universal education, stressing the virtues of initiative, enterprise, invention, and social cooperation

- To strengthen the voluntary, nonstatist social sector by laws and tax incentives favorable to the development of foundations and other private institutes of social welfare, not as a substitute for state-sponsored social welfare programs, but as a fresh source of innovation and public service

- In recognition of their indispensable social contribution to the progress of science and the practical arts: To develop strong copyright and patent laws, which grant to authors and inventors the right to the fruits of their inventions for a limited time. This last element is one of the key turning points of economic revolution. It is decisive for the emergence of capitalism.

102. Ignatieff, 11.

103. *Centesimus Annus*, #43.

104. Thomas L. Pangle, "The Liberal Paradox," *Crisis* (May 1992): 18–25.

6. WAR ON POVERTY

1. Quoted by Acker, *Policy Review* (Winter 1991): 63. Original citation from *The Washington Post* (November 30, 1989).

2. Zhelyo Zhelev, cited in Acker, 64.

3. After having praised the institutions of democracy, personal economic initiative, and religious liberty, the Pope took pains to note:

> The Church's social doctrine *is not* a "third way" between
> *liberal capitalism* and *Marxist collectivism*, nor even a possi-
> ble alternative to other solutions less radically opposed to
> one another: rather, it constitutes a *category of its own*.
> Nor is it an *ideology*, but rather the *accurate formulation* of
> the results of a careful reflection on the complex realities of
> human existence, in society and in the international order,
> in the light of faith and of the Church's tradition. Its main
> aim is to *interpret* these realities, determining their con-
> formity with or divergence from the lines of the Gospel
> teaching on man and his vocation, a vocation which is at
> once earthly and transcendent; its aim is thus *to guide*
> Christian behavior. It therefore belongs to the field, not of
> *ideology*, but of *theology* and particularly of moral theology
> (*Sollicitudo Rei Socialis*, #41; emphasis in original).

4. St. Thomas Aquinas writes: "Our will can reach higher than can our intelligence when we are confronted by things that are above us. Whereas our notions about moral matters, which are below man, are enlightened by a cognitive habit—for prudence informs the other moral virtues—when it comes to the divine virtues about God, a will-virtue, namely charity, informs the mind-virtue, namely faith." Disputations, *de Caritate* III, ad 13.

5. See Thomas Aquinas on the interplay of justice and mercy:

> Mercy is supremely God's effectively rather than affec-
> tively. . . . The work of divine justice always presupposes
> the work of mercy and is founded thereon. Creatures have
> no rights except because of something pre-existing or pre-

considered in them, and since we cannot go back and back, we must come to something founded on the sole generosity of the divine will, which is the ultimate end. . . . Mercy is the root in each and every divine work, and its virtue persists in everything that grows out of that, and even more vehemently flourishes there. . . . [The] order of justice would be served by much less than in fact is granted by divine generosity, which far exceeds what is owing (St. Thomas Aquinas, *Summa Theologica*, I, q. 21, art. 3–4. Cf. John Paul II's encyclical *Dives in Misericordia*).

6. *Sollicitudo Rei Socialis*, #42. In the footnote accompanying this text, the Pope cites as background Vatican II's decree *Gaudium et Spes*, #69, Paul VI's encyclical *Populorum Progressio*, #22, and St. Thomas Aquinas, *Summa Theologica* I–II, q. 66, art. 2.
7. *Gaudium et Spes*, #69. The text continues:

Whatever the forms of ownership may be, as adapted to the legitimate institutions of people according to diverse and changeable circumstances, attention must always be paid to the universal purpose for which created goods are meant. In using them, therefore, a man should regard his lawful possessions not merely as his own but also as a common property in the sense that they should accrue to the benefit of not only himself but of others.

8. *Populorum Progressio*, #23.
9. *Summa Theologica* I–II, q. 66, art. 2.
10. He provides a personalist argument:

The person who works desires not only due remuneration for his work; he also wishes that within the production process provision be made for him to be able to know that in his work, even on something that is owned in common, he is working "for himself." This awareness is extinguished within him in a system of excessive bureaucratic centralization, which makes the worker feel that he is just a cog in a huge machine moved from above, that he is for more reasons than one a mere production instrument rather than a true subject of work with an initiative of his own. . . . In the mind of St. Thomas Aquinas, this is the principal reason in favor of private ownership of the means of production. . . . The personalist argument still holds good both on the level of principles and on the practical level. If it is to be rational and fruitful, any socialization of the means of production must be made to ensure that in this kind of system also the human person can preserve his awareness of working "for himself" (*Laborem Exercens,* #15).

Cf. Leo XIII in *Rerum Novarum*: "Private possessions are clearly in accord with nature" (#15). "To own goods privately . . . is a right natural to man, and to exercise this right, especially in life in society, is not only lawful, but clearly necessary" (#36). Pope Leo then quotes St. Thomas Aquinas: "It is lawful for man to own his own things. It is even necessary for human life." *Summa Theologica,* II–II, q. 66, art. 2.

11. "In other cases the land is still the central element in the economic process, but those who cultivate it are excluded from ownership and are reduced to a state of quasiservitude. In these cases it is still possible today, as in the days of *Rerum Novarum,* to speak of inhuman exploitation. . . . Unfortunately, the great majority of people in the Third World still live in such conditions." *Centesimus Annus,* #33.

12. Locke argues from both reason and revelation:

> Whether we consider natural *Reason,* which tells us, that
> Men, being once born, have a right to their Preservation
> and consequently to Meat and Drink, and such other
> things, as Nature affords for their subsistence: or *Revelation,* which gives us an account of those Grants God made
> of the World to *Adam,* and to *Noah,* and his Sons, 'tis very
> clear, that God, as King *David* says, *Psalm.* CXV.xvi. *has
> given the Earth to the Children of Men,* given it to Mankind in common (John Locke, *Two Treatises of Government,* ed. Peter Laslett, Second Treatise, sec. 25, 327;
> emphasis in original).

For an analysis of chapter 5 of Locke's Second Treatise see Robert A. Goldwin, "A Reading of Locke's Chapter 'Of Property'," in *Why Blacks, Women, and Jews are not Mentioned in the Constitution, and Other Unorthodox Views* (Washington, DC: The AEI Press, 1990), 99–109.

Cf. Hollenbach, 84:

> As John Paul puts it, "The original source of all that is
> good is the very act of God, who created both the earth
> and man so that he might have dominion over it by his
> work and enjoy its fruits [Gen. 1:28]. God gave the earth
> to the whole human race for the sustenance of all its members without excluding anyone." It is only through their in-

telligence and work, however, that human beings make the earth fruitful. John Paul, echoing Locke and Leo XIII, affirms that persons make part of the earth their own through work. "This is the origin of individual property." But its accumulation is limited by "the responsibility not to hinder others from having their own part of God's gift" [*Centesimus Annus*, #31]. This again echoes Locke, who maintained that the natural law limited the acquisition of property by the requirement that there be "as much as good left in common for others" [Locke, 18].

In a footnote, Hollenbach goes on to say:

> The degree to which Locke took this requirement seriously is disputed. Those who, like C. B. MacPherson, see Locke as a paradigmatic "possessive individualist" think he did not. A recent interpretation that argues Locke believed in strict limits on property and that his views are closer to Thomas Aquinas than to modern individualism is that of Andrew Lustig, "Natural Law, Property, and Justice: The General Justification of Property in Aquinas and Locke," *Journal of Religious Ethics* 19 (1991): 119–49. To the extent that John Paul echoes Locke, it is Lustig's rather than MacPherson's Locke that is at issue.

13. As Locke says:

> He who appropriates land to himself by his labour, does not lessen but increase the common stock of mankind. For the provisions serving to the support of humane life, produced by one acre of inclosed and cultivated land, are (to speak much within compasse) ten times more, than those, which are yielded by an acre of land, of an equal richness, lying wast in common. . . . I have here rated the improved land very low in making its product but as ten to one, when it is much nearer an hundred to one (Locke, *Two Treatises*, 336).

14. In this respect Mill writes:

> Whenever, in any country, the proprietor, generally speaking, ceases to be the improver, political economy has nothing to say in defense of private property, as there es-

tablished. . . . No man made the land. It is the original inheritance of the whole species. Its appropriation is wholly a
question of general expediency. When private property in
land is not expedient, it is unjust. . . . Even in the case of
cultivated land, a man whom, though only one among millions, the law permits to hold thousands of acres as his single share, is not entitled to think that all this is given to
him to use and abuse, and deal with as if it concerned nobody but himself. . . . The rents of profits which he can
obtain for it are at his sole disposal; but with regard to the
land, in everything which he does with it, and in everything
which he abstains from doing, he is morally bound, and
should whenever the case admits, be legally compelled to
make his interest and pleasure consistent with the public
good (John Stuart Mill, *Principles of Political Economy*, ed.
Sir William Ashley [New York: Augustus M. Kelley,
1969], 231, 233–35).

15. "There is no touchstone, except the treatment of childhood, which
reveals the true character of a social philosophy more clearly than the
spirit in which it regards the misfortunes of those of its members who
fall by the way." R. H. Tawney, *Religion and the Rise of Capitalism*
(Gloucester, Mass.: Peter Smith, 1962), 268. See also Chap. 5, n. 89,
above.

16. See Roger Heckel, S.J., *Self-Reliance* (Vatican City: Pontifical
Commission "Justice and Peace," 1978), 4–5:

Self-reliance does not project the idea of "falling back upon
oneself" or of isolation, but rather of a genuine return to
the living subject and his/her dynamism. The connotation,
therefore, is of an eminently positive nature. The full meaning of the concept appears less in the *noun* (self-reliance)
and more in the *adjective* (self-reliant) coupled to the word
development with which it finds its full meaning. . . . [Self-
reliance] is of the same order as *freedom*. It is through voluntary and reasoned action that a people becomes aware of
its own law of development and implements it as a vital capacity or power. Self-reliance would therefore be an internal vital principle which manifests its presence under the
guise of a power. It is the ever-increasing capacity of a people to assume its past, decide upon its future, and, on a
level of equality, contribute to the shaping of humankind
and the universe of which it is part.

17. According to a 1989 report by the Morgan Guaranty Trust Company, at the end of 1987 Latin American foreign investment was as follows: Brazil, $31 billion; Mexico, $84 billion; Venezuela, $58 billion; Argentina, $46 billion. According to Mark Falcoff, these amounts would cover the following percentages of foreign debt for each country if invested at home: Brazil, 30–40%; Mexico, 60%; and Argentina and Venezuela, 100%. See also Nicholas Eberstadt, *Foreign Aid and American Purpose* (Washington, DC: AEI Press, 1989); and *Centesimus Annus*, #35.

18. See, e.g., the remarks of Lord Bauer:

> Foreign aid does not in fact go to the pitiable figures we see
> on aid posters, in aid advertisements, and in other aid prop-
> aganda in the media. It goes to the governments, that is to
> the rulers, and the policies of the rulers who receive aid are
> sometimes directly responsible for conditions such as those
> depicted. But even in less extreme instances, it is still the
> case that aid goes to the rulers; and their policies, including
> the pattern of public spending, are determined by their own
> personal and political interests, among which the position
> of the poorest has a very low priority (P. T. Bauer, *Reality
> and Rhetoric: Studies in the Economics of Development*
> [Cambridge, MA: Harvard University Press, 1984], 50).

19. See chap. 5, p. 281 above.

20. See Michael Novak, "Liberation Theology—What's Left," *First Things*, No. 14 (June/July 1991): 10–12; and the new introduction to the paperback edition of *Will It Liberate?* (Lanham, MD: University Press of America, 1992).

21. See de Soto, *The Other Path*: In Peru, "48 percent of the economically active population and 61.2 percent of work hours are devoted to informal activities which contribute 38.9 percent of the gross domestic product recorded in the national accounts" (p. 12). "Informals have managed to gain control of 93 percent of the urban transport fleet" (p. 13).

22. "Only 3.5 percent of Peruvian homes are titled. One should not be amazed therefore that Peruvians don't get ahead. They have no way of converting secure property rights, even when they've obtained them, into credit—without which it is impossible to conceive a business." Hernando De Soto, "What's Wrong with Latin American Economies?" *Reason* (October 1989): 40.

23. *Centesimus Annus*, #33.

24. See Michael Novak, *Free Persons and the Common Good* (Lanham, MD: Madison Books, 1989), esp. 108–109.

25. *Centesimus Annus*, ## 33–35.

26. *Gaudium et Spes*, #69.

27. See Michael Novak et al., *The New Consensus on Family and Welfare* (Washington, DC: American Enterprise Institute for Public Policy Research, 1987; and Milwaukee: Marquette University, 1987).

28. See chap. 2, n. 46, above.

29. "The 1984 survey by the Bureau of Labor Statistics, based on complete income figures submitted by several thousand nationally representative households, shows that the poorest 20 percent of households had average reported income before taxes of $3,200 and annual expenditures of $10,800." U.S. Department of Labor, Bureau of Labor Statistics, *1984 Consumer Expenditure Survey*, in *New Consensus*, 70.

30. David Wessell, "Rep. Weber's Plan for a Time Limit on Welfare Draws Criticism from Some of His Usual Allies," *Wall Street Journal* (June 17, 1992): A18.

31. The Pope's words on the welfare state were not entirely unanticipated. See the Lay Letter on the U.S. Economy, *Toward the Future: Catholic Social Thought and the U.S. Economy* (1984), 58–66.

32. "To be attached to the subdivision, to love the little platoon we belong to in society, is the first principle (the germ as it were) of public affections. It is the first link in the series by which we proceed toward a love to our country and to mankind." Edmund Burke, *Reflections on the Revolution in France* (Indianapolis: Bobbs–Merrill, 1955), 53.

33. *Centesimus Annus*, #48.

34. Tocqueville, 691–92.

35. "The dependency of the 5 million or so who are in that situation [both poor and concentrated in cities in which 20 percent of the population is also poor] is of a depth not exhausted by the catch-all phrase 'below the poverty line'." *New Consensus*, 25–26. This is based on data presented by Richard P. Nathan, in "The Underclass: Will It Always Be With Us?" presented at the New School for Social Research, November 14, 1986.

Cf. Charles Murray:

> "Underclass" is an ugly word, with its whiff of Marx and the lumpenproletariat. . . . So let us get it straight from the outset: the "underclass" does not refer to degree of poverty, but to type of poverty.
>
> It is not a new concept. I grew up knowing what the underclass was; we just didn't call it that in those days. In the small Iowa town where I lived, I was taught by my middle-class parents that there were two kinds of poor people. One class of poor people was never even called "poor." I came to understand that they simply lived with

low incomes, as my own parents had done when they were
young. Then there was another set of poor people, just a
handful of them. These poor people didn't lack just money.
They were defined by their behavior. Their homes were lit-
tered and unkempt. The men in the family were unable to
hold a job for more than a few weeks at a time. Drunken-
ness was common. The children grew up ill-schooled and
ill-behaved and contributed a disproportionate share of the
local juvenile delinquents (Charles Murray, *The Emerging
British Underclass* [London: The IEA Health and Welfare
Unit, 1990], 1).

36. See Charles Murray with Deborah Laren, "According to Age:
Longitudinal Profiles of AFDC Recipients and the Poor by Age Group,"
paper presented at the Working Seminar on the Family and American
Welfare Policy, Washington, DC, September 23, 1986. Murray cites a
Michigan study which shows that of all men ages 20 to 64 who had
completed high school—with no more education—fewer than 1 percent
are poor. See also Lawrence M. Mead, *The New Politics of Poverty* (New
York: Basic Books, 1992).

37. Basing its findings on the 1989 "American Housing Survey," U.S.
Department of Commerce, Bureau of the Census, and U.S. Department
of Housing and Urban Development, Office of Policy Development and
Research, *American Housing Survey for the United States in 1989*, Current Housing Reports H150/89 (Washington, DC: U.S. Government
Printing Office, July 1991), the Heritage Foundation issued the following
report about poor housing:

- Nearly 40 percent of all "poor" households actually own their
own homes. The median value of the homes of these households
is 58 percent of the median value of all homes owned in America.
Over one million poor households owned homes worth over
$80,000.

- The average home owned by persons classified as poor in the
U.S. is a three-bedroom house with a garage and porch or patio.
Contrary to popular impression, the majority of these households
who own their own homes are not elderly.

- According to the Census Bureau, only 8 percent of poor
households are overcrowded. Nearly two-thirds have more than
two rooms per person.

- The average American defined as poor has twice as much
living space as the average Japanese and four times as much living

space as the average Russian. Note: These comparisons are to the average citizens in these countries, not to those classified as poor.

■ The homes and apartments of the poor typically are in good condition. The Census Bureau reports that only 5 percent of all housing of the poor have even "moderate upkeep" problems.

■ Some 53 percent of poor households, owners as well as renters, have air conditioning. By contrast, just 20 years ago only 36 percent of the entire U.S population enjoyed air conditioning.

■ Contrary to popular impression, housing costs for many poor households are quite low; half of all poor households either live in taxpayer-subsidized public housing or own their own homes with mortgages fully paid.

38. Lawrence Mead, "The Work Problem in Workforce," paper presented at the Working Seminar on the Family and American Welfare Policy. See also his *New Politics of Poverty*. "For example, the poverty rate for black families with no workers, is 69 percent; with one worker, 35 percent; with two workers, 8 percent. Clearly, work is an effective path out of poverty, and the number of workers per family matters a great deal." *New Consensus*, 59.

39. "Apart from the family, other intermediate communities exercise primary functions and give life to specific networks of solidarity. These develop as real communities of persons and strengthen the social fabric, preventing society from becoming an anonymous and impersonal mass, as unfortunately often happens today. It is in interrelationships on many levels that a person lives, and that society becomes more 'personalized'." *Centesimus Annus*, #49.

40. Charles Murray, *In Pursuit of Happiness and Good Government* (New York: Simon & Schuster, 1988). See especially Part Three: Toward the Best of All Possible Worlds.

41. Speech, National Conference of Black Mayors, Kansas City, Missouri, April 23, 1992.

42. Ibid.

43. "Don't Give Up: Poverty Programs That Work," *Washington Monthly* (June 1988): 28–40.

44. Roger J. Vaughan, "Sell More Salsa," Ibid., 36.

45. Ibid., 28, 31–32.

46. See Robert L. Woodson, "Transform Inner Cities from the Grass Roots Up," *Wall Street Journal*, June 3, 1992.

47. *Centesimus Annus*, #33.

48. For example, the Working Seminar made the following recommendations on the given topics:

Families

■ Religious institutions, schools, and voluntary institutions should make the moral, cultural, and educational enrichment of home life a primary focus of efforts to reduce dependency. Classes in child care, handbooks designed for parents who seek help in doing better, and outreach services should be developed.

■ Parental responsibility for the support of children should be reinforced. Although the nation pays considerable homage to the notion that parents are responsible for the support and upbringing of their children, our practice in recent decades has fallen increasingly short of that ideal. Public policies have failed to support the exercise of this responsibility.

■ Political and administrative pressure should be brought to bear to improve that record. Some would advocate allowing lawyers to accept child-support cases on a contingent-fee basis. Others argue that changes in the property aspects of divorce laws will be needed to undo provisions adopted in the past decade.

■ The fathers of out-of-wedlock chidren receiving AFDC should be identified by mandatory paternity findings; all fathers should be held to child-support obligations, and efforts should be made to collect from them; and community leaders ought to hold up for esteem only those fathers who fulfill their family responsibilities.

■ Young mothers receiving AFDC benefits should be required to complete their high school degrees or equivalency and then seek work.

■ Voluntary institutions should help these young mothers through classes in child care and child education, and other efforts that bring these mothers out of isolation, in social settings that provide child care and instruction and also prepare them for employment. Such initiatives are underway in several states.

■ In regard to young teenage mothers, welfare policy should not confuse their legal status as parents with the physical and emotional standing, which may be less than adult. It is self-deception to suppose that allowing teenagers to establish their own homes enables them to exercise parental responsibility. Consequently, unless there is a finding that their safety so requires, welfare benefits should not be paid to recipients under age 18 living in independent households. Rather, recipients should be aided either in the homes of their own parents or in supervised congregate homes, such as those now being run by voluntary civil, religious, or other social service groups.

■ Child abuse and child neglect are serious national problems. There is a tendency, however, to treat the symptoms of poverty as a form of "child neglect." A large number of our poor children now being placed in foster care could be safely left with their parents.

■ Support should be given to organized private efforts such as one recently announced by a national coalition of black churches to encourage their members to open their homes for the adoption of parentless black children who would otherwise be sent to state foster care.

■ Parent–teacher associations should develop materials and counseling services especially designed for parents in high-poverty areas to help them to strengthen the educational environment of the home, to design home study areas, and to prescribe hours for homework.

■ Experiments in various localities to link schools to homes, especially among the dependent poor, should be studied for ideas that work, as should those experiments in early childhood education for the poor that have proved particularly effective.

■ Instruction in the probable long-term effects of illegitimacy and early parenthood upon both children and their unprepared parents should be made available to families and schools, lest irresponsible pregnancies contribute to long-term dependency.

Schools

■ Communities should be encouraged and assisted in setting high standards for their schools, recognizing that the key factors are strong principals, an orderly but not rigid school atmosphere, a schoolwide commitment of resources to and focus on basic skills, a highly visible expectation that every child can learn, and frequent monitoring of the performance of each student.

■ Great care should be taken in choosing principals, and rewards should go to those who are particularly successful in setting high standards and in leading students to achieve them.

■ The training of principals should be a high community priority.

- Fear of lawsuits claiming the violation of "student rights" has deprived some school officials of a spirit of initiative and has led others to take the course of least resistance, for example, by not enforcing standards of behavior that they know have been violated. Federal law should be amended so that, within appropriate limits, principals have greater good-faith discretion in setting and enforcing schoolwide standards of behavior, without fear of lawsuits.

- Since there is abundant evidence that family life has a profound—even decisive—impact on what a child learns, educators must make a more serious and sustained effort to involve parents in the education of their children. To be successful with disadvantaged children, in particular, schools must involve families in the day-to-day business of education: doing homework, specifying expectations, maintaining intellectual and physical discipline, and monitoring performance. In addition, parents must ensure that the climate of home complements and reinforces that at school and that both together reward solid achievement and excellence.

- An important step in this direction, consistent with racial integration and systemwide order, would be to give parents a greater measure of choice regarding which public schools their children attend, as is now done with "magnet" or specialized schools.

- The choice of an appropriate educational program for their children is especially important for low-income families. Some members of the Working Seminar favor a voucher or an open enrollment plan; others doubt the practicality of such plans. All agree in seeking ways to give poor parents more of the flexibility and freedom others already have and to make the public schools more accountable for their performance among the poor.

- Although most of the burden for improving education lies with state governments and local communities, the federal government has expressed its own concern through various programs. There is some evidence to suggest that these efforts have had at least some good effects, not as deep and lasting as had been hoped, but warranting experiments and demonstrations designed to do better than the early ventures.

- Since teenage pregnancy is a significant cause of dropping out of high school (as well as of a future of welfare dependency), much recent discussion has been devoted to what schools might be able to do to prevent it. For behavioral dependency, illegitimacy is a crucial issue. Some suggest earlier and more thorough sex education classes; others favor providing advice on contraceptives through school health services; some advocate moral education and character formation; still others believe that only strict methods such as expulsion from regular classes can have the needed impact on the values of all.

Neighborhoods

■ Innovative methods of policing, aimed at maintaining order, not just solving crimes, should be introduced.

■ Court procedures, particularly with regard to bail, sentencing, and parole, should be tightened.

■ The illegal drug trade in poverty-stricken communities should be controlled. In this task, broad community support at every level is necessary, including national leadership and massive support from the media of popular entertainment.

■ Government can act differently and effectively to better neighborhood conditions by amending the rules regarding public housing. At present, these regulations make it extremely difficult to exclude or to evict tenants who do not meet minimally acceptable standards of conduct. This situation should be remedied.

■ In some places, groups of public housing residents have been able to organize and enforce standards that have dramatically improved living conditions and safety. Public policy should encourage neighborhood crime patrols, sanitary code enforcement drives, school associations, and the like. Most communities, when challenged, do possess the leadership to sustain such activities; but beyond attaining immediate goals, successful local self-organization reinforces habits of social imagination and perseverance.

Voluntary Associations

■ The mass media, for example, have vast (but not unlimited) power to shape the national ethos and to focus public awareness on important problems, as they have done successfully with regard to world famine, fitness, smoking, and other issues. In the values they transmit, in the heroes they hold up for public acclaim, in the lessons they convey through songs and stories, and in other ways, the media can help nourish a moral environment in which the habits crucial to exiting from poverty are socially reinforced. The media must lead the way to a new national commitment to reducing dependency if that commitment is to succeed. Some of the young are more likely to derive their cultural heroes from the media than from their parents, teachers, religious traditions, or other local authorities.

- Since many of the poor, as well as the nonpoor, are devoutly religious, religious institutions are among the most effective institutions in impoverished communities, and have the potential to provide considerable personal guidance and practical help. When true to their own inherent power, few institutions can better inculcate those habits of cooperation and self-reliance, of responsibility, self-control, and community service that best express human dignity. Few can better address the current breakdown of religious ideals of marriage, fidelity, and commitment, which is not only wreaking unprecedented devastation among the poor, but also steadily increasing their numbers (even during periods of economic growth).

- Religious social agencies should help to focus the resources of society upon the moral dimensions of dependency. But at the same time, working from principles different from those of government officials, they should challenge the poor and empower them through spiritual determination, inner strength, and community involvement.

- Religious institutions should inspire the nonpoor to reach out to the poor in private and local ways. Whereas making up for income shortfalls is necessarily a task in which government must play by far the larger role, religious and other voluntary institutions can focus both philanthropy and charity on the family life of the vulnerable, the personal development of youth, and social cooperation in neighborhoods.

- Voluntary and professional associations—fraternal organizations, foundations, service clubs, citizens' committees, neighborhood organizations, businesses in their civic and philanthropic roles, and other social bodies—should strive to make up for the inevitable limitations of public policy.

- Using the talent and resources that are their glory, voluntary associations should continue to take inventory of the problems of the poor and the dependent in their communities and seek to invent new ways of coming to their aid. This should include diagnosing where government programs fall short, examining local civic resources, and restructuring local methods of meeting human needs, so that efforts now wasted (or not being undertaken at all) might be redirected in a more systematic and productive way.

■ Beyond providing those charitable donations of goods and services that will always be necessary in any society, associations with particular skills should make contributions, flowing from their own strengths, that no one else is likely to meet.

■ Lawyers and medical professionals have special obligations to the homeless, many of whom are clearly incapable of self-reliance and in need of medical treatment. Using private initiatives, bankers, builders, and realtors should address the housing needs of low-income families and encourage the private upgrading and improvement of the existing housing of the poor. One example of such projects is to sponsor neighborhood teams of craftsmen— who might not otherwise find credit—to purchase, rehabilitate, and resell or rent older buildings. As some are already doing, food distributors in metropolitan centers should devise private sector ways to make otherwise wasted food available to food banks for the hungry.

■ Last, but not least, is the important role of specific organizations of ethnic and racial minorities. Although blacks and Hispanics are still disproportionately represented among the dependent, it is less plausible today than it was a generation ago to assert that poverty is especially connected with race. Today, nonetheless, the scholars, leaders, and rank-and-file members of black and other minority-group organizations are speaking frankly about behavioral dependency and devising realistic ways of dealing with it. Their leadership is indispensable to the social progress of all groups. They establish the tone and context of much public discussion. The nation relies heavily upon them.

■ For all voluntary institutions, from religious institutions through philanthropic organizations to businesses, it is more than ever necessary to reach into the areas in which dependency is concentrated. Apart from habits of self-reliance, citizens in those areas cannot better their condition; yet interventions from government are likely to deepen them in dependency unless other citizens reach into their lives and draw them into the ethos of cooperation and self-reliance. It would be wrong now, more than ever, to abandon the underclass. Since federal programs are not sufficient to end dependency (and, when done badly, may permit it to thrive), it is crucial that other agencies become involved.

Welfare

- Young mothers should be required to complete high school (or its equivalent) and prepare themselves for future employment.

- Older mothers with previous experience in the labor force should be expected to find work in the private sector or (as a last resort) to accept an assignment in the public sector.

- Those involved in work programs, whether staff or participants, should be expected to regard every job, even part time and at a minimum wage, as an obligation to society, as important to future work experience, and as an occasion of self-development. Without this conviction current efforts to provide new services to welfare recipients could, like many previous ones, become a substitute for work.

- A minimum of emphasis should be placed on public service jobs; the overriding emphasis should fall on personal responsibility for finding jobs in the private sector. Social service agencies, with strong political leadership, should develop programs to involve private sector employers in placement efforts. Jobs in government should be accepted reluctantly and only in areas so depressed that there are clearly insufficient jobs of any kind. In the growing service economy of the 1990s, entry-level jobs are likely to become increasingly abundant as labor shortages develop because of demographic factors. The coming decade may be unusually favorable for moving large numbers of recipients from welfare to work.

- For women of mature age thrown into temporary poverty by divorce or separation, transitional aid is in line with the purposes of AFDC. Many such women possess the educational resources, skills, and determination to enable them to become independent within a short time. Programs assisting them, accordingly, should not compromise their independence.

- Those, however, who need preliminary training in personal habits and work skills should be required to enroll for a time in work-training programs or, if necessary and appropriate, to complete work for their high-school diploma or equivalent.

- After a specific time limit (such as two years), a recipient of AFDC should be required, as a condition of further assistance, either to find employment or to accept employment in a public job.

- At a minimum, taxes should not drive low-income workers below the poverty line. By raising exemptions and the standard deduction, the tax bill of 1986 has essentially lifted the burden of the federal income tax from the working poor. State and local income taxes should be adjusted similarly.

- The working poor remain liable for payroll taxes for social security, which the earned income tax credit (EITC) only partially offsets. Thus some in the Working Seminar favor raising the levels of EITC. Others strongly oppose this, predicting that it would spread some of the dependency-inducing characteristics of current cash-assistance welfare programs to a broader range of citizens. Hence EITC should not be expanded without a detailed calculation of its costs and probable behavioral consequences.

- The Working Seminar did not undertake a study of health care. Yet our concern about dependency led us to note a central problem: on the one hand, about 15 percent of the population, among whom are many who have worked their way out of poverty, lack medical coverage; on the other hand, there is evidence that some persons now stay on welfare primarily to keep Medicaid coverage. Major programmatic experiments are now under way, and a sustained investigation of their results will shortly be in order.

- Finally, although it is self-evident, it seems worth repeating that government most fundamentally helps the working poor by pursuing policies that foster economic growth, deal with labor market inefficiencies, improve education and job-related training, and lead to rising real incomes.

(*The New Consensus on Family and Welfare* [Washington, DC: American Enterprise Institute, 1987], 101–117).

49. Jack Kemp, "A New Agenda for Ending Poverty," *Washington Post*, May 3, 1992.

50. Stuart Butler, "Razing the Liberal Plantation," *National Review* 41 (November 10, 1989): 27–30.

51. Guy Sorman, *Barefoot Capitalism: A Solution for India* (New Delhi: Vikas Publishing [Distributed by Advent Books, New York], 1989).

7. ETHNICITY, RACE, AND SOCIAL JUSTICE

1. Nathan Glazer and Daniel Patrick Moynihan, *Beyond the Melting Pot: The Negroes, Puerto Ricans, Jews, Italians, and Irish of New York City*, 2d rev. ed. (Cambridge, MA: MIT Press, 1970).

2. Michael Novak, *The Rise of the Unmeltable Ethnics* (New York: Macmillan, 1972).

3. Gabriel Marcel, *The Mystery of Being*, 2 vols. (Chicago: Gateway, 1960), 1:154–181; id., *Creative Fidelity* (New York: Farrar, Straus, 1964), 109–119.

4. Ben J. Wattenberg, *The First Universal Nation: Leading Indicators and Ideas about the Surge of America in the 1990s* (New York: Free Press, 1991).

5. Richard Brookhiser, *The Way of the WASP: How It Made America, and How It Can Save It, So To Speak* (New York: Free Press, 1991), 1–17.

6. William Julius Wilson, "The Right Message," *New York Times*, May 17, 1992, A25.

7. U.S. Bureau of the Census, Current Population Reports, Series P–60, No. 174, *Money Income of Households, Families, and Persons in the United States: 1990*, U.S. Government Printing Office, Washington, D.C., 1991, 54.

8. Ibid., 17.

9. Ibid., 5.

10. U.S. Bureau of the Census, *Statistical Abstract of the United States: 1991* (111th ed.), Washington, DC, 1991.

11. David J. Dent, "The New Black Suburbs," *The New York Times Magazine* (July 14, 1992): 20.

12. John F. Kennedy, "Special Message to the Congress on Public Welfare Programs," *Public Papers of the Presidents of the United States* (Washington, DC: Office of the *Federal Register*, National Archives and Record Service, 1953–   ), 102–103.

13. U.S. Department of Commerce, Economics and Statistics Administration, Bureau of the Census, *Poverty in the United States: 1990*, Current Population Reports, Consumer Income, Series P-60, No. 175.

14. Arthur Hu, "Us and Them," *The New Republic* (June 1, 1992): 12, 14.

15. Ibid.

16. For example, John D. Kasarda says:

> In the wake of the L.A. riots, many people are demanding massive government aid for the cities. But government can do little to address the root of the urban problem—values. . . .

Almost by definition, the moral authority for a change in the values that create these conditions must come from . . . emphasis on the family, disciplined economic self-support, and anti-drug, anti-crime programs. As Malcom X liked to say, only a revolution in mentality will change anything (John D. Kasarda, "Why Asians Can Prosper Where Blacks Fail," *Wall Street Journal* [May 28, 1992]).

See also Lawrence E. Harrison, *Who Prospers?* (New York: Basic Books, 1992). For my part, I hold, with Aristotle, that the structures of the polity do affect values and must be designed in the light of the latter.

17. Aquinas observes:

Man is a social animal, having many wants he cannot supply for himself. He is born into a group by nature. By living with others he is helped to the good life. And this on two heads.

First, as regards necessities without which life cannot be lived, he is supported by the domestic group. He depends on his parents for his birth, feeding, upbringing. Each member of the family helps the others.

Secondly, as regards the conveniences without which life cannot be lived well, he is helped by the civil group, both for material benefit, for the State provides public services beyond the means of one household, and for moral advantage, thus public authority can check young criminals when paternal warnings go unheeded [*Commentary, I Ethics,* lect. 1].

Well-adjusted home and social relationships are indispensable for the proper welfare of each singular person. Nevertheless, domestic and political prudence do not supply the want of personal prudence [*Commentary, VI Ethics,* lect. 7].

To be a social and political animal living in a crowd is even more natural to man than to the other animals. His inherited needs declare this dependence. Nature provides food for other animals, covering, weapons of defense, teeth and claws, or at least swiftness of flight. But with man it is different; instead he is endowed with his reason by which he can contrive these aids. Yet to see to all of them is beyond any one man's power; alone he cannot dispatch the business of living. Consequently that he should dwell in association with many is according to his nature.

Furthermore, other animals have an inborn ingenuity with regard to what is beneficial or harmful; a sheep instinctively recognizes that a wolf is a menace, and other animals similarly take advantage of medicinal herbs and other things needful to life. But man's inbred knowledge about these matters is limited to general principles; he has to take pains to work from them to the provision of his needs in each and every case. One solitary man cannot discover everything for himself. He must combine in a team, so that one may help another and different men be reasonably engaged in different jobs, one in medicine, another in this, another in that.

This is made plain by the fact that it is peculiar to man to use language, through which he can adequately disclose his thoughts to another. Other animals may express their common emotions to one another, a dog by barking and other animals by appropriate signs. But man is more communicative, even more so than the gregarious animals, such as storks, ants, and bees. With this in mind, Solomon says: *It is better that two should be together than solitary; for they gain by their mutual companionship* [*Opusc. XI, I de Regimine Principum ad Regem Cypri*, I] (*St. Thomas Aquinas: Philosophical Texts*, trans. Thomas Gilby [New York: Oxford University Press, 1960], 371–74).

18. The Alan Guttmacher Institute, *Facts in Brief*, April 1992, Abortion in the United States. See also, from the same institute, *Abortion Factbook, 1992 Edition: Readings, Trends, and State and Local Data to 1988* (New York: Alan Guttmacher Institute, 1992).

19. Jason DeParle, "Young Black Men in Capital: Study Finds 42% in Courts," *New York Times* (April 18, 1992).

20. David Popenoe writes:

The Swedish marriage rate is now the lowest in the industrialized world, and the average age at first marriage is probably the highest. The rate of nomarital cohabitation, or consensual unions, outranks that of all other advanced nations; such unions, rather than being a mere prelude to marriage (as is more often the case in the United States now), have become a parallel institution alongside legal marriage. About 25 percent of all couples in Sweden today are living in consensual unions (up from 1 percent in 1960), compared with about 5 percent in the United States. The growth of nonmarital cohabitation among childbearing couples has given Sweden one of the highest percentages of children born out of wedlock in the industrial world—over 50 percent of all children, compared with about 22 percent in the United States.

There is one thing about growing up in Sweden today that should give pause even to those sympathetic to the welfare state. There is a strong likelihood that the family has grown weaker there than anywhere else in the world. What has happened to the family in Sweden over the past few decades lends strong support to the proposition that as the welfare state advances, the family declines. If unchecked, this decline could eventually undermine the very welfare that the state seeks to promote.

The modern welfare state was founded with the goal of helping families to function better as decentralized welfare agencies. It sought to strengthen families, not to weaken them. Over time, however, welfare states have increasingly tended not so much to assist families as to replace them; people's dependence on the state has grown while their reliance on families has weakened. In a classic illustration of the law of unintended consequences, the family under the welfare state is gradually losing both the ability and the will to care for itself (David Popenoe, "Family Decline in the Swedish Welfare State," *Public Interest*, No. 102 [Winter 1991]: 65–66).

21. *Centesimus Annus*, #48.
22. Ibid.
23. This civilizing process must contend against powerful natural tendencies:

Males commit more crimes than females, young males more crime than older males. These age and gender differences dwarf all other factors associated with individual variations in criminality (for example, ethnicity and social class). . . . The most careful of the available studies . . . leave little doubt that a significant portion of male aggressiveness has a constitutional origin: it arises from a temperament that predisposes boys as young as two or three years of age to behaviors that in their milder forms we describe as roughhousing, assertiveness, and independence and in the more extreme forms we characterize as hostility, conduct disorders, and antisocial personality (James Q. Wilson, *On Character* [Washington, DC: AEI Press, 1991], 45).

8. AGAINST THE ADVERSARY CULTURE

1. Of one of his intellectual predecessors Rorty approvingly notes: "Wittgenstein . . . cheerfully tosses out half-a-dozen incompatible metaphilosophical views in the course of the *Investigations.*" *Consequences of Pragmatism* (Minneapolis: University of Minnesota Press, 1982), 23. Rorty draws an explicitly historicist consequence from this: "We Deweyan historicists . . . think that 'first principles' are abbreviations of, rather than justifications for, a set of beliefs about the desirability of certain concrete alternatives over others; the source of those beliefs is not 'reason' or 'nature', but rather the prevalence of certain institutions or modes of life in the past." Richard Rorty, "That Old-Time Philosophy," *New Republic* (April 4, 1988): 30. See also: "No specific doctrine is much of a danger, but the idea that democracy depends on adhesion to some such doctrine is." Richard Rorty, "Taking Philosophy Seriously," *New Republic* (April 11, 1988): 33.

2. Schlesinger once wrote:

> The American mind is by nature and tradition skeptical, irreverent, pluralistic and relativistic. . . . Our relative values are not matters of whim and happenstance. History has given them to us. They are anchored in our national experience, in our great national documents, in our national heroes, in our folkways, traditions, standards. Some of these values seem to us so self-evident that even relativists think they have, or ought to have, universal application: the right to life, liberty and the pursuit of happiness, for example; the duty to treat persons as ends in themselves; the prohibition of slavery, torture, genocide. People with different history will have different values. But we believe that our own are better for us. They work for us; and, for that reason, we live and die by them (Arthur Schlesinger, Jr., "The Opening of the American Mind," *New York Times Book Review* [July 23, 1989]: 26).

See my reply, "Relativism or Absolutes: Which is the American Way?" *National Catholic Register* (October 29, 1989).

3. Richard Rorty, *Philosophy and the Mirror of Nature* (Princeton: Princeton University Press, 1979).

4. Richard Rorty, "The Seer of Prague," *The New Republic* (July 1, 1991): 39.

5. For Schlesinger's second thoughts, see his *Disuniting of America: Reflections of a Multicultural Society* (New York: Norton, 1992).

6. See the following remarks of Murray and Maritain:

Because it was conceived in the tradition of natural law the American Republic was rescued from the fate, still not overcome, that fell upon the European nations in which Continental Liberalism, a deformation of the liberal tradition, lodged itself. . . . It is indeed one of the ironies of history that the tradition [of natural law] should have so largely languished in the so-called Catholic nations of Europe at the same time that its enduring vigor was launching a new Republic across the broad ocean. There is also some paradox in the fact that a nation which has (rightly or wrongly) thought of its own genius in Protestant terms should have owed its origins and the stability of its political structure to a tradition whose genius is alien to current intellectualized versions of the Protestant religion, and even to certain individualistic exigencies of Protestant religiosity. . . . Catholic participation in the American consensus has been full and free, unreserved and unembarrassed, because the contents of this consensus—the ethical and political principles drawn from the tradition of natural law— approve themselves to the Catholic intelligence and conscience (John Courtney Murray, S.J., *We Hold These Truths* [New York: Sheed & Ward, 1960], 31, 41).

Not only does the democratic state of mind stem from the inspiration of the Gospel, but it cannot exist without it. To keep faith in the forward march of humanity despite all the temptations to despair of man that are furnished by history, and particularly contemporary history; to have faith in the dignity of the person and of common humanity, in human rights and in justice—that is, in essentially spiritual values; to have, not in formulas but in reality, the sense of and respect for the dignity of the people, which is a spiritual dignity and is revealed to whoever knows how to love it; to sustain and revive the sense of equality without sinking into egalitarianism; to respect authority, knowing that its wielders are only men, like those they rule, and derive their trust from the consent or the will of the people whose vicars or representatives they are; to believe in the sanctity of law and in the efficacious virtue—efficacious at long range—of political justice in face of the scandalous triumphs of falsehood and violence; to have faith in liberty and in fraternity, an heroical inspiration and an heroical belief are needed which fortify and vivify reason, and which none other than Jesus of Nazareth brought forth in the world (Jacques Maritain, *Christianity and Democracy* [New York: Charles Scribner's Sons, 1950], 59–60).

7. See Lippman's remarks on public philosophy:

> Freedom of religion and of thought and of speech were achieved by denying both to the state and to the established church a sovereign monopoly in the field of religion, philosophy, morals, science, learning, opinion and conscience. The liberal constitutions, with their bills of rights, fixed the boundaries past which the sovereign—the King, the Parliament, the Congress, the voters—were forbidden to go.
> Yet the men of the seventeenth and eighteenth centuries who established these great salutary rules would certainly have denied that a community could do without a general public philosophy. They were themselves the adherents of a public philosophy—of the doctrine of natural law, which held that there was law "above the ruler and the sovereign people . . . above the whole community of morals" (Walter Lippmann, *The Public Philosophy* [New York: New American Library, 1956], 76, 77–78).

8. Leo Strauss, *The Rebirth of Classical Political Rationalism* (Chicago: University of Chicago Press, 1989); Allan Bloom, *The Closing of the American Mind* (New York: Simon & Schuster, 1987); Allan Bloom, ed., *Confronting the Constitution: The Challenge to Locke, Montesquieu, Jefferson, and the Federalists from Utilitarianism, Historicism, Marxism, Freudianism, Pragmatism, Existentialism* (Washington, DC: AEI Press, 1990); Francis Fukuyama, *The End of History and the Last Man* (New York: Free Press, 1992); Harry V. Jaffa, *American Conservatism and the American Founding* (Winston–Salem, NC: Carolina Academic Press, 1984); and Harry V. Jaffa, *How to Think About The American Revolution* (Winston–Salem, NC: Carolina Academic Press, 1978).

9. One such reconstruction has been attempted by Hollenbach:

> The thesis proposed here is that Catholic teaching on human rights today presupposes a reconstruction of the classical liberal understanding of what these rights are. The pivot on which this reconstruction turns is the traditional natural law conviction that the human person is an essentially social being. Catholic thought and action in the human rights sphere, in other words, are rooted in a communitarian alternative to classical liberal human rights theory. At the same time, by adopting certain key ideas about

constitutional democracy originally developed by classical liberalism, recent Catholic thought has brought about a notable new development of the longer tradition of the church while simultaneously offering an alternative to the standard liberal theory of democratic government (David Hollenbach, S.J., "A Communitarian Reconstruction of Human Rights: Contributions from Catholic Tradition," 2 [paper prepared for a project on "Liberalism, Catholicism, and American Public Philosophy" at the Woodstock Theological Center, Georgetown University, forthcoming in a book by Fr. Hollenbach]).

Some objections, however, to this synthesis have been raised:

> For centuries, the cornerstone of Catholic moral theology was not the natural or human *rights* doctrine but something quite different, called the natural *law*. Rights, to the extent that they were mentioned at least by implication, were contingent on the fulfillment of prior duties. . . . Simply stated, what the church taught and tried to inculcate was an ethic of virtue as distinct from an ethic of rights. . . .
>
> The bishops may have confused some of their readers by using language that looks in two different directions at once: that of rights or freedom on the one hand, and of virtue, character formation, and the common good on the other. They would certainly be ill-advised to give up their vigorous defense of rights, especially since the pseudo-morphic collapse of Neo-Thomism in the wake of Vatican II has left them without any alternative on which to fall back; but they have yet to tell us, or tell us more clearly, how the two ends are supposed to meet (Ernest L. Fortin, "The Trouble with Catholic Social Thought," *Boston College Magazine* [Summer 1988]: 38, 42).

10. E. J. Dionne has remarked:

> Because of our flight from public life, our common citizenship no longer fosters a sense of community or common purpose. Social gaps, notably the divide between blacks and whites, grow wider. The very language and music heard in the inner city is increasingly estranged from the words and melodies of the affluent suburbs. We have less and less to do with each other, meaning that we feel few obligations to each other and are less and less inclined to vindicate each

other's rights (E. J. Dionne, Jr., *Why Americans Hate Politics* [New York: A Touchstone Book published by Simon & Schuster, 1991]).

11. Michael Novak, *Free Persons and the Common Good* (Lanham, MD: Madison Books, 1989). See also *Centesimus Annus*, ##11, 17, 40. See esp. #43:

> The Church offers her social teaching as an *indispensable and ideal orientation*, a teaching which, as already mentioned, recognizes the positive value of the market and of enterprise, but which at the same time points out that these need to be oriented towards the common good. This teaching also recognizes the legitimacy of workers' efforts to obtain full respect for their dignity and to gain broader areas of participation in the life of industrial enterprises so that, while cooperating with others and under the direction of others, they can in a certain sense "work for themselves" through the exercise of their intelligence and freedom.

12. Even so, Jacques Maritain reminds us that we need not be completely despairing. Every age sees itself as falling off in morals ("*O Tempora, O Mores*"). In a chapter called "The Old Tag of American Materialism," Maritain says:

> The American people are the least materialist among the modern peoples which have attained the industrial stage. . . .
> Americans like to give. . . . The ancient Greek and Roman idea of the *civis praeclarus*, the dedicated citizen who spends his money in the service of the common good, plays an essential part in American consciousness. And let me observe that more often than not the gifts in question are made for the sake of education and knowledge. . . .
> There is no materialism, I think, in the astonishing countless initiatives of fraternal help which are the daily bread of the American people. . . .
> There is no materialism in the fact that the American charities, drawing money from every purse, and notably to assist people abroad, run every year into such enormous sums that charity ranks among the largest American industries, the second or third in size, according to statisticians. . . . Let us not forget what an immense amount of personal attention to one's neighbor and what personal ef-

fort is unceasingly put forth in all the groups which exist in this country, and which spring up every day, to meet some particular human misfortune or some particular social mal-adjustment. . . .

There is a perpetual self-examination and self-criticism going on everywhere and in every sphere of American life; a phenomenon incomprehensible without a quest for truth of which a materialist cast of mind is incapable (Jacques Maritain, *Reflections on America* [New York: Charles Scribner's Sons, 1958], 29–30, 34–36, 38).

13. *Centesimus Annus*, #36.

14. Joseph A. Schumpeter, *Capitalism, Socialism and Democracy*, 3d ed. (New York: Harper & Row, 1975); and Daniel Bell, *The Cultural Contradictions of Capitalism* (New York: Basic Books, 1976).

15. *Centesimus Annus*, #36.

16. Ibid.

17. Ibid.

18. Ibid., #51.

19. Gabriel Marcel, *Being and Having* (New York: Harper & Row, 1965).

20. Gabriel Marcel, *The Mystery of Being*, 2 vols. (Chicago: Regnery, 1960) and also Gabriel Marcel, *Creative Fidelity* (New York: Farrar, Straus, 1964).

21. *Centesimus Annus*, ##44–47. See Russell Hittinger, "The Problem of the State in *Centesimus Annus*," *Fordham International Law Journal* 15, no. 4 (August 1992).

22. *Centesimus Annus*, #50.

23. "It would be difficult to find in contemporary political debate an issue position regarded as distinctively liberal that does not trace back either to equality of result or to relativism, which at root are the same thing." Jeffrey Bell, *Populism and Elitism: Politics in the Age of Equality* (Washington, DC: Regnery Gateway, 1992), 185.

24. Paul V. Mankowski, "What I Saw at the American Academy of Religion," *First Things* (March 1992): 36–41.

25. Gallup Cross-National Surveys, 1981. Cf. James Davison Hunter, *Culture Wars: The Struggle to Define America* (New York: Basic, 1991).

26. Congregation for the Doctrine of the Faith, "Instruction on Christian Freedom and Liberation" (Vatican City: Vatican Polyglot Press, 1986), 7.

27. Hannah Arendt, *On Revolution* (New York: The Viking Press, 1965), 49.

28. Lionel Trilling, *Beyond Culture: Essays on Literature and Learning* (New York: The Viking Press, 1968).

29. Arendt, 49 (italics added).

30. At a critical point in the Constitutional Convention on June 28, 1787, Franklin suggested the depths of the Framers' struggle to concur on a new order:

> We indeed seem to feel our own want of political wisdom, since we have been running about in search of it. We have gone back to ancient history for models of Government, and examined the different forms of those Republics which having been formed with the seeds of their own dissolution now no longer exist. And we have viewed Modern States all round Europe, but find none of their Constitutions suitable to our circumstances (Speech of Benjamin Franklin to the Federal Convention, June 28, 1787, cited in James Madison, *Notes of Debates in the Federal Convention of 1787* [New York: W. W. Norton & Co., 1987], 209).

31. *The Federalist Papers*, No. 14.

32. Arendt, 15.

33. Crèvecoeur describes the new prosperity:

> The American ought therefore to love this country much better than that wherein either he or his forefathers were born. Here the rewards of his industry follow with equal steps the progress of his labour; his labour is founded on the basis of nature, *self-interest*; can it want a stronger allurement? Wives and children, who before in vain demanded of him a morsel of bread, now, fat and frolicsome, gladly help their father to clear those fields whence exuberant crops are to arise to feed and to clothe them all; without any part being claimed, either by a despotic prince, a rich abbot, or a mighty lord (Hector St. John Crèvecoeur, *Letter from an American Farmer* [1782; reprint ed., New York: Fox, Duffield & Co., 1904], 55).

34. In Tocqueville's words:

> If patient observation and sincere meditation have led men of the present day to recognize that both the past and the future of their history consist in the gradual and measured advance of equality, that discovery in itself gives this progress the sacred character of the will of the Sovereign Master. In that case effort to halt democracy appears as a fight against God Himself, and nations have no alternative but

to acquiesce in the social state imposed by Providence (Alexis de Tocqueville, *Democracy in America*, trans. George Lawrence, ed. J. P. Mayer [Garden City: Anchor Books, 1969], 12).

35. "The Miami Meeting with President Reagan," *Origins* 17 (September 24, 1987): 238.

36. "Is there no virtue among us?" asked Madison defiantly. "If there be not, we are in a wretched situation. No theoretical checks, no form of government, can render us secure. To suppose any form of government will secure liberty or happiness without any virtue in the people, is a chimerical idea." Jonathan Elliot, ed., *Debates in the Several State Conventions on the Adoption of the Federal Constitution* (Philadelphia: Lippincott, 1907), Virginia, June 20, 1788.

37. Russell Kirk, *The Roots of American Order* (Washington, DC: Regnery Gateway, 1992).

38. Hamilton wrote as follows (except for the italicizations) to the people of the United States, in *Federalist* 1:

You are called upon to deliberate on a new Constitution for the United States of America. . . . It has frequently been remarked that it seems to have been reserved to the people of this country, by their conduct and example, to decide the important question, whether societies of men are really capable or not of establishing good government from *reflection* and *choice*, or whether they are forever destined to depend for their political constitutions on accident and force.

39. Arendt, 15.

40. John Adams wrote in 1809:

I will insist that the Hebrews have done more to civilize men than any other nation. If I were an athiest, and believed in blind eternal fate, I should still believe that fate had ordained the Jews to be the most essential instrument for civilizing the nations. If I were an athiest of the other sect, who believe or pretend to believe that all is ordered by chance, I should believe that chance had ordered the Jews to preserve and propagate to all mankind the doctrine of a supreme, intelligent, wise, almighty sovereign of the universe, which I believe to be the great essential principle of all morality, and consequently of all civilization (John Adams to F. A. Vanderkemp, February 16, 1809, in C. F.

Adams, ed., *The Works of John Adams* [Boston: Little,
Brown, 1854], 9: 609–10).

41. "The basis of our governments being the opinion of the people,
the very first object should be to keep that right [a free press]; and were
it left to me to decide whether we should have a government without
newspapers, or newspapers without a government, I should not hesitate
a moment to prefer the latter." Letter to Edward Carrington, January
16, 1787, in *Thomas Jefferson* (New York: Literary Classics of the United
States, Inc., 1984), 880.

42. Sung-Chull Junn, "Why Koreans Think We're Jerks," *Washington Post*, "Outlook," April 9, 1989.

43. Trilling, xii. Irving Kristol adds an important clarification, which
is that the new class is adversarial not just to the practices of the nation
but to its ideals:

> We are so used to this fact of our lives, we take it so for
> granted, that we fail to realize how extraordinary it is. Has
> there ever been in all of recorded history, a civilization
> whose culture was at odds with the values and ideals of that
> civilization itself? It is not uncommon that a culture will be
> critical of the civilization that sustains it—and always critical of the failure of this civilization to realize perfectly the
> ideals that it claims as inspiration. Such criticism is implicit
> or explicit in Aristophanes and Euripides, Dante and Shakespeare. But to take an adversary posture toward the ideals
> themselves? That is unprecedented. . . . The more "cultivated" a person is in our society, the more disaffected and
> malcontent he is likely to be—a disaffection, moreover, directed not only at the actuality of our society but at the
> ideality as well. Indeed, the ideality may be more strenuously opposed than the actuality (Irving Kristol, *Reflections of a Neoconservative: Looking Back, Looking Ahead*
> [New York: Basic Books, 1983], 27–28).

44. Trilling, xii.
45. Ibid., xiv–xv.
46. A useful introduction to the "new class" may be found in B.
Bruce-Briggs, *The New Class?* (New Brunswick: Transaction Books,
1979). In *Beyond Culture*, Lionel Trilling showed the influence of the
new class in literature; for the influence of the new class on politics and
economics see, respectively, Jeane J. Kirkpatrick, "Politics and the 'New
Class'," *Dictatorship and Double Standards: Rationalism and Reason in
Politics* (New York: American Enterprise Institute and Simon and Schus-

ter, 1982), 186–203; and Irving Kristol, *Two Cheers for Capitalism* (New York: Basic Books, 1978), chap. 2, "Business and the 'New Class'," 25–31.

In Marxist countries the danger of a new class was discerned as early as 1939 by Bruno Rizzi; see his *The Bureaucratization of the World*, trans. with intro. by Adam Westoby (New York: The Free Press, 1986). Almost simultaneously, James Burnham discerned an equivalent to the new class in *The Managerial Revolution* (New York: John Day Co., 1941). The concept became prominent on the left with the publication of Milovan Djilas's *The New Class* (New York: Praeger, 1957). In the United States writers on the left, such as John Kenneth Galbraith, David T. Bazelon, and Michael Harrington began to point to the "new class" as a potential ally of—if not a replacement for—the proletariat. See Galbraith, *The Affluent Society* (Boston: Houghton Mifflin, 1967), and Harrington, *Toward a Democratic Left* (New York: Macmillan, 1968), 265–97.

47. See *Antonio Gramsci: Selections from Political Writings, 1910–1920*, trans. John Mathews (Ann Arbor: Books on Demand, UMI, 1976). See also Jaime Antunez, "Socialism Chic," *Crisis* 7 (April 1989): 38–40.

48. See Bell, xvi.

49. Michael Novak, "The Secular Saint," *Illinois State University Journal* 30 (September 1967): 3–35; id., *A Theology for Radical Politics* (New York: Herder & Herder, 1969).

50. Bell, xvi.

51. Ibid., xvii.

52. Kristol distinguishes two poles in the tradition:

> The terms "prophetic" and "rabbinic" which come, of course, from the Jewis tradition, indicate the two poles within which the Jewish tradition operates. They are not two equal poles: The rabbinic is the stronger pole, always. In an Orthodox Hebrew school, the prophets are read only by those who are far advanced. The rest of the students read the first five books of the Bible, and no more. They learn the Law. The prophets are only for people who are advanced in their learning and not likely to be misled by prophetic fever (Kristol, *Reflections of a Neoconservative*, 316–17).

53. See Ronald A. Knox, *Enthusiasm* (Westminster, MD: Christian Classics, 1983).

54. "It cannot be repeated too often: nothing is more fertile in marvels than the art of being free, but nothing is harder than freedom's appren-

ticeship. . . . But liberty is generally born in stormy weather, growing with difficulty amid civil discords, and only when it is already old does one see the blessings it has brought." Tocqueville, 240.

Living on the boundary between the traditional society and the democratic society, Tocqueville himself saw more clearly than most the differences in the virtues required in the democratic, as opposed to aristocratic, societies. (He saw these as differences more clearly with respect to political institutions than he did with respect to economic institutions.)

55. "Yet more serious is the destruction of the *human environment*. People are rightly worried about the extinction of animal species, but too little effort is made to *safeguard the moral conditions for an authentic 'human ecology.'* " *Centesimus Annus*, #38.

56. "There is," writes Cotton Mather, "a *liberty* of corrupt nature, which is affected by *men* and *beasts* to do what they list; and this *liberty* is inconsistent with *authority*, impatient of all restraint; by this *liberty*, *Sumus Omnes Deteriores*, 'tis the grand enemy of *truth* and *peace*, and all the *ordinances* of God are bent against it. But there is a civil, a moral, a federal *liberty* . . . for that only which is *just* and *good*; for this *liberty* you are to stand with the hazard of your very *lives*." Cited in Tocqueville, 46.

57. This is clearly recognized in the recent encyclical:

> A person who is concerned solely or primarily with possessing and enjoying, who is no longer able to control his instincts and passions, or to subordinate them by obedience to the truth, cannot be free: *obedience to the truth* about God and man is the first condition of freedom, making it possible for a person to order his needs and desires and to choose the means of satisfying them according to a correct scale of values, so that the ownership of things may become an occasion of growth for him (*Centesimus Annus*, #41).

For the inseparability of obedience and freedom as understood by the Pope, see Karol Cardinal Wojtyla, "The Eucharist and Man's Hunger for Freedom," Homily given at the Forty-first International Eucharistic Congress in Philadelphia, August 3, 1976 (Daughters of St. Paul Pamphlets, 1978):

> Freedom has been given to him by his Creator not in order to commit what is evil (cf. Gal. 5:13), but to do good. God also bestowed upon man understanding and conscience to show him what is good and what ought to be done, what is

wrong and what ought to be avoided. God's commandments help our understanding and our conscience on their
way. The greatest commandment—that of love—leads the
way to the fullest use of liberty (cf. 1 Cor. 9:19–22; 13:1–
13). Freedom has been given to man in order to love, to
love true good: to love God above all, to love man as his
neighbor and brother (cf. Dt. 6:5; Lv. 19:18; Mk. 12:30–
33). Those who obey this truth, this Gospel, the real disci-
ples of eternal Wisdom, achieve thus, as the Council puts
it, a state of "royal freedom," for they follow "that King
whom to serve is to reign."

Freedom is therefore offered to man and given to him as
a task. He must not only possess it, but also conquer it. He
must recognize the work of his life in a good use, in an increasingly good use of his liberty. This is the truly essential, the fundamental work on which the value and the
sense of his whole life depend (7–8).

On this same occasion in Philadelphia, the Pope noted the common
aspirations of the colonial Americans and his own Polish compatriots:

This year is the bicentennial of the day when the hunger for
freedom ripened in the American society and revealed itself
in liberation and the Declaration of Independence of the
United States. Tadeusz Kosciuszko and Kazimierz Pulaski,
my compatriots, participated in this fight for independence.
The heroes of the Polish nation became heroes of American
independence. And all this took place at the time when the
Polish Kingdom, a big state consisting of three nations, the
Poles, the Lithuanians and the Ruthenians, was beginning
to lose its independence, and by degrees became the prey of
its rapacious neighbors, Russia, Germany and Austria. At
the same time while the United States of America was gaining independence, we were losing it for a period of more
than a hundred years. And many heroic efforts and sacri-
fices, similar to those of Kosciuszko and Pulaski, had been
necessary to ripen anew the freedom of the nation, to test it
before all the world and to express it in time by the independence of our country (10–11).

58. See Michael Novak, "Christ: The Great Divide," *Crisis* (July–
August 1992): 2–3.
59. *Centesimus Annus*, #60.

EPILOGUE

1. Hans Urs von Balthasar, *Theo-Drama*, trans. Graham Harrison (Harrison, NY: Ignatius Press, 1988).

2. But see Leo Strauss, *Persecution and the Art of Writing* (Chicago: University of Chicago Press, 1988).

3. See *Centesimus Annus*, #32, second paragraph.

4. According to Berger:

> The mythic deprivation of capitalism is, very likely, grounded in the fact that capitalism is an economic system and nothing else (by contrast, socialism is a comprehensive view of human society). All economic realities are essentially *prosaic*, as against the poetry that inspires, moves, and converts human minds. Max Weber, in his well-known analysis of charisma as a force in history, describes charisma as *wirtschaftsfremd*—as inimical to economic concerns. Without doing violence to Weber's thinking, one may reverse the proposition: Economic reality is inimical to charisma, or, put in Sorelian language, economics is averse to myth. Economic rationality and the mythopoetic impetus occupy very different compartments of human consciousness. Efforts to combine the two are unlikely to be successful, in the sense of success as plausibility to significant numbers of people.
>
> This is not a new problem in the history of capitalism. From its inception, capitalism legitimated itself indirectly—by being linked up with other legitimations, *not* of the economic system as such but rather of other, more myth-prone realities of human life (Peter L. Berger, *The Capitalist Revolution* [New York: Basic Books, 1986], 206).

Berger (now at 208) summarizes his analysis of this issue in the following proposition: "Capitalism has a built-in incapacity to generate legitimations of itself, and it is particularly deprived of mythic potency; consequently, it depends upon the legitimating effects of its sheer facticity or upon association with other, noneconomic legitimating symbols."

For his part, Johnson confesses:

> I prefer to see the entrepreneurial spirit, of which capitalism is the result, not as positively virtuous, or for that matter as intrinsically sinful, but as morally neutral. It seems to me that capitalism is an impersonal force and therefore inca-

pable of moral choices. Capitalism, including the market system which gives it its efficiency and its power, is single-minded in its thrust, and that is why it is so productive. Focused solely on its own materialistic objectives, it has no room for idealism. It responds with great speed and accuracy to all the market factors. In a way it is like a marvelous natural computer. But it cannot make distinctions for which it is not programmed. Acutely responsive to market factors, it is blind to all others—blind to class, race, and color, to religion and sex, to nationality and creed, to good and evil (Paul Johnson, "The Capitalist Commandments: Ten Ways for Businessmen to Promote Social Justice," *Crisis* [November 1989], 10–16).

5. Michael Novak, "Boredom, Virtue and Democratic Capitalism," *Commentary* 88 (September 1989): 34–37.

6. Alan Peacock and Hans Willgerodt, eds., *Germany's Social Market Economy: Origins and Evolution* (New York: St. Martin's Press, 1989).

7. David Little, *Religion, Order, and Law: A Study in Pre-Revolutionary England* (Chicago and London: University of Chicago Press, 1969).

8. Ibid., 6–32, 226–37.

9. H. R. Trevor-Roper, "Religion, the Reformation and Social Change" in *The European Witch-Craze of the Sixteenth and Seventeenth Centuries and Other Essays* (New York: Harper & Row, 1969), 1–45.

10. David Martin, *Tongues of Fire: The Explosion of Protestantism in Latin America* (Oxford: Basil Blackwell, 1990).

11. Ibid., 290–91.

12. Jacob Viner, *Religious Thought and Economic Society: Four Chapters of an Unfinished Work*, ed. Jacques Melitz and Donald Winch (Durham, NC: Duke University Press, 1978), 151–89.

13. See, e.g., *Law, Legislation and Liberty* and *The Constitution of Liberty*.

14. This was recognized by, e.g., Bernard Bosanquet:

In any discussion regarding the nationalization of an industry, the true issue, at once of principle and of practice, turns on the possibility of creating an administration which shall fulfill the requirements of personal responsibility, invention, initiative, and energy. For it is these, and not self-interest, as both sides are too apt to assume, which form the spur and the delight of what is known as private enterprise, and which ordinary bureaucracy destroys (Bernard Bosanquet, *The Philosophical Theory of the State* [London: Macmillan, 1951], xii–xiii).

15. *Centesimus Annus, #32.*

ACKNOWLEDGMENTS

The author wishes to thank Derek Cross, Research Associate at the American Enterprise Institute, who took responsibility for the endnotes and whose editorial influence can be felt on every page of this book; Kenneth R. Craycraft, Jr., who helped with the endnotes in an earlier draft of some parts; and such extraordinary AEI interns (over two summers) as Daniel Gordon, David Robinson, Benjamin Schwartz, Robert Lakind, Marcy Friedlander, William J. Fidurko, and Kathryn Madden. Catherine M. Love typed (and retyped) the manuscript. Peter J. Dougherty of The Free Press offered sound structural advice and raised questions that thickened the texture of the argument; he was a congenial and good-natured midwife of a better book than he first saw. As copy editor, George A. Rowland offered many splendid suggestions. My colleagues Russell Hittinger, Charles Murray, and Douglas Besharov and other friends such as Richard John Neuhaus, George Weigel, David Green, Rocco Buttiglione, and Michael Cromartie offered helpful advice and saved me from many errors. All these provided an example of the communitarian effort normal to modern creative activities.

My gratitude is also due to the Ethics and Public Policy Center (Washington, DC); the University of Notre Dame (Notre Dame, IN); Rosemont College (Villanova, PA); the Centro di Ricerca e Documentazione "Luigi Einaudi" (Turin, Italy); The Karl Brunner Symposium (Interlaken, Switzerland); the Institute of Economic Affairs (London, England); the Von Hügel Institute at St. Edmund's College (Cambridge, England); Lancaster University (Lancaster, England); the Université d'Été de la Nouvelle Economie, Aix-en-Provence; and Christendom College (Front Royal, Virginia) for inviting me to deliver the papers that became the early nucleus of this book and for helping me to improve them through criticism. I thank them, too, for (in some cases) publishing the original lectures and allowing me to draw upon them for the fuller statements of this book. I also thank the University of Notre Dame Press for inviting me to write an introduction to a new edition of *Catholicism, Protestantism and Capitalism*, and for allowing me to reprint it here in rather different form.

Earlier versions of several chapters appeared in the following translations and reprints: Chapter 1 in "The Catholic Anti-Capitalism Bias," Introduction to Amintore Fanfani, *Catholicism, Protestantism, and Capitalism* (Notre Dame, IN: Notre Dame Press, 1984), xxix–lv. Chapter 4 in "Liberté religieuse et liberté economique," *Revue des Etudes Humaines* (Sept.–Dec. 1991): 22–26; "The Great Convergence: A New Consensus in Favor of Economic and Religious Liberty," *Crisis* 9 (December 1991): 28–33; "La seconda liberta: libertá religiosa e libertá economica," *Biblioteca della libertá* 26 (July–September 1991): 84–91. Chapter 5 in "El Capitalismo Correctamente Entendido: La Vision del Humanismo Cristiano," *Estudios Publicos* (Spring 1992): 29–59; and "Capitalism Rightly Understood: The Vision of Christian Humanism," *Faith and Reason* 17 (Winter 1991): 317–52. Chapter 6 in "La transformation de la revolution capitaliste/democratique," *Journal des Economistes et des Etudes Humaines* 11 (December 1991): 513–57; "Transforming the Democratic/Capitalist Revolution," *International Journal of Value-Based Management* 4 (1991): 9–56; "Transforming the Democratic/Capitalist Revolution," in *Proceedings, First International Conference on Social Values*, Vol. 2 (Cambridge, England: Cambridge University, Von Hügel Institute, 1991), 1–28; and "Trasformare la rivoluzione democratico-capitalista," *Studi Sociali* (April 1991): 9–42. Chapter 8 in "Countering the Adversary Culture," in *The Making of an Economic Vision*, Oliver F. Williams and John W. Houck, eds. (Lanham, MD: University Press of America, 1991), 99–120. Some paragraphs of the epilogue in "Persona e creativitá," *Studi Sociali* (February 1991): 7–13; and "Osoba Tworoza," *Tygodnik Powszechny* 45 (1991).

Finally, I am grateful to the following authors and/or publishers for permission to reprint excerpts from their works:

- Peter Berger, *The Capitalist Revolution.* Copyright © 1986 by Basic Books, Inc. Reprinted by permission of Basic Books, a division of HarperCollins Publishers.

- Ernest Fortin, "The Trouble with Catholic Social Thought," *Boston College Magazine* (Summer 1988). Copyright © *Boston College Magazine.*

- F.A. Hayek, *Law, Legislation and Liberty*, Vol. 2. Copyright © 1976 by University of Chicago Press. Reprinted by permission of University of Chicago Press.

- Irving Kristol, *Reflections of a Neoconservative.* Copyright © 1983 by Basic Books, Inc. Reprinted by permission of Basic Books, a division of HarperCollins Publishers.

- Jacques Maritain, *Reflections on America.* Reprinted with the permission of Charles Scribner's Sons, an imprint of Macmillan Publishing Company. Copyright © 1958, Jacques Maritain.

- John Courtney Murray, S.J. *We Hold These Truths.* Copyright © 1960, Sheed & Ward, Kansas City.

- Robert Heilbroner, "The World After Communism," *Dissent* (Fall 1990). Reprinted with permission of Robert Heilbroner.

- Arthur Hu, "Us and Them," *The New Republic* (June 1, 1992). Reprinted by permission of *The New Republic.* Copyright © 1992, The New Republic, Inc.

- John D. Kasarda, "Why Asians Can Prosper Where Blacks Fail," *Wall Street Journal* (May 28, 1992). Reprinted by permission of *Wall Street Journal.* Copyright © 1992 Dow Jones & Company, Inc. All Rights Reserved Worldwide.

- Roy Porter, "The Heart of the Country," *The New Republic* (May 4, 1992). Reprinted by permission of *The*

INDEX